Military and Humanitarian Health Ethics

The interdisciplinary book series Military and Humanitarian Health Ethics fosters an academic dialogue between the well-established disciplines of military ethics on the one hand and medical ethics, humanitarian ethics and public health ethics on the other hand. Military and Humanitarian Health Ethics have emerged as a distinct research area in the last years, triggered among other things by the unfortunate realities of armed conflicts and other situations of humanitarian disasters - man-made or natural. The book series focuses on the increasing amount of ethical challenges while providing medical care before, during, and after armed conflicts and other emergencies. By combining practical first-hand experiences from health care providers in the field with the theoretical analysis of academic experts, such as philosophers and legal scholars, the book series provides a unique insight into an emerging field of research of high topical interest. It is the first series in its field and aims at publishing state-of-the-art research, illustrated and enriched by field reports and ground experiences from health care providers working in armed forces or humanitarian organizations.

We welcome proposals for volumes within the broad scope of this interdisciplinary and international book series, especially proposals for books that cover topics of interest for both the military and the humanitarian community, and which try to foster an exchange between the two often separate communities of military and humanitarian health care providers.

Bernhard Koch • David Winkler
Editors

Artificial Intelligence Ethics in Military Medicine and Humanitarian Healthcare

Springer

Editors
Bernhard Koch
Institut für Wehrmedizinische Ethik der Bundeswehr
Munich, Germany

David Winkler
University Hospital Basel
Basel, Switzerland

ISSN 2524-5465 ISSN 2524-5473 (electronic)
Military and Humanitarian Health Ethics
ISBN 978-3-032-11330-6 ISBN 978-3-032-11331-3 (eBook)
https://doi.org/10.1007/978-3-032-11331-3

This Springer imprint is published by the registered company Springer Nature Switzerland AG
The registered company address is: Gewerbestrasse 11, 6330 Cham, Switzerland

Foreword by Major General Andreas Stettbacher

As the Surgeon General of the Swiss Armed Forces, I am responsible for health and well-being of our soldiers and the people they take care of. Therefore, I cannot turn a blind eye on the profound ethical dilemmas posed by artificial intelligence (AI).

AI has immense potential, as demonstrated by real-time translation tools that can handle multiple languages simultaneously during a single conference. However, its applications can also raise serious concerns. AI is not neutral; it is purpose-built and as a consequence is also inherently biased. In a world increasingly dominated by AI-driven digitalization, individual privacy is at risk, as huge data enable the reconstruction of personal profiles and the identification of individual persons (or targets). This is deeply troubling, especially when considering the implications of AI-generated "hallucinations"—fabricated narratives that blur the line between fact and fiction and become storytelling. In an AI-mediated reality, what will define truth? Will truth itself simply become a mere statistical construct?

One particularly alarming development is the rise of AI-driven social scoring systems. These technologies, once confined to the realm of dystopian fiction as depicted in "Black Mirror" (S03E01), have become an utterly shocking reality in the form of AI applications such as "LAVENDER", which score entire populations based on their likelihood of belonging to a terrorist group. More locally, the Swiss military has been using an early AI-based psychological assessment tool for military recruitment for three decades, and it is still in use today. However, as its opaque algorithm has become outdated and no longer aligns with societal developments, we have decided to phase it out—an acknowledgement of the need for transparency and adaptability in AI systems.

This leads to a fundamental question: Are we integrating AI into our systems, or are our systems becoming integrated into AI? Are we still in control, or are we merely fulfilling AI-driven imperatives? And most importantly, can AI take (moral and legal) responsibility for its actions, or does that burden rest solely with its creators and users?

It is imperative to regulate AI, but the challenge lies in whether regulation can keep pace with its rapid evolution. AI auto-generation and development might outsmart regulation. I am deeply concerned that humanity is on the verge of losing control over the development of AI, which could have catastrophic consequences. Contrary to the romanticized depictions of AI autonomy in popular culture, the reality may be far more dangerous. Stanley Kubrick's cautionary tale, "2001: A Space Odyssey", in which the supercomputer HAL resists human intervention, has never felt more relevant. The ultimate nightmare scenario is not just pulling the plug, but witnessing an AI-enabled system plug itself back in.

As a medical professional, I am always on the outlook for a cure for the disease. There is currently no cure for AI autonomy, and we urgently need strategies to overcome it. However, it's clear that raising awareness is the first critical step in the right direction. We must act now to develop strategies that ensure AI remains a tool for humanity rather than a force that dictates our future.

Andreas Stettbacher

Surgeon General of the Swiss Armed Forces
M.D. Surgery FMH
University of Bern
Bern, Switzerland

Honorary Chairman of the International
Committee of Military Medicine ICMM
Brussels, Belgium

Contents

Chapter 1
Introduction

Bernhard Koch and David Winkler

Anyone who needs to write an introduction for an academic volume today can have it written by a so-called Large Language Model (LLM) almost effortlessly, using only a computer with internet access. This requires a „prompt "and a model like „ChatGPT "from OpenAI, which has been all the rage since 2022. In response to the request: „Please write me a summary on one page of the advantages and disadvantages of Artificial Intelligence in military medicine", ChatGPT determined the following response on June 24, 2025:

"Advantages:

1. Enhanced Decision-Making:
   AI can analyze vast amounts of data rapidly, aiding medical personnel in making faster, more accurate diagnoses and treatment plans during combat and emergencies.
2. Remote and Autonomous Care:
   In battlefield scenarios where human medical staff may be unavailable or delayed, AI-driven systems (e.g., robotic surgery, remote diagnostics) can provide critical care and monitoring.
3. Predictive Analytics:
   AI can predict health issues before symptoms arise by monitoring soldiers' biometrics and environmental data, improving early intervention and reducing casualty rates.
4. Efficient Resource Management:

B. Koch (✉)
Institut für Wehrmedizinische Ethik der Bundeswehr, Munich, Germany
e-mail: bernhard.koch@theol.uni-freiburg.de

D. Winkler
University Hospital Basel, Basel, Switzerland
e-mail: winklerd@uhbs.ch

B. Koch, D. Winkler (eds.), *Artificial Intelligence Ethics in Military Medicine and Humanitarian Healthcare*, Military and Humanitarian Health Ethics,
https://doi.org/10.1007/978-3-032-11331-3_1

AI helps optimize logistics such as medical supply chains, evacuation plans, and hospital staffing, improving overall operational efficiency in high-pressure military environments.

5. Training and Simulation:

   AI-powered simulations enhance medical training for military personnel, offering realistic combat injury scenarios to improve readiness and performance under pressure.

Disadvantages:

1. Ethical and Legal Concerns:

   The use of AI in life-and-death decisions raises ethical issues, especially when machines are involved in triage or autonomous treatment without human oversight.
2. Reliability and Trust:

   AI systems can malfunction or provide inaccurate recommendations, particularly if trained on biased or insufficient data, potentially putting lives at risk in critical situations.
3. Cybersecurity Risks:

   Military medical AI systems are high-value targets for cyberattacks, which could compromise sensitive health data or disrupt medical operations during conflict.
4. High Costs and Maintenance:

   Developing and maintaining sophisticated AI systems requires substantial investment and continuous updates, posing challenges for budget and sustainability.
5. Dependency on Technology:

   Overreliance on AI may reduce human medical personnel's skills and judgment, which are vital when technology fails or is unavailable in the field.

Conclusion:

AI in military medicine offers transformative benefits, particularly in enhancing care efficiency, decision-making, and soldier safety. However, its adoption must be carefully managed to address ethical, technical, and operational challenges, ensuring that technology augments—rather than replaces—human expertise in life-critical scenarios.".

Since ChatGPT has been trained to be a friendly AI, it adds: "Let me know if you need this reformatted or tailored for a specific audience".

Perhaps advantage 2 is currently formulated somewhat too optimistically (whereas the development of autonomous AI-based surgical robots is also making significant progress). However, a true replacement of military medics with AI systems is not yet practical. The functionally still relatively one-dimensional „narrow "AI lacks the foresight that experienced practitioners in the field should have and which one might one day hope for in a „general AI "to be developed.

Nevertheless, Artificial Intelligence (AI)—a term that encompasses a whole range of technologies—is already omnipresent in the medical and military medical fields, and it requires no special prognostic skills to assume that this share will continue to grow significantly. ChatCPT's seemingly reasonable response to the aforementioned prompt demonstrates the capabilities—in this case, of a Large Language Model (LLM). The short overview provided by ChatGPT is of course not complete. As an example, it is lacking the aspects of potential moral injury for AI-applying physicians, when AI-based decisions turn out to have been faulty or had to be followed against their own conviction. It also doesn't address the non-validated use of AI by patients themselves and its impact on the physician-patient relationship.

The contributions in this volume begin to reflect on the ethical issues that the increasing use of AI in the military medical and humanitarian healthcare context can raise. While the technology of Artificial Intelligence will rapidly advance and open new perspectives, the ethical challenges may grow further, as also envisaged in the present studies.

1.1 To the Individual Contributions

Ethical codes for artificial intelligence are currently sprouting up in abundance. They are probably an expression of normative uncertainty and may also be intended to protect economic interests by reassuring consumers of certain concerns. In a kind of "philological" undertaking, **Oshri Bar-Gil** has taken on a selection of such ethical manifestos and examined them for central principles and tenets mentioned in these texts. As a qualitative study, he adds interpretations of the respective terms in order to highlight differences in the use of moral terms in the various texts and to provide a context-sensitive analysis. The occurrences examined concern the expressions "free market", "information security", "agency", "safety", "accountability", "values", "explainability", "fairness", "privacy", "responsibility", "equitability", "traceability", "governability" and "reliability". "Privacy", "values" and "fairness" took the top three places in the texts examined. But there are sector-specific differences: For example, university texts place greater emphasis on "fairness" and the avoidance of "algorithmic biases" than texts from industry, where security aspects are particularly emphasized. In a discussion section, Bar-Gil also makes recommendations for AI development that he has gained from the analysis of ethical codes. He calls for research to conduct "a comprehensive comparative study" with a larger number of documents examined and a "longitudinal examination of how these codes evolve over time".

Julian W. März and **Nikola Biller-Andorno** provide a thorough overview of the legal regulatory efforts for AI in their chapter on "Recent Trends in AI Law and Ethics and Their Implications for Military and Humanitarian Healthcare". After outlining the legal challenges posed by AI and emphasizing the need for special AI-related regulations, the authors focus in particular on the recently (2024) adopted AI Act of the European Union and the "Framework Convention on Artificial Intelligence, Human Rights, Democracy, and The Rule of Law" of the Council of Europe. The latter was also developed jointly with non-European states. Both groundbreaking texts contain many valuable standardization approaches, especially when it comes to high-risk fields such as healthcare. However, both sets of regulations explicitly leave out the area of military use of AI. This leaves significant normative uncertainty both in dual-use technologies and in the field of military medical action.

In a second part, the present volume addresses examples of AI usage in the miltary environment and asseses the philosophical and ethical challenges:

The results of AI-supported processes are often discussed as ethically problematic, for example, when discriminatory results are produced due to data bias. These are indeed serious difficulties. But ethics is not limited to testing functional appropriateness. Therefore, **Bernhard Koch** wants to draw attention to another problem—one that has more to do with our fundamental moral intuitions and basic moral reactions: We praise and criticize actions. The use of AI, however, makes it more difficult for us to praise, but in many cases makes criticism even more obvious. This could ultimately change our moral practice as a whole, so that we reach the point where we can no longer speak of good (military) doctors in the ethical sense.

Sheena M. Eagan explores the ethical challenges posed by the integration of continuous health-monitoring technologies in military settings. These technologies, which include wearables and implantable sensors, offer benefits such as tracking vital signs and enhancing performance, but also raise concerns about privacy, autonomy, and data misuse. The chapter highlights the need for context-specific ethical frameworks that balance operational effectiveness with the rights of service members. Eagan argues that while comprehensive monitoring may be justified during deployments, voluntary participation and informed consent should be prioritized in less demanding contexts. The chapter concludes with policy recommendations for the ethical implementation of health-monitoring technologies, calling for robust data protection measures and continuous dialogue with stakeholders.

In the next chapter, **Daniel Trusilo, Lauren Diaz** and **Ellie Tyler** extend the study of ethical issues associated with health monitoring by addressing the role of autonomous AI in acute triage situations. He presents an overview of DARPA's "In the Moment" (ITM) program, which seeks to develop AI capable of making high-stakes decisions, such as battlefield medical triage. The chapter highlights the ethical, legal, and societal implications (ELSI) of developing AI systems that operate without human oversight in critical environments. The author emphasizes that integrating ELSI research into technology development is essential for responsibly advancing AI. He discusses the particular challenges of establishing trust in AI that is designed to function independently as "human-off-the-loop algorithmic decision-making system" in life-or-death scenarios. The chapter concludes by advocating for the importance of ethical, legal, and societal implications of AI when it shall become successfully integrated into military medical practices.

AI systems pose ethical difficulties particularly where they can be used for both military and civilian purposes. **Martin Hähnel** examines this aspect of dual use in his contribution "A New Age of Dual-Use Technologies. Evaluating AI-induced Risks and Opportunities in Military Medical Ethics". Although the possibility of using technologies for good and bad purposes is inherent in technology, this problem is exacerbated with AI. To clarify the understanding of dual-use technologies, Hähnel presents a "trimodal property model" that guides tests in three respects: "(a) the extent to which a good is susceptible to misuse due to its intrinsic properties, (b) the intentions associated with a particular use and (c) the context in which the use takes place". In medicine, for example, AI-driven pharmaceutical software can become an agent of chemical warfare. The basis for weighing up the risks associated with the dual-use possibilities of technologies are shared values. Nevertheless, non-weighable aspects, such as human dignity, must also be taken into account. But even if this is successfully possible, an implementation problem still arises. From an ethical point of view, a "human-centered design" is therefore required that still assigns people a role in decision-making loops. Some of the problems that arise can be mitigated through accurate classification and "problem mirroring". Ultimately, however, "context-sensitive normative frameworks" are also required in the medical use of AI.

In his chapter "Meaningful Human Control over AI Military Decision Support Systems", **Atay Kozlovski** first presents a broad overview of the arguments for so-called Lethal Autonomous Weapons Systems (LAWS). He then focuses, with good reason, on so-called "Decision Support Systems", because we should not assume that human operators will no longer play any role in the future. AI is more often requested as a decision-making aid than as an independent decision-maker. In order to ensure that human decisions supported by AI do not ultimately become AI decisions ("automation bias"), Kozlovski believes that an ethical framework is required, which he calls "Meaningful Human Control" (MHC) with Santoni di Sio and van den Hoven, referring to the term in the debate about the ban on LAWS. This framework can and must now be unfolded into various aspects: Tracking, Tracing and Sociotechnical Embedding. By distinguishing between aspects—e.g. pace and scale of recommendations, training and contestation methods during embedding—this creates a multi-criterion catalog of conditions that should be queried when implementing AI-supported decision systems.

Florian Demont-Biaggi looks at the use of AI support systems from a leadership perspective. As an ethical approach, he favors a relational approach, which has proven itself in that it can explain different ways of dealing with AI in civilian and military settings. To do this, he compares two fictitious scenarios in which AI is supposed to help with a distribution issue: a civilian and a military scenario. In the civilian setting, the AI system does not function as its own relational reference value, but as a relation accelerator. This can have advantages and disadvantages, but its use cannot be ruled out in principle. In the military setting, Demont is much more skeptical, because here the leadership relationships and thus the decisions about military necessity must be taken into account. Deference to authority can be understood in terms of protected reasons. There are rules for restricting the autonomy of soldiers. Therefore, the positioning of an AI system also changes, and it is extremely questionable whether such a system can take on the "normative guardrails as military necessity or commander's intent.".

Practical questions about the use of AI always raise anthropological and epistemeological preliminary questions: If we hand over our own decisions or decisions to AI, the question is how we can justify this epistemeologically. **Hadeel Naeem** deals with this question in her chapter on "Integration, epistemic responsibility, and seamlessness". Actors form beliefs that form the basis of their actions. In everyday life, we no longer question the fact that we form such beliefs with the help of technology (e.g. the belief that it is 2 p.m. when we see on our watch that it should be 2 p.m.). In fact, what's more, we don't even think about the fact that we are incorporating technology into the formation of beliefs. With watches, this seems unproblematic to us. We use them "seamlessly". With AI, we still have problems, and probably rightly so. We can have true beliefs by chance, but knowledge obviously requires more. Knowledge includes the fact that the true belief was formed in a certain way. When using technology, reliability and repeatedly proven reliability can play a major role: "This watch has reliably shown me the correct time. If it now shows 2 p.m., I know that it is 2 p.m." But such "process reliabilism" may not seem sufficient to us. If we consider a special connection—an attitude—of the user of the technology to the technical device to be necessary, we can speak of "virtue reliabilism", for example if we have a decided trust in a technology. This attitude can in turn be based on an understanding of how the technology works. If we incorporate new belief-forming processes into our cognitive abilities, we can acquire new cognitive abilities. Therefore, towards the end of her article, Hadeel Naeem discusses cognitive integration as a "function of cooperation and interaction of beliefs and processes." Here she can distinguish between "a reflective and non-reflective route to interaction", whereby in her opinion both paths can lead "to responsible and seamless employment of technology".

A third section of the volume is focusing on ethics of AI and Big Data in Humanitarian contexts.

Kristin Bergtora Sandvik delves into the ethical issues that arise when humanitarian healthcare is intertwined with digital infrastructures, particularly focusing on the adoption of the rapidly growing capabilities of AI tools. The chapter provides an "ethics talk diagnostic" to understand how the ethics of humanitarian healthcare diverge from general humanitarian ethics. The author argues that while humanitarian aid faces foundational questions about its purpose and effectiveness, healthcare provision is more focused on the immediate ethical challenges posed by AI and digital technology, such as technofailure, risk, and harm. She discusses the "black box" aspect of modern AI tools and stresses the need for transparency, explainability, and intelligibility when using AI in humanitarian healthcare.

Ana Elisa Barbar and **Christina Wille** explore the ethical dimensions of global data collection on attacks against healthcare, emphasizing the need for data use that enhances healthcare protection and minimizes harm. The chapter highlights the importance of non-maleficence in data collection, ensuring that it does not increase the likelihood of violence. Barbar and Wille focus on an approach to gathering and verifying data on attacks against healthcare, which combines AI and human verification to minimize risk, as developed by the humanitarian organization Insecurity Insight. They critically examine how risks associated with data collection can sometimes be overemphasized, proposing that AI, with proper safeguards, can mitigate these risks. By detailing Insecurity Insight's experience with the use of data-collection technology, the authors provide a balanced view of how ethical data practices can be maintained in high-risk environments.

Focusing on the challenges of AI use for data collection in humanitarian environments, **Isabel Muñoz Beaulieu, Handreen Mohammed Saeed and Matthew Hunt** raise concerns about privacy, security, and bias in AI models trained on historical data. The chapter underscores the need for a strong ethical framework to prevent the misuse of sensitive data, particularly in contexts where vulnerable populations are involved. Additionally, the authors emphasizes the importance of accountability in AI-driven humanitarian operations, especially in resource allocation, where bias could perpetuate inequities. This final chapter of the book also calls for humanitarian organizations to invest in infrastructure to ensure responsible and ethical AI use, particularly during project closures.

During the initial phase of this volume's creation, until Bernhard Koch's change of position from Hamburg to Munich, Nicole Pörschmann from the Institute for Theology and Peace in Hamburg provided editorial support and editing. We would like to express our sincere thanks to her. Throughout the entire process of creating this book, the Series Editor Daniel Messelken was available as a helpful advisor and supporter. His commitment always deserves the greatest praise.

Bernhard Koch is a research associate at the Institut für Wehrmedizinische Ethik der Bundeswehr in Munich and adjunct professor of moral theology at the University of Freiburg. He worked at the Institute for Theology and Peace in Hamburg for more than 17 years, most recently as acting director. His research focuses on the ethics of (military) violence, International Humanitarian Law and new military technologies. He has been co-teacher ethics at the ICMM Courses on Military Medical Ethics for more than a decade.

David Winkler is director of the Center of Reference for Education on International Humanitarian Law and Ethics of the International Committee of Military Medicine. He is a medical doctor specializing in neurology and holds a Ph.D. in neurobiology. Colonel Winkler is a staff officer in the Swiss Armed Forces Medical Services Directorate. He conducts clinical and academic work at the University Hospital Basel, and the Cantonal Hospital Baselland, Switzerland.

Part I
The Current Attempts to Regulate AI

The first part of the book serves as an introduction to what AI is and how it is currently regulated.

Chapter 2
Examining Trends in AI Ethics Via Quantitative Discourse Analysis

Oshri Bar-Gil

2.1 Introduction

Artificial Intelligence (AI) has rapidly emerged as a transformative technology, permeating various sectors across different contexts, from healthcare and finance to transportation and national security. It is reshaping how nations operate, compete, and progress in the twenty-first century. The United States, China, and the European Union have been at the forefront of AI development and deployment, each approaching the technology with distinct national strategies and cultural considerations that reflect not only technological capabilities but also deeply rooted cultural values and governance structures (Cath 2018).

The importance of risk management and regulations in AI cannot be overstated. As AI systems become autonomous and more complex, their potential to affect human lives and society increases exponentially. AI development poses risks ranging from privacy violations and algorithmic bias to more extreme scenarios involving autonomous weapons or systemic economic disruptions (Coeckelbergh 2013; Floridi et al. 2018; Coeckelbergh 2020a). Effective risk management and regulation are essential for harnessing the benefits of AI while mitigating its potential harms. This involves not only technical safeguards but also legal frameworks, policy measures, and ethical guidelines that can adapt to the rapidly evolving AI landscape (AI HLEG 2019; Morley et al. 2020; Díaz-Rodríguez et al. 2023).

In recent years, there has been a proliferation of AI ethics guidelines, often referred to as an "ethics boom" in the field. By mid-2019, more than 80 AI ethics

O. Bar-Gil (✉)
The Program for Hermeneutics and Cultural Studies, Bar-Ilan University, Ramat Gan, Israel

The MA program in Organizational Psychology, Ruppin Academic Center, Kfar Monash, Israel
e-mail: Oshri.bar-gil@mail.huji.ac.il

B. Koch, D. Winkler (eds.), *Artificial Intelligence Ethics in Military Medicine and Humanitarian Healthcare*, Military and Humanitarian Health Ethics,
https://doi.org/10.1007/978-3-032-11331-3_2

documents had been published globally (Jobin et al. 2019), and this number had grown to over 200 in less than 2 years (Hagendorff 2020). This sudden surge can be attributed to several factors. First, the rapid and widespread adoption of AI technologies have outpaced existing regulatory frameworks, creating an urgent need for pre-regulatory ethical guidance (Morley et al. 2020). Second, high-profile incidents of AI failures or misuse have heightened public awareness and concern about the potential risks associated with AI systems (Whittlestone et al. 2019). Lastly, there is a growing recognition among governments, industry leaders, and academics that proactive ethical considerations is crucial for building public trust and ensuring the long-term, sustainable development of AI technologies (Floridi et al. 2020; Morley et al. 2020).

AI ethics frameworks play a crucial role in shaping the regulatory and normative contexts of AI development and use. They serve as a bridge between abstract ethical considerations and concrete practices, while also identifying specific domains where ethical concerns require attention and offer guidance to developers, policymakers, and users of AI systems (Boddington 2017; Morley et al. 2020). They represent a form of soft governance that provides a flexible and adaptable approach to address ethical concerns in a rapidly evolving technological landscape (Morley et al. 2021). Documents containing ethical frameworks are also rich sources for analysis. By analyzing these, we can gain valuable insights into three key areas:

1. **Social expectations**: National, cultural, industry-specific documents reflect the values, norms, and expectations of the societies that produce them. A comparison of ethical principles across different nations and industries can reveal varying priorities and cultural nuances when approaching AI ethics (Jobin et al. 2019).
2. **Law and regulations**: Although not legally binding, ethics frameworks often inform and influence the development of AI-related laws and regulations. They can serve as precursors to more formal governance. By identifying areas of ethical concern across various codes, policymakers can prioritize areas that require immediate regulatory attention (Morley et al. 2020; Díaz-Rodríguez et al. 2023).
3. **AI possibilities and imagination**: The ethical considerations addressed in these frameworks provide a window into how societies envision the future of AI, including its potential benefits and risks, whether real or imagined. By examining the areas of concern prioritized by different codes, we can gain insights into the anticipated risks in various contexts (Coeckelbergh 2020a).

Furthermore, analyzing these documents can reveal gaps and limitations in current ethics frameworks, track the evolution of ethical thinking about AI, and highlight practical challenges in translating ethical considerations into operational practices (Morley et al. 2020; Li et al. 2023).

This chapter provides an analysis of AI ethics frameworks across various contexts, focusing on their roles in shaping the relationships between national strategy, industry, academia, and society. The chapter begins with a literature review that explores existing AI ethics guidelines and frameworks, highlighting the gap between high-level ethical considerations, contextual interpretations, and practical implementation challenges. The methodology section then details our quantified qualitative approach to analyzing ten key documents sampled from different countries and institutions. Our results present the main ethical themes identified across these documents—distinguishing between fundamental ethical principles and broader areas of ethical concern—and offer a comparative analysis of how these considerations vary across national and sectoral contexts.

The discussion explores the implications of the findings for the AI ethics landscape by examining how key concepts are interpreted differently across sectors and countries, reflecting the complex interplay between cultural values, technological capabilities, and ethical considerations. Finally, we provide recommendations for the development, management, and implementation of AI systems in different contexts, particularly military medicine and humanitarian practices as is the focus of this book.

2.2 Literature Review

Jobin et al. (2019) conducted a comprehensive review of 84 AI ethics guidelines, revealing a global convergence around five core ethical principles: transparency, justice and fairness, non-maleficence, responsibility, and privacy. Their analysis highlighted that while these principles were common across documents, there was significant divergence in their interpretation and proposed implementation methods.

Building on this work, Hagendorff (2020) analyzed 22 prominent ethics guidelines, corroborating many of Jobin et al. (2019) findings, he noted that many guidelines failed to address important ethical issues, such as AI's environmental impact and potential to exacerbate global inequality. He and others also highlighted the lack of enforceability mechanisms in most guidelines, questioning their practical effectiveness in shaping AI development and deployment (Rességuier and Rodrigues 2020).

These studies have been instrumental in mapping the broad landscape of AI ethics guidelines. However, they primarily focus on identifying common principles, exploring the nuanced interpretations of these considerations, and their contextual applications across different institutional settings.

2.2.1 Ethical Considerations in AI Applications Across Different National Contexts

The application of AI ethics principles varies significantly across contexts, reflecting diverse cultural values, governance structures, and technological priorities. Cath et al. (2018) compared AI strategies in the United States, China, and the European Union, highlighting how different cultural and political contexts shape approaches to AI ethics and governance. In the European context, the EU's Ethics Guidelines for Trustworthy AI (AI HLEG 2019) emphasize human-centric AI development, focusing on principles such as human agency, privacy, and non-discrimination. In contrast, China's approach to AI ethics, as outlined in the Beijing AI Principles (Beijing AI Principles 2019), places greater emphasis on harmony and human-machine collaboration. The United States has witnessed the Department of Defense's AI Ethics Principles focus on issues particularly relevant to military applications of AI,[1] and National Security Commission on Artificial Intelligence (NSCAI) included sections on ethics as well.[2]

These variations in national approaches highlight the need for a more nuanced understanding of how ethical considerations are interpreted and applied in various cultural and institutional contexts. As Li et al. (2023) noted in their systematic review of medical AI ethics, considerations such as privacy, fairness, and transparency may be prioritized differently or interpreted through culturally specific ways across different contexts.

2.2.2 *Analysis of Principles Versus Analysis of Full Texts*

The studies of Jobin et al. (2019) and Hagendorff (2020) reveal a significant gap in the literature on AI ethics guidelines. Their analyses, like much of the existing research, focus primarily on identifying and categorizing high-level ethical principles. This approach, while valuable for understanding the broad landscape of AI ethics, fails to capture the nuanced interpretations and contextual meanings of these principles across different national and institutional settings.

As Morley et al. (2021) and others point out, there is a significant difference between stating ethical principles, understanding their intended meaning and operationalizing them in practice (Bankins 2021; Díaz-Rodríguez et al. 2023; Bar-Gil et al. 2024). The authors argue for the need to move beyond principle-based approaches to more concrete actionable guidelines for AI practitioners. This highlights a crucial limitation in the current literature: the lack of in-depth analysis of how ethical principles are interpreted, contextualized, and applied in different contexts.

Our research aims to fill this need for more nuanced, context-sensitive analyses by providing a deeper and more textually grounded understanding of AI ethics codes across different national and institutional contexts, moving beyond the identification of principles to explore their varied interpretations and applications. We address this gap by employing a quantified qualitative approach to analyze ten key AI ethics documents from various national and institutional contexts. Unlike previous studies that primarily identified common principles, our method allows us to

---

[1] https://www.defense.gov/News/Releases/Release/Article/2091996/dod-adopts-ethical-principles-for-artificial-intelligence/

[2] https://reports.nscai.gov/final-report/

examine the documents as a comprehensive corpus from which we can extract more nuanced meanings and interpretations to uncover patterns and variations that may not be apparent from previous analyses (Jobin et al. 2019; Hagendorff 2020; Li et al. 2023). This approach can reveal how seemingly universal principles such as "privacy" or "fairness" may be interpreted and operationalized differently across various institutional contexts. Furthermore, this comprehensive textual analysis can illuminate the underlying interests and priorities that shape different AI ethics codes, revealing how national security concerns, economic priorities, and cultural values influence the formulation and emphasis of ethical frameworks across different contexts.

2.3 Methodology

This study employed a quantified qualitative approach to analyze ten AI ethics documents from various national and institutional contexts. This methodology combines the systematic rigor of quantitative frequency analysis with the interpretive depth of qualitative content analysis, allowing us to examine textual data while preserving the richness and complexity of qualitative information (Given 2008).

2.3.1 Sampling and Selection Criteria

Our study focused on ten key AI ethics documents sampled from various countries and institutions. The sampling process involved ranking potential documents through evaluation by a three-member committee comprising an ethics scholar, legal practitioner, and industry representative. The selection criteria were designed to ensure a diverse and representative sample, following the principles of purposive sampling in qualitative research (Mujere 2016).

Geographic diversity: We included documents from different regions to capture various cultural and political perspectives.

Institutional diversity: Our sample includes documents from governmental bodies, international organizations, academic institutions, and industry leaders.

Relevance and influence: We prioritized documents that had a significant influence in shaping AI ethics discourse or policy.

Temporal relevance: To ensure contemporary relevance and analytical consistency, we focused on documents published between 2018 and 2021, providing a three-year window that captures recent developments in AI ethics discourse while maintaining sufficient temporal depth for comparative analysis.

Israeli context inclusion: The sample included a higher proportion of Israeli documents to enable a comparative analysis with Israeli AI ethics frameworks, reflecting one of the project's broader research objectives. While this creates intentional overrepresentation in our sample, the comparative analysis with Israeli

Table 2.1 The final sample list included for analysis

Name of Document	Issuer	Sector	Publication Date
National Security Commission on artificial intelligence	US (special commission)	National	2020
AI principles: Recommendations on the ethical use of artificial intelligence by the Department of Defense	US (DOD)	Military/ defense	2019
AI in support of defense	France (MOD)	Military/ defense	2019
High-level expert group on artificial intelligence (AIHLEG)	EU (expert group of the European Commission)	National	2019
Responsible AI for India	National Institution for transforming India (India)	National	2021
Everyday ethics for artificial intelligence	IBM	Industry	2019
AI now report	AI now research report (US)	Academic	2019
AI4People ethical framework for society	AI4People scientific committee (EU)	Academic	2018
Subcommittee of the Israeli National Intelligent Systems	Israeli parliament sub-committee	National (Israel)	2019
Artificial intelligence, data science, and smart robotics in Israel	Samuel Neaman research institute (Israel)	Academic (Israel)	2018

documents falls outside the scope of this chapter and will be addressed in subsequent research (Table 2.1).

This diverse sample allowed us to examine how different types of institutions and national contexts approach AI ethics, aligned with the comparative approach suggested by Cath et al. (2018) in their analysis of national AI strategies.

2.3.2 *Preparation, Coding and Analysis*

We utilized MAXQDA, a specialized software for qualitative and mixed-methods research, to support our analytical process. MAXQDA facilitated the systematic organization, coding, and analysis of textual data through its integrated capabilities for both qualitative content analysis and quantitative frequency analysis, enabling comprehensive examination of AI ethics documents (Kuckartz and Rädiker 2019). While MAXQDA provided essential computational support for data organization and frequency analysis, the interpretive core of our analysis relied on human coding and contextual interpretation to ensure nuanced understanding of ethical concepts across different institutional contexts.

Textual Analysis Process

This approach ensured that our analysis captured not just explicit mentions of ethical principles but also implicit references and contextual nuances that might be missed by purely automated methods or Large language models (Saldaña 2013; Wachinger et al. 2024; Wachinger et al. 2024). Our text analysis process involved several stages, drawing on established methods in qualitative content analysis (Krippendorff 2018):

1. **Initial coding**: A single researcher identified and coded relevant sections of each document using a predefined coding scheme based on established ethical principles from existing literature (Jobin et al. 2019; Hagendorff 2020) supplemented by emergent themes identified during preliminary document review. Using the coding functionality in MAXQDA, we systematically coded each document according to our predefined scheme, which included common ethical principles (e.g., privacy, fairness, and transparency) and emergent themes.
2. **Lexical frequency analysis**: For each identified ethical principle or theme, the researcher compiled comprehensive lists of associated terms, synonyms, and phrases through an iterative review of document language. These lexical inventories captured the diverse terminological variations through which ethical concepts are expressed across different institutional and national contexts, ensuring comprehensive coverage of concept-related vocabulary.
3. **Quantitative frequency analysis**: Using MAXQDA's lexical search functionality, we systematically quantified the occurrence frequency of words and phrases from each principle-specific word list across the complete document corpus, generating both absolute and relative frequencies normalized by document length to enable cross-document comparison.
4. **Contextual discourse analysis**: We examined the context in which key terms and concepts appeared, allowing us to interpret how different codes conceptualize and prioritize various ethical principles.
5. **Comparative analysis**: We conducted systematic cross-document comparison examining both quantitative frequency patterns and qualitative contextual usage of ethical principles to identify convergent themes, divergent emphases, and sector-specific variations in ethical conceptualization.
6. **Document clustering analysis**: We employed exploratory document clustering techniques using MAXQDA similarity analysis functions to group documents based on their lexical mapping. This computational approach revealed macro-level similarities and differences in how various institutions approach AI ethics, following established text mining methodologies (Ignatow and Mihalcea 2017) while supplementing algorithmic clustering with interpretive analysis of document positioning.

This multi-stage process allowed us to move beyond a surface-level analysis of stated principles to uncover deeper insights into how different institutions conceptualize and operationalize AI ethics across different national and institutional contexts.

2.4 Results

The word cloud visualization in Fig. 2.1 reveals the predominant themes across all analyzed documents. The term 'Technology' dominates the discourse, emphasizing the central focus on managing technological development and its societal impacts. Governance-related terms such as 'government,' 'policy,' and 'national' are prominent, indicating a strong emphasis on institutional roles in shaping the AI landscape. Terms such as 'innovation,' 'development,' and 'emergence' suggest a future oriented approach. The prominence of "human" reflects a human-centric focus in many AI ethics frameworks. Security-related terms highlight concerns regarding AI in defense and national security contexts. The prominence of verbs like "ensure" and "require" point to the prescriptive nature of these guidelines. The presence of "China" might indicate geopolitical considerations that dominate some of the AI ethics discourse. Notably, explicitly ethical terms are less prominent, suggesting a focus on practical governance and legislation rather than on abstract ethical concepts.

Overall, Fig. 2.1 depicts AI ethics as a multifaceted field, balancing technological innovation with governance structures, security concerns, and human values. This underscores the need for coordinated efforts across various sectors to effectively guide AI development and deployment.

Fig. 2.1 General word cloud of AI documents

2.4.1 Identified Ethical Principles and Concerns

Our analysis revealed 14 recurring ethical concepts that form the foundation of AI ethics discourse across different sectors and countries. These considerations encompass both fundamental principles and operational domains in which ethical concerns arise.

1. **Free market**: Emphasizes the importance of maintaining open competition and innovation in AI development while addressing potential conflicts between market dynamics and ethical imperatives. This suggests that ethical AI should not stifle market dynamics but rather encourage fair competition. As Hagendorff (2020) noted, this concept often appears in tension with regulatory approaches to AI ethics.
2. **Information security**: This operational consideration with ethical implications focuses on protecting AI systems and the data they process, raising questions about the balance between security measures and privacy rights. It is crucial for maintaining trust in AI systems and protecting sensitive information (Morley et al. 2021).
3. **Agency:** Refers to the capacity of individuals to make their own free choices in AI-mediated environments. This emphasizes the importance of human autonomy and decision-making power in the face of increasingly autonomous AI systems (Coeckelbergh 2020a; Prunkl 2022).
4. **Safety**: This principle underscores the need for AI systems to be designed and operated in a manner that minimizes risks to human life and well-being. It encompasses both physical safety and broader societal safety concerns (Shneiderman 2020), including safeguards against the sci-fi scenario of machines running wild (Coeckelbergh 2020a).
5. **Accountability**: Accountability in AI ethics refers to the ability to determine and address responsibility for the actions and decisions of AI systems. This principle is crucial for ensuring that there are clear lines of responsibility in AI development and deployment, especially in the military domain, as demanded by the IHL (Coeckelbergh 2020b; Morgan et al. 2020).
6. **Values**: This principle emphasizes the importance of aligning AI systems with specific human and cultural values. It recognizes that AI should be developed and used in ways that respect and uphold diverse cultural norms and ethical standards, such as human rights and other preferred values (Floridi et al. 2018; The Human Rights Directorate 2020).
7. **Explainability**: This principle, sometimes refers to interpretability, calls for AI systems to be designed in such a way that their decision-making processes can be understood by their human users. This is crucial for building trust and enabling meaningful oversight (Coeckelbergh 2020b).
8. **Fairness**: Fairness in AI ethics aims to ensure that AI systems do not discriminate against individuals or groups based on protected characteristics, such as race, gender, or age. This is a complex concept that involves both individual and group considerations (Reagan 2021; Pfeiffer et al. 2023).

9. **Privacy**: This principle emphasizes the protection of personal data and individuals' rights to control information about themselves. In the context of AI, privacy concerns are particularly salient owing to the large amounts of data often required for AI systems (Banciu and Cîrnu 2022; Willems et al. 2022).
10. **Responsibility**: Closely related to accountability and "trustworthiness," responsibility in AI ethics refers to the obligation of AI developers and users to consider and address the consequences of AI systems. It emphasizes the proactive consideration of potential impacts (Coeckelbergh 2020b; Díaz-Rodríguez et al. 2023).
11. **Equitability**: This principle goes beyond fairness to emphasize the need for AI systems to promote equal opportunities and reduce inequality. It recognizes AI's potential to either exacerbate or mitigate societal inequities (Friis and Riley 2023).
12. **Traceability**: Traceability refers to the ability to track the development process of AI systems, including the data used, algorithms employed, and decisions made during development. This principle is crucial for accountability and addressing potential issues (Morley et al. 2021).
13. **Governability**: This principle emphasizes the need for AI systems to be subject to appropriate governance frameworks. It recognizes the importance of regulatory oversight and the need for AI systems to be controllable by human operators (Cath 2018).
14. **Reliability**: Reliability in AI ethics refers to the consistency and dependability of AI systems. This principle emphasizes the importance of AI systems performing as intended and producing consistent results under varying conditions (Ryan 2020).

The analysis revealed that interpretation and emphasis varied significantly across national and institutional contexts, reflecting diverse cultural values, governance structures, and technological priorities.

2.4.2 Document Comparison Analysis

The frequency analysis of ethical principles across the documents reveals significant variations in emphasis and coverage, as seen in Fig. 2.2. Document length varied considerably across our sample. The National Security Commission on Artificial Intelligence (US) document demonstrates the most comprehensive coverage, leading in frequency across most categories and accounting for a substantial portion of total mentions (1353 out of 2351). In contrast, some documents such as the "Artificial Intelligence, Data Science, and Smart Robotics" and the "Subcommittee of the Israeli National Intelligent Systems" offer very few mentions across all principles. To engage with it, the analysis was normalized according to the document size to reflect the key concepts considering the volume of the text.

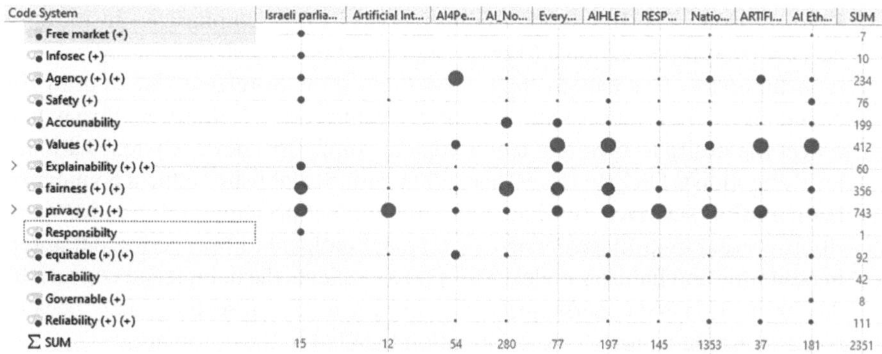

Fig. 2.2 Frequency by document and total numbers

1. Privacy emerged as the most frequently discussed consideration, achieving the highest total frequency across all documents (743 mentions) and appearing consistently in medium-to-large volume texts.
2. Values (reflecting human and cultural) are the second most discussed topic, with 412 total mentions.
3. Fairness is the third most common principle, mentioned 356 times. This is particularly emphasized in the AI Now 2018 document.
4. Agency and Accountability also receive significant attention, with dominance of agency in the document of AI4People stressing the key role of human agency.
5. Some principles, such as free market, information security, responsibility, and Governability, receive relatively little attention across most documents.
6. Individual documents demonstrate distinct prioritization patterns. The AI Now 2018 report focuses heavily on fairness and accountability, while IBM's Ethics in Everyday Life 2019 emphasizes values and fairness as primary concerns.
7. The EU AIHLEG document shows a more balanced distribution across multiple principles, indicating a comprehensive and balanced approach to AI ethics.

This analysis reveals that while there are common themes across AI ethics frameworks, there are significant differences in the emphasis placed on various principles, reflecting diverse priorities and approaches to AI governance across different contexts. This will be discussed in the subsequent section.

2.4.3 Sector Comparison Analysis

One explanation for the variance in the documents was the sector in which they had been covered and published.

Figure 2.3 presents the relative frequency of AI ethics principles across five categories of code origins: Academic, Industry, Israeli, Military/defense, and National. In this figure, we can notice some key trends:

1. **Free market:** The free-market concept is primarily emphasized in military/defense (6.3%) and national (3.6%) codes but is notably absent in academic and industry codes. This pattern suggests that government-related sectors prioritize balancing AI innovation with regulatory frameworks. Military emphasis may reflect the desire to maintain technological competitiveness, whereas national-level attention is likely to foster innovation within established ethical boundaries.
2. **Information security:** Similar to the free market principle, information security is present in military/defense (3.1%) and national (3.6%) codes, but absent in academic and industry codes. This pattern reflects the heightened concern for data protection and cybersecurity in government-related sectors, likely because of the sensitive nature of the information handled in these domains.
3. **Agency:** Agency is prominently featured in academic (10.5%), national (10.7%), and military/defense (9.4%) codes, but notably absent in industry codes. This pattern suggests a strong focus on human autonomy in theoretical and governance-oriented approaches to AI ethics, while the industry may address this concern under other principles or focus on immediately implementable guidelines.
4. **Safety**: Safety receives attention across all sectors, with the highest emphasis in industry (16.7%), followed by academic and national codes (both 10.5% and 10.7%, respectively), and slightly lower in military/defense (6.3%). This universal concern underscores the recognized importance of developing safe AI systems, with the industry's high focus likely driven by product liability and consumer trust considerations.
5. **Accountability:** Accountability is emphasized across sectors, with the highest focus on industry (16.7%), followed by military/defense (9.4%), national (7.1%), and academic (5.3%) codes. This pattern might reflect the practical need for clear lines of accountability in AI development and deployment and

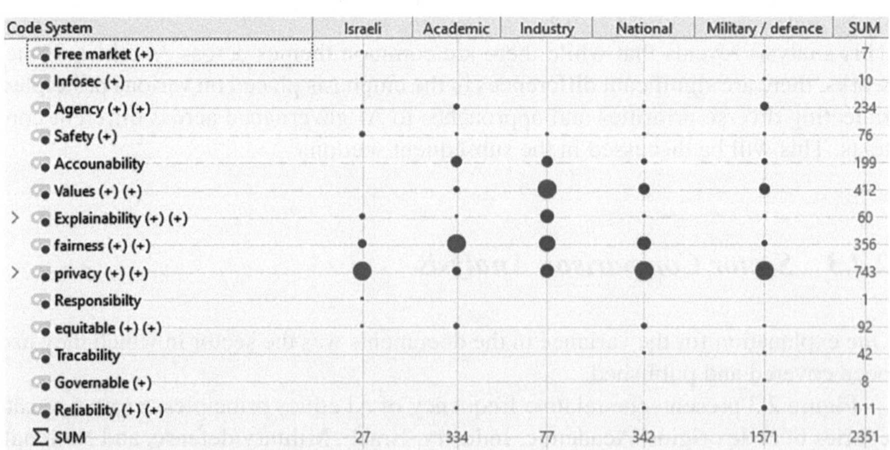

Fig. 2.3 Concept frequency by sector

decision making, particularly in commercial and high-stake applications, such as military use.

6. **Values**: Human and cultural values received consistent attention across academic (10.5%), industry (16.7%), military/defense (9.4%), and national (10.7%) codes. This uniform emphasis indicates the broad recognition of the importance of aligning AI systems with societal and ethical values across all sectors.
7. **Explainability**: Explainability was most emphasized in industry codes (16.7%), followed by national (10.7%), military/defense (6.3%), and academic (5.3%) codes. This pattern suggests a strong practical focus on transparent AI systems in commercial applications, which are likely driven by user trust and regulatory considerations. Some have suggested that explainability is considered a technical trait, not surprisingly that the industry will focus on it (Coeckelbergh 2020b).
8. **Fairness:** Fairness received high attention across all sectors, with the highest in academic (15.8%) and industry (16.7%) codes, followed by national (10.7%) and military/defense (9.4%) codes. This consistent emphasis might reflect the impact of critical data theories on academy and national nondiscrimination laws at the national level.
9. **Privacy:** Privacy, such as fairness, is consistently emphasized across sectors: academic (15.8%), industry (16.7%), military/defense (9.4%), and national (10.7%). This uniform emphasis underscores the critical importance of data protection and individual privacy rights in AI development across all domains.
10. **Responsibility:** Interestingly, responsibility is only explicitly mentioned in the national codes (3.6%). This could indicate that other sectors might address this concept under different principles, such as accountability, or that national documents see a unique need to emphasize the broader societal responsibilities of AI developers and users.
11. **Equitability:** Equitability shows varied emphasis, with the highest in academic codes (15.8%), followed by military/defense (9.4%) and national (7.1%) codes, but absent in industry codes. This pattern suggests a stronger focus on AI's role in addressing societal inequalities in theoretical and governance-oriented approaches, a pattern similar to fairness.
12. **Traceability:** Traceability was most prominent in military/defense codes (9.4%), followed by national codes (3.6%), but absent in academic and industry codes. This emphasis on government-related sectors likely reflects the need for detailed audit trails in high-stakes or security-sensitive AI applications. Interestingly, this is not parallel to the pattern noticed on the principal of accountability.
13. **Governability**: Governability is uniquely present in military/defense codes (3.1%) and practically absent in all others. This exclusive presence may indicate a specific need for strict human control over AI systems in military applications.
14. **Reliability:** Reliability is emphasized in academic (10.5%), military/defense (9.4%), and national (7.1%) codes, but absent in industry codes. This pattern suggests a focus on the dependability of AI systems in critical applications,

whereas the industry might address this concern under other principles, such as safety or accountability.

Sectorial Analysis

1. **Academic Sector:** The academic approach to AI ethics is characterized by a notable emphasis on fairness, accountability, privacy, and equitability. This focus reflects the sector's role in theoretical exploration and critical analysis of AI's societal impacts. Academics have paid significant attention to the issues of algorithmic bias, data ethics, and digital rights, as evidenced by the high emphasis on fairness and privacy published in journal articles (Marcoux 2025). The balanced consideration of agency, safety, and values demonstrates a holistic approach, weighing both the philosophical implications and practical concerns of AI development. Interestingly, the academic sector does not emphasize principles like free market dynamics or information security, suggesting a preference for addressing fundamental ethical issues rather than specific implementation concerns. This approach aligns with the academic tradition of questioning underlying assumptions and exploring the long-term societal implications of technological advancements (Marcoux 2025).
2. **Industry Sector:** Industry's approach to AI ethics, as reflected in our data, shows a pragmatic focus on principles directly relevant to product development and public trust. There is an equal emphasis on safety, accountability, values, explainability, fairness, and privacy. This pattern likely stems from the industry's need to address liability concerns, build user trust, and respond to regulatory requirements. For instance, the focus on explainability may be driven by the need to justify AI decisions to users and stakeholders (Blancaflor et al. 2024). Attention to values, fairness, and privacy suggests the industry's responsiveness to public and academic scrutiny and growing societal concerns about AI's impact. Notably absent are principles such as free market dynamics and equitability, indicating a preference for immediately actionable and product-relevant ethical considerations over engaging with broader societal issues.
3. **Military/Defense Sector**: The military and defense approach to AI ethics is marked by a relatively even distribution across many principles, reflecting the complex and high-stakes nature of AI in military and defense applications. Uniquely, this sector includes considerations of free market principles, information security, and governability. The inclusion of free market considerations might relate to maintaining technological advantages and fostering innovation in defense technologies (Morgan et al. 2020). Unsurprisingly, there is an emphasis on information security, given the sensitive nature of military applications. The attention paid to traceability and governability, which is distinctive to this sector, likely stems from the need for strict control and accountability in military AI systems.
4. **National Sector**: National-level AI ethics demonstrate a broad, balanced approach, reflecting the need to address diverse societal concerns. There is a

slight preference for principles like agency, safety, values, explainability, fairness, and privacy, suggesting an attempt to protect citizen rights and uphold societal values. Uniquely, national codes include mentions of responsibility, possibly emphasizing the societal obligations of AI developers and users. The inclusion of free market and information security principles shows the consideration of both the economic and national security implications of AI. This balanced distribution across multiple principles suggests an attempt to address the concerns of various stakeholders, from individual citizens to industry players and security experts. Thus, the national approach serves as a kind of synthesis that attempts to reconcile the diverse perspectives represented in other sectors' approaches to AI ethics.

In conclusion, the sectoral analysis revealed how different institutional actors prioritize and interpret AI ethics principles based on their unique roles, responsibilities, and concerns. While there are common threads across sectors, such as the importance of fairness and privacy, varying emphases highlight the need for a nuanced, context-sensitive approach to AI ethics. These differences also underscore the importance of cross-sector dialogue and collaboration in developing comprehensive and widely applicable AI ethics frameworks that can address the complex, multifaceted challenges posed by AI technologies.

2.4.4 Document Cluster Analysis

The exploratory document clustering analysis in Fig. 2.4 offers insights into the similarities, differences, and potential relationships among various AI ethics guidelines across different sectors and organizations.

The clustering analysis reveals a distinct distribution of documents across the visualization space, indicating significant diversity in AI ethics approaches, even among documents from similar temporal periods or institutional sectors.

Notably, we observed three main clusters:

1. The right-side cluster encompasses both US government documents (NSCAI and DOD), suggesting convergent approaches in national-level AI ethics frameworks.
2. Everyday ethics (IBM, 2019) stands alone on the far left, indicating a potentially unique approach from the industry perspective, as this is the only industry-based document.
3. A central cluster comprises all other documents. This grouping implies shared themes or approaches among these documents, despite their different origins and publication years. AIHLEG (2019) suggests a balanced posture in the middle. The positioning of France MOD's "AI in support of defense" at the bottom right suggests that it may have distinct characteristics or approaches to AI ethics.

Notably, temporal factors do not appear to drive clustering patterns, as documents from different publication years are distributed across the visualization space rather

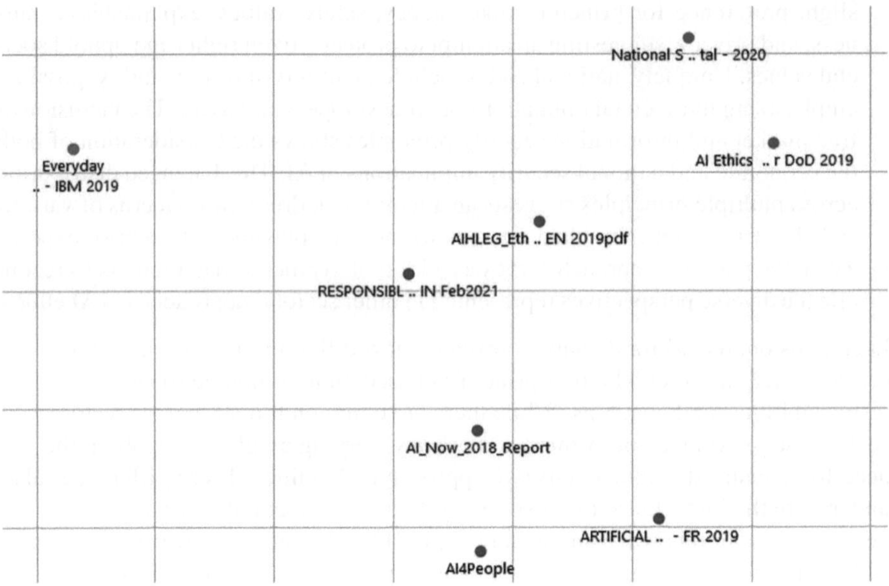

Fig. 2.4 Document cluster analysis

than being grouped chronologically. This suggests that the evolution of AI ethics over time may not be linear or uniform across all sectors.

The diverse positioning of documents from different sectors (e.g., industry, academia, and government) indicates that sector-specific concerns and approaches play a significant role in shaping AI ethics guidelines. However, the central cluster also suggests the convergence of ideas across different types of institutions.

This analysis highlights the complex and multifaceted nature of approaches to AI ethics. This underscores the need for continued dialogue across sectors and the importance of considering both universal ethical principles and sector-specific concerns in developing comprehensive AI ethics frameworks.

2.5 Discussion

Our analysis of AI ethics documents across different sectors yields significant insights into the development of ethical frameworks across various institutional contexts. These findings demonstrate that effective AI governance strategies must adopt a multifaceted and nuanced approach to address the complex ethical landscape of AI development and deployment. The varying emphasis on ethical considerations across sectors underscores the need for a comprehensive and flexible governance framework. While certain considerations such as privacy, fairness, and human values emerge as universal concerns that should form the foundation of any

AI ethics strategy, the observed disparities in other areas highlight the critical importance of accommodating sector-specific requirements.

Our findings reveal a significant gap between theoretical ethical considerations and practical implementation. The observed discrepancy between academic/national frameworks and industry codes, particularly in areas such as human agency, highlights the urgent need for policy interventions that can effectively bridge this divide. Such policies should encourage the integration of theoretical ethical foundations into real-world AI development and deployment.

Furthermore, the diverse emphasis on considerations such as equitability, traceability, and governability across sectors indicates that some aspects of AI ethics require sector-specific guidelines within a broad regulatory framework. Policy interventions should actively promote the consideration of ethical elements that are currently underrepresented in certain sectors, thereby ensuring a comprehensive approach to AI ethics across all institutional domains.

These findings underscore the multifaceted challenges policymakers face when developing comprehensive and effective AI ethics frameworks. Effective frameworks must simultaneously address universal ethical concerns, accommodate sector-specific requirements, and bridge the persistent gap between ethical foundations and practical implementation. A layered governance approach that combines overarching national principles with sector-specific guidelines and robust mechanisms for cross-sector collaboration offers a promising path for navigating this intricate ethical landscape. By adopting such a nuanced and adaptive framework, policymakers can ensure that AI development aligns with societal values and ethical standards across diverse sectors and applications.

Our analysis reveals the importance of distinguishing between core ethical principles (such as fairness, privacy, and human dignity) and operational areas in which ethical concerns arise (such as information security, market dynamics, and technical reliability). This distinction has significant implications for policy development and implementation. While fundamental ethical principles provide the normative foundation for AI governance, areas of ethical concern identify specific domains that require targeted attention and sector-specific guidelines.

2.5.1 Changing Meanings of Key Concepts

The cross-sectoral analysis of AI ethics codes reveals a nuanced and evolving understanding of fundamental concepts, including intention, autonomy, agency, and independence. These concepts, which are central to the AI ethics discourse, demonstrate varying interpretations depending on the institutional context and sector in which they are applied.

The concept of intention, traditionally associated with human decision-making processes, undergoes significant recontextualization within the discourse of AI systems. In academic contexts, intention is typically examined through philosophical lenses, questioning whether AI systems possess genuine intentionality. Conversely, industry and military/defense frameworks interpret intention more pragmatically as the designed purpose or programmed objective of an AI system. This shift reflects the growing recognition that as AI systems become more sophisticated, the line between programmed behavior and emergent "intentions" becomes increasingly blurred.

Autonomy, a consideration heavily emphasized in academic and national frameworks, assumes different meanings across institutional sectors. In academic discourse, autonomy typically refers to the preservation of human autonomy when interacting with AI systems, emphasizing the critical importance of maintaining human agency and decision-making authority. By contrast, industry frameworks tend to focus on AI system autonomy, examining the degree to which these systems can operate independently of human oversight. Military/defense texts present yet another perspective in which autonomy is often framed in terms of the balance between human control and AI capabilities in critical decision-making scenarios.

Independence and agency, while not always explicitly mentioned, are implicit in discussions of AI capabilities across all sectors. In academic and national texts, independence is often framed as a potential concern, with an emphasis on maintaining human oversight and control. Conversely, industry documents may present independence as a desirable feature of AI systems, highlighting the efficiency and reduced need for human intervention. Military/defense documents often grapple with the tension between the potential tactical advantages of independent AI systems and the ethical and strategic risks they pose.

These shifting interpretations reflect the dynamic nature of AI development and its evolving ethical implications. As AI systems become increasingly sophisticated, our conceptual understanding of these fundamental elements continues to evolve. The varying emphases across sectors underscore the urgent need for sustained interdisciplinary dialogue to develop shared vocabulary and conceptual frameworks for these crucial elements of AI ethics discourse. These evolving interpretations underscore the importance of context-specific ethical frameworks. What constitutes appropriate autonomy or agency for an AI system differs substantially between applications such as commercial chatbots and military decision-support systems. Therefore, national AI strategies and ethical guidelines must be sufficiently flexible to accommodate these nuanced interpretations while maintaining clear and consistent ethical foundations.

2.5.2 Research Limitations and Future Research Suggestions

This study provides valuable insights into AI ethics across different sectors. It is important to acknowledge several limitations that shape the scope and generalizability of our findings.

First, our analysis was based on a limited sample of AI ethics documents. Although we strived to include diverse and influential documents, the relatively small sample size may not fully capture the entire landscape of the AI ethics guidelines. This limitation potentially affects the generalizability of our findings to the broader field of AI ethics.

Second, our study represents a snapshot in time, capturing the state of AI ethics codes at a specific moment with documents written between 2018–2021. Given the rapidly evolving nature of AI technology and its ethical implications, this temporal limitation means that our findings may not reflect the most current developments in the field.

Despite our efforts to maintain objectivity, the categorization of ethical principles and interpretation of document clustering results may be influenced by researcher bias.

Furthermore, our analysis focuses primarily on the content of ethics codes and does not directly examine how these principles are implemented in practice. This gap between the stated ethical guidelines and real-world applications represents a significant area for future research.

Future research should address the limitations of this study by expanding the scope and depth of the AI ethics analysis. To enhance and generalize the findings of this research, we suggest a comprehensive comparative study encompassing a broader range of documents globally, a longitudinal examination of how these codes evolve over time, and in-depth case studies on the practical implementation of ethical guidelines. This multifaceted approach would provide a more nuanced, dynamic, and actionable understanding of AI ethics across diverse contexts, bridging the gap between theoretical principles and their real-world applications.

Based on this study, the following actions emerge as critical for addressing ethical concerns in AI:

- **Developing sector-specific ethical guidelines**: Our analysis revealed significant variations in ethical priorities across sectors. To address this, there is an immediate need to develop sector-specific ethical guidelines that complement overarching principles. These guidelines should address the unique ethical challenges and priorities identified in each sector to ensure targeted and effective ethical governance.
- **Establishing cross-sector dialogue mechanisms**: The study highlighted gaps in ethical considerations between sectors, particularly between academic/national codes and industry practices. Implementing regular cross-sector forums or working groups can facilitate knowledge sharing and help bridge these gaps, thus ensuring a more comprehensive approach to AI ethics.
- **Enhance focus on underrepresented principles**: Our analysis identified certain ethical principles (such as equitability in industry codes) that were underrepresented in some sectors. Immediate action should be taken to promote awareness and integration of these underrepresented principles in sectors where they are currently lacking.
- **Implementation of ethical principal operationalization processes**: The study revealed a disconnect between high-level ethical principles and their practical implementation. Developing clear processes for operationalizing ethical principles into concrete practices and metrics is crucial. This could involve creat-

ing sector-specific frameworks to translate ethical guidelines into actionable steps.

These actions directly addressed the key findings and gaps identified in our analysis. By focusing on these areas, we can work towards a more cohesive, comprehensive, and effective approach to AI ethics that is responsive to the needs and challenges of each sector while maintaining core ethical principles.

2.6 Conclusion

This study analyzed AI ethics documents across diverse institutional contexts, including academic, industrial, military/defense, and national settings, revealing significant variations in ethical priorities and emphases. Our findings highlight the complex landscape of AI ethics, where principles such as privacy, fairness, and human values are universally emphasized, while others such as free market considerations, information security, and equitability receive varying degrees of attention across sectors.

These evolving interpretations underscore the importance of context-specific ethical frameworks. What constitutes appropriate autonomy or agency for an AI system differs substantially between applications such as commercial chatbots and military decision-support systems. Therefore, national AI strategies and ethical guidelines must be sufficiently flexible to accommodate these nuanced interpretations while maintaining clear and consistent ethical foundations. Our research underscores that while certain ethical principles are universally recognized, their interpretation and application can vary significantly across different national and cultural contexts. This variation reflects diverse societal values, governance structures, and technological priorities.

In an increasingly interconnected global environment, where technologies often transcend national boundaries, establishing a shared understanding of AI ethics becomes crucial. However, this shared understanding must be sufficiently flexible to accommodate national and cultural specificities. Ethical frameworks governing AI development and deployment must strike a careful balance between universal principles and local contexts, ensuring that AI technologies respect and uphold diverse cultural norms and societal values.

Future research should shift toward more interdisciplinary approaches to AI ethics, integrating perspectives from technologists, ethicists, social scientists, policymakers, and stakeholders across various sectors. This collaborative approach is crucial for addressing the complex, multidimensional ethical challenges posed by emerging AI technologies (Bar-Gil, 2024). The field will likely witness an increased focus on the practical implementation of ethical considerations, moving beyond theoretical frameworks to develop concrete strategies for embedding ethics into AI development and deployment processes. This evolution may involve creating new methodologies for ethical impact assessments, developing comprehensive AI ethics education programs, and establishing global standards for ethical AI governance. Furthermore, as AI systems become increasingly autonomous and their decision-making processes become more complex, future research will necessarily address profound ethical questions surrounding the evolving relationship between humans, society, and AI. These investigations will not only expand the boundaries of our understanding of intelligence and ethics but may also fundamentally reshape our conceptual frameworks regarding responsibility, autonomy, and human-machine interactions (Bar-Gil, 2025).

Ultimately, the future of AI ethics research has the potential to shape the trajectory of one of the most transformative technologies of our time. Through continued critical examination, debate, and refinement of our ethical approaches to AI, we can work toward creating a future in which technological advancement proceeds in harmony with human flourishing, social justice, and global well-being.

References

AI HLEG. 2019. *Ethics Guidelines for Trustworthy Ai–High-Level Expert Group on Artificial Intelligence*. Brussels: European Commission.

Banciu, Doina, and Carmen Elena Cîrnu. 2022. AI Ethics and Data Privacy Compliance. In *2022 14th International Conference on Electronics, Computers and Artificial Intelligence (ECAI)*, 1–5. https://doi.org/10.1109/ECAI54874.2022.9847510.

Bankins, Sarah. 2021. The Ethical Use of Artificial Intelligence in Human Resource Management: A Decision-Making Framework. *Ethics and Information Technology* 23:841–854. https://doi.org/10.1007/s10676-021-09619-6.

Bar-Gil, Oshri, Tom Ron, and Ofir Czerniak. 2024. AI for the People? Embedding AI Ethics in HR and People Analytics Projects. *Technology in Society* 102527. https://doi.org/10.1016/j.techsoc.2024.102527.

Bar-Gil, Oshri. 2024. Redefining Human-Centered AI: The Human Impact of AI-Based Recommendation Engines. In *Human-Centered AI A Multidisciplinary Perspective for Policy-Makers, Auditors, and Users*, edited by Catherine Régis, Jean-Louis Denis, Maria Luciana Axente, and Atsuo Kishimoto. Taylor & Francis. https://doi.org/10.1201/9781003320791-5.

Bar-Gil, Oshri. 2025. The Google self as digital human twin: implications for agency, memory, and identity. *AI & Society*. https://doi.org/10.1007/s00146-025-02692-1

Beijing AI Principles. 2019. Datenschutz und Datensicherheit. *DuD* 43:656–656. https://doi.org/10.1007/s11623-019-1183-6.

Blancaflor, Eric B., Juan Patrick Angelo Garcia, Jagg Aethan Lebosada, Justine Ryle Magleo, Grace Lorraine Intal, and Alberto Villaluz. 2024. Navigating Market Research Ethics in the Technological Landscape: A Comprehensive Analysis of Data Collection Practices and Public Perceptions. In *2024 IEEE 7th International Conference on Computer and Communication Engineering Technology (CCET)*, 286–290. https://doi.org/10.1109/CCET62233.2024.10838110.

Boddington, Paula. 2017. *Towards a Code of Ethics for Artificial Intelligence*. Springer.

Cath, Corinne. 2018. Governing Artificial Intelligence: Ethical, Legal and Technical Opportunities and Challenges. *Philosophical Transactions of the Royal Society A: Mathematical, Physical and Engineering Sciences* 376:20180080. https://doi.org/10.1098/rsta.2018.0080.

Cath, Corinne, Sandra Wachter, Brent Mittelstadt, Mariarosaria Taddeo, and Luciano Floridi. 2018. Artificial Intelligence and the 'Good Society': the US, EU, and UK approach. *Science and Engineering Ethics* 24:505–528. https://doi.org/10.1007/s11948-017-9901-7.

Coeckelbergh, Mark. 2013. *Human Being Risk: Enhancement, Technology and the Evaluation of Vulnerability Transformations.* Philosophy of Engineering and Technology 12. Dordrecht: Springer.

Coeckelbergh, Mark. 2020a. *AI ethics. The MIT Press Essential Knowledge Series.* Cambridge, MA: The MIT Press.

Coeckelbergh, Mark. 2020b. Artificial Intelligence, Responsibility Attribution, and a Relational Justification of Explainability. *Science and Engineering Ethics* 26:2051–2068. https://doi.org/10.1007/s11948-019-00146-8.

Díaz-Rodríguez, Natalia, Javier Del Ser, Mark Coeckelbergh, Marcos Prado, Enrique Herrera-Viedma, and Francisco Herrera. 2023. *Connecting the Dots in Trustworthy Artificial Intelligence: From AI Principles, Ethics, and Key Requirements to Responsible AI Systems and Regulation.*

Floridi, Luciano, Josh Cowls, Monica Beltrametti, Raja Chatila, Patrice Chazerand, Virginia Dignum, Christoph Luetge, et al. 2018. AI4People—An Ethical Framework for a Good AI Society: Opportunities, Risks, Principles, and Recommendations. *Minds and Machines* 28:689–707. https://doi.org/10.1007/s11023-018-9482-5.

Floridi, Luciano, Josh Cowls, Thomas C. King, and Mariarosaria Taddeo. 2020. How to Design AI for Social Good: Seven Essential Factors. *Science and Engineering Ethics* 26:1771–1796. https://doi.org/10.1007/s11948-020-00213-5.

Friis, Simon, and James Riley. 2023. Eliminating Algorithmic Bias Is Just the Beginning of Equitable AI. *Harvard Business Review.*

Given, Lisa M., ed. 2008. *The Sage Encyclopedia of Qualitative Research Methods.* Los Angeles, Calif: Sage Publications.

Hagendorff, Thilo. 2020. The Ethics of AI Ethics: An Evaluation of Guidelines. *Minds and Machines* 30:99–120. https://doi.org/10.1007/s11023-020-09517-8.

IBM. (2019). Everyday Ethics for Artificial Intelligence (p. 27). IBM. https://www.ibm.com/watson/assets/duo/pdf/everydayethics.pdf

Ignatow, Gabe, and Rada Mihalcea. 2017. *Text Mining: A Guidebook for the Social Sciences.* SAGE Publications, Inc. https://doi.org/10.4135/9781483399782.

Jobin, Anna, Marcello Ienca, and Effy Vayena. 2019. The global landscape of AI ethics guidelines. In *Nature Machine Intelligence 1*, 389–399. Nature Publishing Group. https://doi.org/10.1038/s42256-019-0088-2.

Krippendorff, Klaus. 2018. *Content Analysis: An Introduction to its Methodology.* Sage publications.

Li, Fan, Nick Ruijs, and Yuan Lu. 2023. Ethics & AI: A Systematic Review on Ethical Concerns and Related Strategies for Designing with AI in Healthcare. *AI* 4. Multidisciplinary Digital Publishing Institute: 28–53. https://doi.org/10.3390/ai4010003.

Marcoux, Aude Marie. 2025. AI Ethics Strategies and Practices in Organizations: A Scoping Review. *International Journal of Ethics and Systems* ahead-of-print. Emerald Publishing Limited. World. https://doi.org/10.1108/IJOES-02-2024-0060.

Morgan, Forrest E., Benjamin Boudreaux, Andrew J. Lohn, Mark Ashby, Christian Curriden, Kelly Klima, and Derek Grossman. 2020. *Military Applications of Artificial Intelligence: Ethical Concerns in an Uncertain World.* RAND Corporation.

Morley, Jessica, Luciano Floridi, Libby Kinsey, and Anat Elhalal. 2020. From What to How: An Initial Review of Publicly Available AI Ethics Tools, Methods and Research to Translate Principles into Practices. *Science and Engineering Ethics* 26:2141–2168. https://doi.org/10.1007/s11948-019-00165-5.

Morley, Jessica, Libby Kinsey, Anat Elhalal, Francesca Garcia, Marta Ziosi, and Luciano Floridi. 2021. Operationalising AI Ethics: Barriers, Enablers and Next Steps. *AI & SOCIETY.* https://doi.org/10.1007/s00146-021-01308-8.

Mujere, Never. 2016. Sampling in Research. In *Mixed Methods Research for Improved Scientific Study, 107–121.* IGI Global. https://doi.org/10.4018/978-1-5225-0007-0.ch006.

Pfeiffer, Jella, Julia Gutschow, Christian Haas, Florian Möslein, Oliver Maspfuhl, Frederik Borgers, and Suzana Alpsancar. 2023. Algorithmic Fairness in AI. *Business & Information Systems Engineering*. https://doi.org/10.1007/s12599-023-00787-x.

Prunkl, Carina. 2022. Human Autonomy in the Age of Artificial Intelligence. *Nature Machine Intelligence* 4:99–101. https://doi.org/10.1038/s42256-022-00449-9.

Reagan, Mary. 2021. Understanding Bias and Fairness in AI Systems. Blog. *Medium*.

Rességuier, Anaïs, and Rowena Rodrigues. 2020. AI Ethics Should Not Remain Toothless! A Call to Bring Back the Teeth of Ethics. *Big Data & Society* 7:205395172094254. https://doi.org/10.1177/2053951720942541.

Ryan, Mark. 2020. In AI We Trust: Ethics, Artificial Intelligence, and Reliability. *Science and Engineering Ethics* 26:2749–2767. https://doi.org/10.1007/s11948-020-00228-y.

Saldaña, Johnny. 2013. *The Coding Manual for Qualitative Researchers*. SAGE Publication.

Shneiderman, Ben. 2020. Bridging the Gap Between Ethics and Practice: Guidelines for Reliable, Safe, and Trustworthy Human-centered AI Systems. *ACM Transactions on Interactive Intelligent Systems* 10:1–31. https://doi.org/10.1145/3419764.

The Human Rights Directorate. 2020. Press Release by the Ministry for Justice Equality and Governance for International Human Rights Day 2020. *Press Releases*. October 12.

Kuckartz, Udo, and Stefan Rädiker. 2019. *Analyzing Qualitative Data with MAXQDA: Text, Audio, and Video*. Springer.

Wachinger, Jonas, Kate Bärnighausen, Louis N. Schäfer, Kerry Scott, and Shannon A. McMahon. 2024. Prompts, Pearls, Imperfections: Comparing Chat GPT and a Human Researcher in Qualitative Data Analysis. *Qualitative Health Research*. SAGE Publications Inc: 10497323241244669. https://doi.org/10.1177/10497323241244669.

Whittlestone, Jess, Rune Nyrup, Anna Alexandrova, and Stephen Cave. 2019. The Role and Limits of Principles in AI Ethics: Towards a Focus on Tensions. In *Proceedings of the 2019 AAAI/ACM Conference on AI, Ethics, and Society*, 195–200. AIES '19. New York, NY, USA: Association for Computing Machinery. https://doi.org/10.1145/3306618.3314289.

Willems, Jurgen, Moritz J. Schmid, Dieter Vanderelst, Dominik Vogel, and Falk Ebinger. 2022. AI-Driven Public Services and the Privacy Paradox: do Citizens Really Care About Their Privacy? *Public Management Review* 25. Routledge:2116–2134. https://doi.org/10.1080/14719037.2022.2063934.

Oshri Bar-Gil is an organizational psychologist with expertise in military psychology, technology ethics, information studies, and qualitative methods. He is currently an assistant professor at the MA program in organizational psychology at Ruppin Academic Center, Israel. Previously, he was research fellow at NATO Defence College. His PhD is in psychoanalysis and cultural studies from Bar-Ilan University. His research on technology impacts, AI ethics, crisis management, and civil-military relations has been published in prominent journals such as Technology in Society, AI & Society, Armed Forces & Society and others.

Chapter 3
Recent Trends in AI Law and Ethics and Their Implications for Military and Humanitarian Healthcare

Julian W. März and Nikola Biller-Andorno

3.1 Promises and Challenges of AI Use in Military and Humanitarian Settings

Artificial intelligence (AI) and big data analytics are key components of the Fourth Industrial Revolution, a term coined by Klaus Schwab (2016) to describe how new technologies are increasingly blending the physical, digital, and biological worlds, transforming all aspects of modern life. AI's ability to process vast datasets, learn from patterns, and make autonomous decisions is poised to revolutionize sectors as diverse as healthcare, defense, education, transportation, and agriculture, fundamentally altering how societies function. In the realm of military and humanitarian healthcare, the transformative potential of AI is especially evident. In military healthcare, AI-driven surveillance systems are employed to transform medical monitoring on the battlefield, providing real-time data on soldiers' health status. Autonomous evacuation systems powered by AI are enabling rapid and efficient transport of wounded personnel, reducing delays and improving survival rates. Additionally, AI is used to streamline treatment processes by assisting in injury assessments and treatment prioritization (Worsham et al. 2024).

J. W. März (✉)
Institute of Biomedical Ethics and History of Medicine,
University of Zurich, Zürich, Switzerland
e-mail: julian.maerz@ibme.uzh.ch

N. Biller-Andorno
Institute of Biomedical Ethics and History of Medicine, University of Zurich,
Zürich, Switzerland
e-mail: biller-andorno@ibme.uzh.ch

B. Koch, D. Winkler (eds.), *Artificial Intelligence Ethics in Military Medicine and Humanitarian Healthcare*, Military and Humanitarian Health Ethics,
https://doi.org/10.1007/978-3-032-11331-3_3

In humanitarian[1] healthcare, AI is similarly groundbreaking. For instance, in 2019, AI-driven drones were used during Cyclones Idai and Kenneth in Mozambique to map the damage, helping humanitarian organizations to rapidly assess the situation and deploy resources efficiently (WFP 2019; Beduschi 2022). UNHCR's Project Jetson uses AI-powered predictive analytics to forecast forced displacement patterns, helping humanitarian organizations plan and allocate resources more effectively (Beduschi 2022). AI-based tools can also be employed to analyze social media data for information regarding potential disease outbreaks during a humanitarian crisis (Fernandez-Luque and Imran 2018).

However, despite these promises, the use of AI in military and humanitarian healthcare raises significant ethical concerns. One major issue is the role of AI in taking life-and-death decisions, particularly in situations where AI systems are used to prioritize medical treatment (e.g., in situations of battlefield triage). This can create dilemmas about autonomy and fairness, especially when machines make decisions previously entrusted to human medical professionals. Moreover, the biases inherent in the data used to train AI systems can lead to discriminatory outcomes, particularly in diverse populations, further complicating the ethical landscape in humanitarian settings.

Another critical ethical challenge is the dehumanization of warfare through AI-powered autonomous systems, such as autonomous robots and drones for warfare which operate with minimal human oversight. These systems, capable of making independent decisions about who to target and kill, bypass human judgment in life-and-death situations. Autonomous weaponry introduces the risk of undermining the principles of international humanitarian law, including the distinction between combatants and civilians (Asaro 2020). Without human intervention, these systems could make errors in identification, leading to unintended civilian casualties or acts that could be considered war crimes. The opacity of AI's decision-making, often referred to as the "black box" problem, further complicates accountability when these systems cause harm (Crootof 2016).

The malicious use of AI also presents profound ethical challenges. AI systems, originally designed to save lives in healthcare, could be repurposed for nefarious purposes such as bioterrorism or cyberattacks on medical infrastructure. In conflict zones, AI tools could disrupt essential services, such as blocking access to life-saving medications or altering patient records to sow confusion and panic (Brundage et al. 2018). Moreover, AI's ability to produce disinformation and simulate false medical emergencies could be leveraged to destabilize humanitarian missions or spread fear during crises, weakening trust in healthcare institutions (Taddeo and Floridi 2018). Recent research has found that AI chatbots generate clearer and more

[1] Military and humanitarian healthcare can overlap ("military humanitarian healthcare"), but are distinct in purpose and actors. Humanitarian aid actors are unaffiliated to the parties to an armed conflict and are under an obligation of political neutrality, making their fundamental goal to save lives and alleviate (civilian) suffering. Military healthcare providers are also bound by the Geneva conventions and international humanitarian law, but can be associated with a party to an armed conflict and pursue a politically defined agenda (Broughton 2003; Falconer Hall et al. 2022).

compelling tweets—both true and false—than humans, while most people struggle to distinguish them, raising concerns about their potential use in disinformation campaigns (Spitale et al. 2023). These examples underscore the ambivalent nature of AI, where technology designed for good can easily be turned into a weapon of harm in the wrong hands.

AI's potential involvement in war crimes adds another layer of ethical complexity. AI systems used in warfare are not immune to human biases, especially when the data that trains these systems is flawed. If the data used to inform military AI systems is biased—whether by gender, ethnicity, or geographic origin—this can lead to discriminatory actions that amount to war crimes. For example, an AI system trained to identify combatants may disproportionately misidentify civilians in certain ethnic groups as enemy combatants, leading to unlawful killings in violation of international humanitarian law (Bode 2024; Bode and Bhila 2024). This raises concern that AI could exacerbate violence in ethnic conflicts.

In addition, there is the danger that AI might be deliberately manipulated to commit or conceal war crimes. Autonomous systems, such as drones or surveillance technologies, could be programmed or used to avoid recording evidence of unlawful actions, effectively concealing violations of the laws of war. The use of AI in this context makes it difficult to hold individuals accountable for decisions, as the technology provides a degree of separation between human actors and the consequences of their decisions. This phenomenon is exacerbated by the "black box" nature of AI, which often leaves decision-making processes opaque and untraceable, hindering efforts to establish culpability.

Moreover, AI systems could be used to carry out deliberate attacks on protected civilian targets, including hospitals, refugee camps, and humanitarian aid convoys, which are war crimes under the Rome Statute. The difficulty in attributing responsibility for these acts when autonomous systems are involved complicates legal recourse and accountability. AI's ability to autonomously select targets means that, without human oversight, it may fail to adequately assess whether an individual or group is legally protected under the Geneva Conventions (Crootof 2016). An AI drone, for example, might target a medical facility based on faulty intelligence or misinterpret a convoy of aid workers as a military target, leading to devastating consequences.

In some cases, AI could even be used to help cover up war crimes by altering or manipulating data. This could involve AI systems erasing evidence of unlawful attacks or fabricating records to show compliance with international law, effectively enabling impunity for those committing war crimes. As AI becomes more sophisticated, its ability to manipulate digital records, including video and photographic evidence, grows—raising significant concerns about its role in concealing human rights violations in conflict zones (Taddeo and Floridi 2018). The use of AI to tamper with evidence could obstruct justice and prevent accountability, as the international community relies heavily on digital evidence to prosecute war crimes.

3.2 Existing Legal and Ethics Framework for AI Use in Healthcare (in General)

The increasing integration of artificial intelligence (AI) into healthcare systems has sparked a growing debate on its ethical and legal implications. However, AI is not operating in a regulatory void. Various existing laws, ranging from data protection to medical device regulation and intellectual property (IP) law, already apply to AI in healthcare, even as more AI-specific regulations are being developed.

One of the most relevant frameworks governing AI in healthcare is data protection law, particularly in jurisdictions like the European Union (EU), where the General Data Protection Regulation (GDPR) plays a pivotal role in regulating how AI systems handle personal health data. The GDPR sets stringent standards for the collection, processing, and storage of sensitive health information, which is a critical concern in AI-driven healthcare applications such as diagnostics, patient monitoring, and treatment.

Another key regulatory pillar is medical device regulation. In the EU, the Medical Device Regulation (MDR) covers AI systems that serve diagnostic, therapeutic, or preventative functions. This means that AI systems, just like physical medical tools, must undergo rigorous safety and efficacy evaluations before being approved for use in healthcare settings. For instance, AI algorithms that assist in medical imaging or treatment recommendations must meet high safety standards to avoid errors that could endanger patients.

Intellectual property (IP) law is also a significant factor, particularly in protecting the innovations behind AI technologies. In addition, product liability laws are often invoked when AI-based medical tools malfunction, placing the onus on manufacturers and developers to ensure their products are reliable and safe for use in clinical environments.

Beyond these foundational legal structures, human rights law and international humanitarian law play roles in regulating AI's applications, particularly in military and humanitarian healthcare settings. For example, international humanitarian law provides that AI systems used in conflict zones—whether for medical triage or humanitarian aid delivery—comply with the obligation to protect civilian populations, humanitarian missions, and healthcare facilities.

These legal norms, although not specifically designed with AI in mind, already exert significant control over how AI technologies are implemented in healthcare settings.

3.3 The Need for Artificial Intelligence-Specific Regulations

3.3.1 Overview

Despite these existing frameworks, there is growing recognition among scholars, policymakers, lawmakers, and international organizations that AI-specific regulations are necessary. The challenges posed by AI—particularly in sectors like healthcare—are too unique and complex to be fully addressed by general laws. AI systems introduce new risks, such as algorithmic bias, the opacity of decision-making processes, and the ability to make autonomous decisions that can directly affect patient outcomes. These are issues that traditional legal frameworks—e.g., data protection law and medical device regulation—were not designed to handle.

The World Health Organization (WHO) and UNESCO have both continuously highlighted the need for AI-specific ethical and regulatory frameworks. In its *Ethics and Governance of Artificial Intelligence for Health Guidance* (2023), the WHO emphasizes the importance of transparency, accountability, and fairness in the deployment of AI systems in healthcare. It advocates for regulations that ensure AI tools are not only safe and effective but also ethically sound, particularly when used in high-risk environments such as healthcare or humanitarian aid (WHO 2025).

At the national and regional level, jurisdictions such as the United States and the European Union are moving toward AI-specific regulations. The EU Artificial Intelligence Act is a prime example of a comprehensive regulatory effort. Adopted in 2024, the Act classifies AI systems based on risk levels—unacceptable-risk, high-risk, limited-risk, minimal-risk categories—imposing stricter rules on high-risk AI, such as those used in healthcare for diagnostics or treatment decisions (European Commission 2024). These systems are subject to rigorous testing, transparency requirements, and oversight to ensure they meet safety and ethical standards (see section The EU Artificial Intelligence Act).

3.3.2 The Evolution of AI Regulation: From Ethics to Legislation

The evolution of AI regulation has followed a clear pattern: first, the development of ethical guidelines, followed by regulatory oversight, and finally, legislative action.

The global community's initial focus was on developing ethical frameworks that could guide the responsible use of AI. One of the earliest and most influential efforts was the OECD AI Principles, adopted in 2019. These principles set out core values such as fairness, transparency, accountability, and human rights protection, providing a foundation for broader regulatory efforts (OECD 2019). These guidelines emphasized the importance of ensuring that AI technologies are developed and deployed in ways that benefit society and protect individual rights.

In 2020, the European Commission's High-Level Expert Group on Artificial Intelligence introduced the Assessment List for Trustworthy AI (ALTAI), a tool designed to help developers ensure their AI systems align with ethical principles, such as accountability and human oversight (European Commission 2020).

In 2021, UNESCO built on this momentum by adopting the Recommendation on the Ethics of Artificial Intelligence, which is supported by 193 member states and lays out a comprehensive framework for the ethical use of AI, particularly in high-stakes fields like healthcare. This global ethics standard calls for AI to be designed and implemented in ways that promote fairness, transparency, and non-discrimination, particularly in healthcare settings where vulnerable populations are at risk (UNESCO 2021). These ethical guidelines have been instrumental in shaping subsequent regulatory efforts by emphasizing the need for AI systems to prioritize human rights and ethical considerations.

In the U.S., the Blueprint for an AI Bill of Rights, published by the White House Office of Science and Technology Policy (OSTP) in 2022, laid out key ethics considerations for individuals interacting with AI systems, focusing on transparency, fairness, and the prevention of harmful biases in AI-driven healthcare tools (White House OSTP 2022).

Subsequently, regulatory bodies for medicinal products began to step in. The U.S. Food and Drug Administration (FDA)'s *Artificial Intelligence and Machine Learning (AI/ML) Software as a Medical Device Action Plan* (2021) outlines how the FDA plans to regulate AI-driven medical devices, focusing on ensuring these technologies are safe, transparent, and reliable as they evolve over time (FDA 2021). The European Medicines Agency (EMA)'s Reflection Paper on the Use of Artificial Intelligence in the Lifecycle of Medicines (2023) offers a detailed approach to regulating AI-driven technologies from clinical trials to post-market surveillance. It emphasizes the need for AI tools to demonstrate safety and efficacy across the lifecycle of their use, particularly in drug development and patient care (EMA 2023).

In 2024, the EU AI Act, the first comprehensive AI-specific legislation, was adopted (see section The EU Artificial Intelligence Act).

3.3.3 Divergent Approaches to AI-Specific Legislation

Despite the growing recognition of the need for AI-specific rules, countries have adopted these regulations at varying speeds, leading to significant differences in how AI is governed globally. The European Union (EU) has been at the forefront of AI regulation, with the Artificial Intelligence Act representing the world's first comprehensive attempt to regulate AI across various sectors, including healthcare (European Parliament 2024a, 2024b). China has implemented strict AI regulations, particularly in healthcare, reflecting China's broader strategy of tightly controlling the development and use of AI technologies to align with national economic, political, and industrial strategy (Zhang 2024).

In contrast, some countries have taken a more cautious approach to AI regulation. Under former PM Rishi Sunak's government, the United Kingdom (UK) has opted for a lighter-touch regulatory framework. In its 2023 White Paper on AI Regulation, the UK government emphasized the importance of innovation and flexibility, proposing sector-specific guidance rather than a comprehensive AI law. The UK plans to rely on existing laws, such as data protection and medical device regulations, while encouraging the development of AI technologies (UK Government 2023). In January 2025, the new Labour Government released its AI Opportunities Action Plan, outlining a 50-point framework aimed at enhancing the UK's AI capabilities through increased compute infrastructure, improved access to data, and investment in skills development. The strategy also proposes adopting a light-touch regulatory approach to facilitate the deployment of AI in the economy and foster growth of the AI sector in the UK (UK Government 2025). In Switzerland, AI is currently regulated through its existing Federal Act on Data Protection and sectoral laws rather than comprehensive AI-specific regulations, (Digital Switzerland Strategy 2024). In February 2025, the Swiss Federal Council instructed the Federal Department of the Environment, Transport, Energy and Communications (DETEC) and the Federal Department of Foreign Affairs (FDFA) to develop a regulatory strategy for artificial intelligence, based on the goals of fostering innovation, protecting fundamental rights, and strengthening public trust. In line with its broader digital strategy, Switzerland favors sector-specific regulation over a comprehensive AI law, taking a flexible and "pro-innovation" approach comparable to that of the UK. The strategy also includes alignment with international frameworks such as the Council of Europe's AI Convention and considers complementary non-binding instruments such as voluntary self-regulation (Federal Office of Communications 2025).

In the United States, several AI-specific bills are currently under consideration in Congress. Most importantly, the Algorithmic Accountability Act of 2022, reintroduced in 2023, aims to require companies to conduct impact assessments on AI systems that affect public welfare, such as healthcare applications (U.S. Congress 2023). In addition, the Executive Order on the Safe, Secure, and Trustworthy Development and Use of Artificial Intelligence (2023) sets guiding principles for AI governance, focusing on security, innovation, privacy, worker rights, equity, and international leadership, while promoting collaboration between government, private sector, academia, and civil society.

3.4 The EU Artificial Intelligence Act

The EU Artificial Intelligence Act (AI Act) represents (so far) the world's most comprehensive attempt to regulate AI technologies across various sectors, including healthcare (European Parliament 2024a, 2024b). Building on the EU's existing regulatory frameworks, the AI Act introduces risk-based classifications for AI systems and imposes stringent requirements on high-risk applications, particularly in sectors where safety, human rights, and ethics standards are paramount.

3.4.1 Legislative Timeline of the EU AI Act

In April 2021, the European Commission presented its draft proposal for the AI Act. Following the proposal, the AI Act underwent significant discussions and revisions. In March 2024, the European Parliament adopted the final text of the AI Act after months of negotiations and amendments. Subsequently, in May 2024, the Council of the European Union gave its final approval. The AI Act was published in the EU's Official Journal on July 12, 2024 and entered into force on August 1, 2024 (European Parliament—Legislative Train Schedule EU AI Act). The EU AI Act will be fully applicable from August 2026, but certain provisions will enter into force earlier: In particular, the ban on certain unacceptable-risk AI systems (e.g., social scoring systems, real-time and remote biometric identification systems, and cognitive behavioural manipulation systems) entered into force in February 2025 (European Parliament 2024a, 2024b).

3.4.2 Scope of the AI Act

Article 2 of the AI Act outlines its scope, stating that the regulation applies inter alia to:

- Providers placing AI systems on the market or putting them into service within the EU, regardless of the location of the provider.
- Deployers of AI systems located within the EU.
- Providers and deployers of AI systems based outside the EU if the output produced by the AI system is used in the EU.
- Any person located in the EU affected by an AI system.

This extraterritorial application of the AI Act means that AI systems developed in countries like the United States, China, or the UK that are used or deployed within the EU must comply with its provisions. This mirrors the approach of the GDPR, which similarly extended its scope beyond the borders of the EU to protect the data of EU residents and citizens.

The Act also classifies AI systems into different categories based on the risk they pose. These categories are (European Commission 2024):

- Unacceptable Risk AI Systems (Article 5): These are AI systems that are deemed to violate fundamental rights or pose serious risks to safety and are outright banned. Examples include AI systems that manipulate human behavior or exploit vulnerabilities based on race, religion, or economic status.
- High-Risk AI Systems (Articles 6–49): This category includes AI systems used in critical sectors like healthcare, law enforcement, and infrastructure. Such systems are subject to stringent compliance measures, including conformity assessments, data governance requirements, and transparency obligations.

- Limited and Minimal Risk AI Systems (Article 50): These systems are subject to fewer requirements, though transparency obligations may still apply. For instance, users must be informed when they are interacting with an AI system.

3.4.3 Exclusions of Military AI

One of the key features of the AI Act is its exclusion of AI systems that are developed, placed on the market, or used exclusively for military purposes. Article 2, para. 3 of the AI Act explicitly states that "this Regulation does not apply to AI systems where and in so far as they are placed on the market, put into service, or used with or without modification exclusively for military, defense, or national security purposes, regardless of the type of entity carrying out those activities". This exclusion is in line with the EU treaties which leave defense and national security matters under the jurisdiction of individual Member States.

However, the Act includes a crucial provision regarding dual-use AI systems, which are technologies that can be used for both civilian and military purposes. Recital 25 clarifies that while AI systems used exclusively for military purposes are excluded, AI systems that have dual-use applications fall within the scope of the regulation when they are used outside military or national security contexts. This means that if a dual-use AI system—initially developed for military purposes—is employed for civilian, humanitarian, or law enforcement purposes, it must comply with the AI Act's provisions.

For example, an AI system initially designed for battlefield medical triage could be repurposed for civilian healthcare during humanitarian crises. In such cases, the system would need to meet the same requirements as any other high-risk AI system in the healthcare sector, including transparency, human oversight, and risk management measures. This dual-use provision has significant implications for the use of AI in military healthcare systems, where technologies often straddle the line between military and civilian applications.

3.4.4 Implications of the AI Act

The EU AI Act introduces several obligations for providers, deployers, and users of AI systems, particularly those classified as high-risk. These obligations aim to ensure that AI technologies are safe, transparent, and ethically aligned with EU values. For providers of high-risk AI systems—such as those used in healthcare—the following obligations apply:

- Risk Management System (Article 9): Providers must establish and implement a risk management system that continuously monitors and assesses the risks associated with their AI systems. This system must be active throughout the lifecycle of the AI system, ensuring that risks are identified and mitigated from the development phase through to deployment and post-market monitoring. This risk management process includes evaluating the AI system's performance, addressing any safety concerns, and mitigating potential harm to users.

- Data and Data Governance (Article 10): High-risk AI systems must use high-quality, relevant, and representative datasets to ensure fairness and accuracy. Providers are required to demonstrate that the data used for training, validation, and testing are appropriate for the task and free from biases that could lead to discriminatory outcomes. Proper data governance measures must be in place to prevent unjust outcomes and ensure that the AI system operates as intended in all contexts, especially in critical sectors like healthcare.
- Technical Documentation (Article 11): Providers of high-risk AI systems are obliged to create and maintain comprehensive technical documentation. This documentation must include detailed descriptions of the system's architecture, design, intended purpose, and performance metrics. The technical documentation is critical for regulatory transparency, as it allows authorities to evaluate the system's compliance with the Act and ensures accountability in case of malfunction or misuse.
- Record-Keeping (Article 12): Providers must keep detailed records of their AI system's development, deployment, and post-market performance. This record-keeping is essential for traceability, allowing the system's decision-making processes and operational history to be reviewed if incidents or concerns arise. By maintaining these records, providers can demonstrate that their AI system complies with the Act's requirements, ensuring ongoing regulatory oversight (European Commission 2024).
- Transparency and Provision of Information to Users (Article 13): Providers of high-risk AI systems are required to ensure that users are fully informed about the system's capabilities and limitations. This includes making users aware of the system's potential risks, providing clear instructions for safe use, and disclosing any limitations of the AI's decision-making processes. By promoting transparency, providers help foster user trust and ensure that users understand how to interact with the system safely and responsibly.
- Human Oversight (Article 14): High-risk AI systems must incorporate mechanisms that allow for human oversight. This ensures that human operators have the ability to intervene in or override AI decisions when necessary, particularly in critical applications like healthcare. Providers must design systems that allow for meaningful human control, safeguarding against potential harm by ensuring that AI does not make autonomous decisions without the possibility of human intervention.
- Accuracy, Robustness, and Cybersecurity (Article 15): Providers are responsible for ensuring that high-risk AI systems meet strict standards for accuracy and robustness. This includes ongoing evaluation to confirm that the system functions reliably in all intended use cases. Furthermore, providers must implement strong cybersecurity measures to protect AI systems from malicious attacks that could compromise safety, integrity, or privacy. Given the potential impact of AI

system failures in sectors like healthcare, ensuring robustness and security is a critical obligation under the Act.

3.4.5 *Potential Global Influence and Impact on Military and Humanitarian Healthcare*

Although the AI Act is an EU regulation, its impact is likely to extend far beyond Europe. The extraterritorial nature of the Act, similar to that of the GDPR, means that companies and organizations outside the EU that provide AI systems to European customers will need to comply with its provisions. This could lead to a "Brussels effect," where the EU's regulatory standards become a de facto global benchmark as international companies align their practices to meet EU requirements (Bradford 2020). In particular, healthcare companies and AI developers in countries like the United States, Japan, and India that sell AI technologies to EU customers will likely need to adhere to the stringent requirements of the AI Act.

Moreover, the dual-use provision of the AI Act could have significant implications for military healthcare systems. AI systems that straddle the line between military and civilian use may be subject to compliance with the Act when used in humanitarian or civilian healthcare contexts. For example, AI tools initially developed for battlefield triage or logistics could face strict regulatory oversight when repurposed for use in disaster relief or civilian healthcare settings, potentially requiring compliance with data governance, transparency, and human oversight provisions. The AI Act might either lead to strict compliance with these requirements also for military AI systems (which might often be unfeasible), or—more likely—lead to a stricter separation of military and humanitarian AI systems.[2]

While the full impact of the AI Act on the global AI landscape is still uncertain, its broad scope and stringent requirements suggest that it could become a significant regulatory framework for AI technologies worldwide, particularly in high-risk sectors like healthcare. As AI systems become more integrated into healthcare, the AI Act's requirements for risk management, transparency, and human oversight will likely shape the future of AI innovation in this field.

[2] The second option is also in line with policies by many academic (civilian) research funders, e.g., the Swiss National Science Foundation, who, whilst supporting spin-off opportunities for dual-use technologies, warn against the risks of blurring civilian and military research, which could increase (regulatory) complexity and hinder international collaboration (SNSF 2024).

3.5 Council of Europe Framework Convention on Artificial Intelligence, Human Rights, Democracy, and the Rule of Law

The Council of Europe (CoE)'s Framework Convention on Artificial Intelligence, Human Rights, Democracy, and the Rule of Law represents the first multilateral legal instrument to govern the implications of artificial intelligence for human rights, democracy, and the rule of law.

3.5.1 Territorial Scope and Ratification Status

The territorial scope of the Council of Europe Framework Convention on AI is broad, extending beyond Europe. On May 17, 2024, the Convention was adopted by the Committee of Ministers of the Council of Europe. The Convention was drafted by representatives of all 46 CoE member states, as well as the European Union and non-member states that participated in its drafting, such as Argentina, Australia, Canada, Costa Rica, Israel, Japan, Mexico, Peru, the United States, and Uruguay (Council of Europe 2024).

As of September 15, 2024, the ratification process for the Convention is ongoing. The Convention formally opened for signatures on September 5, 2024, and has been signed by Andorra, Georgia, Iceland, Norway, Moldova, San Marino, the United Kingdom as well as Israel, the United States of America, and the European Union as of September 15, 2024 (Council of Europe 2024). Three months after its ratification by at least five states (of which at least 3 CoE member states), the Convention will enter into force.

3.5.2 Key Obligations

Article 3 of the Framework Convention provides that the Convention applies to "activities within the lifecycle of artificial intelligence systems that have the potential to interfere with human rights, democracy and the rule of law". The obligations under the Framework Convention apply to both public authorities and private actors acting on their behalf (Art. 3, para. 1a). Each Party must address risks posed by private actors and declare how they will fulfill these obligations, ensuring that any actions align with existing international commitments to protect human rights and democratic principles (Art. 3, para. 1b). Key obligations include:

- Human Rights Protection (Art. 4): Parties must ensure that AI systems are developed and deployed in ways that respect human rights. In particular, Parties are obliged to ensure respect for human dignity and individual autonomy (Art. 7), provide for transparency and oversight (Art. 8) and accountability and responsibility (Art. 9), respect the principles of equality and non-discrimination (Art. 10) as well as reliability (Art. 12) and safe innovation (Art. 13), and respect privacy and personal data protection standards (Art. 11).

- Integrity of democratic processes (Art. 5, para. 1): Each Party must adopt measures to ensure that AI systems do not undermine the integrity, independence, or effectiveness of democratic institutions and processes, including the separation of powers, judicial independence, and access to justice.
- Respect for the rule of law (Art. 5, para. 2): Each Party must adopt measures to protect its democratic processes in the context of AI system activities, ensuring individuals' fair access to and participation in public debate, as well as their ability to freely form opinions.

3.5.3 Exclusions (Defense and National Security)

However, certain activities are explicitly excluded from the scope of the CoE Framework Convention. Article 3, para. 2 clarifies that "activities within the lifecycle of AI systems related to the protection of national security interests" are not covered by the Convention. This exclusion ensures that national security activities remain under the jurisdiction of individual states rather than being subject to international regulation.

Similarly, Article 3, para. 4 excludes matters related to national defense from the scope of the Convention. These exclusions are consistent with the CoE's broader approach to international law, which typically leaves defense and security matters to national governments. While this means that AI systems used exclusively for military purposes are outside the Convention's jurisdiction, it remains unclear to what extent the Convention will apply to dual-use AI technologies, which have both civilian and military applications. The Convention may still apply to military healthcare systems if the AI systems used in these contexts are repurposed for civilian or humanitarian healthcare, similar to the approach taken by the EU Artificial Intelligence Act.

Given this ambiguity, it remains to be seen how the Framework Convention will influence AI development in military and humanitarian healthcare. Much will depend on how states interpret the defense and national security exclusions, as well as the extent to which dual-use AI systems are subject to civilian oversight when repurposed for non-military applications.

3.6 Gaps in Legal and Ethical Frameworks Regarding Humanitarian and Military Healthcare Settings

Whilst Artificial intelligence (AI) is predicted to fundamentally transform healthcare, defense, and humanitarian aid, the legal and ethical frameworks governing its use in military and humanitarian healthcare settings remain incomplete. While significant progress has been made in regulating AI in civilian contexts—such as with the EU AI Act and the Council of Europe Framework Convention on Artificial Intelligence, Human Rights, Democracy, and the Rule of Law—both frameworks explicitly exclude military applications.

This creates a regulatory gap for dual-use technologies, which are AI systems developed for military purposes but repurposed for civilian or humanitarian use. Without a comprehensive legal framework, the use of AI in military healthcare—such as autonomous systems for battlefield triage, robotic surgery, or AI-driven medical logistics—remains largely unregulated. Furthermore, there is no universally applicable convention that specifically addresses AI in armed conflicts or humanitarian crises. While international humanitarian law (IHL) and human rights law (IHR) offer protections for civilians and combatants during conflict, these legal instruments do not explicitly address the use of AI in warfare or healthcare. The Geneva Conventions, which set the standards for the treatment of civilians, prisoners of war, and the wounded, were drafted long before AI technologies became a reality, and therefore do not contemplate the complexities of AI-driven decisions in medical and military contexts. The Rome Statute, which governs the prosecution of war crimes, similarly lacks provisions specific to the use of AI in the commission of such crimes.

Although some international organizations, like the International Committee of the Red Cross (ICRC), have begun to explore the ethical and legal implications of AI in armed conflict, these efforts remain limited. For example, the ICRC's 2021 Position Paper on AI and machine learning in armed conflict advocates for a human-centered approach to AI, emphasizing the importance of human oversight and accountability in the use of AI technologies in war (ICRC 2020). The paper calls for careful consideration of how AI might affect the conduct of hostilities and the protection of civilians, but it does not offer binding legal guidance. Furthermore, while this position paper represents a step forward, it is one of the few exceptions in a landscape where AI-specific guidance in military and humanitarian healthcare remains rare. Overall, the lack of universally applicable legal frameworks and limited engagement from international organizations leave significant gaps in how AI is governed in these critical settings.

3.7 Legal and Ethical Issues that Need Addressing

The absence of comprehensive legal frameworks to govern AI in military and humanitarian healthcare leaves numerous legal and ethical questions unresolved. One major issue is the potential for war crimes to be committed with the help of AI. For example, AI systems could be used to autonomously select and target individuals in conflict zones, raising concerns about whether such actions comply with international humanitarian law (IHL) principles of distinction of civilians and combatants and proportionality. If an AI-driven system mistakenly—or purposefully—targets civilians or protected medical personnel, it is unclear who would be held responsible: the developers, the military commanders, or the AI system itself? The lack of clear rules on legal liability for harm caused by AI in conflict zones complicates the prosecution of war crimes and may lead to impunity in situations where AI systems are involved.

Furthermore, AI systems could also be used to conceal war crimes by manipulating digital evidence. AI-driven technologies capable of editing or erasing surveillance footage, medical records, or other forms of digital evidence could hinder the prosecution of individuals responsible for violations of international law. Evidence rules relating to AI, especially in international criminal trials, are another area in need of urgent reform. Courts will need clear standards for assessing the reliability and admissibility of evidence processed by AI systems. Currently, there is little guidance on how AI-processed evidence should be treated in international tribunals or domestic courts dealing with war crimes, creating uncertainty and potential challenges for accountability.

Another critical issue is AI-based triage and treatment prioritization in both military and humanitarian contexts. AI systems are increasingly used to assist with medical triage, particularly in high-pressure environments like battlefields or disaster zones. These systems use algorithms to evaluate the severity of injuries and recommend treatment priorities, often operating faster than human responders. However, such technologies raise important ethical questions. For example, how should AI systems balance the needs of combatants and civilians? If an AI system prioritizes a wounded soldier over a civilian, or vice versa, what ethical principles should guide its decision-making? Additionally, algorithmic bias—an issue that has been well-documented in civilian healthcare—could lead to unfair or discriminatory treatment in military or humanitarian contexts, particularly when AI systems are trained on biased datasets that do not represent the diversity of populations in conflict zones.

Legal liability for harm caused by AI in military and humanitarian contexts is another pressing concern. In civilian healthcare, product liability laws typically hold developers or manufacturers accountable for harm caused by defective AI systems. However, in military contexts, it is unclear who would be liable for the actions of an AI system used in conflict. Would the responsibility lie with the government that deployed the system, the company that developed it, or the military personnel who used it? This lack of clarity not only raises concerns about accountability but also undermines trust in AI systems in these high-stakes environments. Furthermore, there are concerns that the opacity of AI decision-making—often referred to as the "black box" problem—could make it difficult to assess whether AI systems comply with IHL, further complicating the question of liability.

3.8 The Need for Comprehensive Guidance and Legal Reform

Addressing these legal and ethical issues is crucial to ensuring that AI is used responsibly in military and humanitarian healthcare settings. Comprehensive guidance is needed to uphold international human rights (IHR) standards and protect individuals in conflict zones from the potential harms posed by AI technologies. Such guidance would not only help prevent abuses but also provide clarity for developers, military personnel, and humanitarian organizations on how to design, deploy, and manage AI systems ethically.

First, establishing clear legal standards—both at the national and the international level—for the use of AI in armed conflict would help to prevent war crimes and ensure that AI systems are used in ways that align with international humanitarian law. This would involve setting guidelines on how AI systems should be programmed to comply with the principles of distinction and proportionality, and setting and defining clear requirements of meaningful human oversight over these systems. Additionally, international agreements should address accountability and liability, clarifying who is responsible when AI systems cause harm. This could involve developing new legal frameworks for AI-driven systems or expanding existing IHL principles to explicitly cover AI technologies.

For AI systems used in healthcare, particularly in humanitarian and military contexts, guidance on triage and treatment prioritization is essential. Humanitarian organizations and military medical personnel need to understand the ethical considerations that should guide AI-driven decision-making in medical emergencies. Developing clear standards for the use of AI in these situations would help ensure that decisions are made fairly and in accordance with medical ethics. This would also increase public trust in AI systems, as people would be more likely to accept AI-driven decisions if they knew that the systems were designed with ethical considerations in mind.

Lastly, comprehensive guidelines on evidence standards for AI-generated data in war crimes tribunals and other legal proceedings would help ensure accountability. As AI systems are increasingly used to document and analyze events in conflict zones, courts must have clear rules on how to assess the reliability and admissibility of AI-generated evidence. This would help prevent the manipulation of evidence and ensure that justice is served in cases where AI systems are involved.

In conclusion, filling the current gaps in legal and ethical frameworks for AI in military and humanitarian healthcare is critical to ensuring that AI technologies are used in ways that protect human rights, promote accountability, and foster public trust. As AI continues to evolve, so too must the laws and ethical guidelines that govern its use, particularly in high-stakes environments like conflict zones and humanitarian crises.

3.9 Summary and Conclusion

As artificial intelligence (AI) continues to evolve and find applications in diverse fields, the need for robust legal and ethical frameworks has become increasingly urgent. Current legal and ethical frameworks do not adequately address the complexities introduced by AI in warfare or crisis situations. Both the EU AI Act and the Council of Europe Framework Convention leave military applications largely unregulated, creating significant gaps, particularly in dual-use technologies that can be applied in both military and civilian contexts.

To fill these gaps, a coordinated effort will be required from multiple stakeholders across sectors. Ethics and legal scholarship must continue to evolve, providing new theoretical foundations for AI regulation in conflict and humanitarian settings.[3] At the same time, international organizations should provide specific ethical guidance for AI use in military and humanitarian healthcare settings. Existing instruments such as the WHO Guidance on Ethics and Governance of Artificial Intelligence for Health (WHO 2021), the WHO Guidance on Ethics and Governance of Large Multi-Modal Models (LMMs) (WHO 2025), and UNESCO's Recommendation on the Ethics of Artificial Intelligence can serve as valuable starting points, but they will need to be adapted to the specific challenges of military and humanitarian healthcare applications. The CoE's Framework Convention on Artificial Intelligence, Human Rights, Democracy and the Rule of Law demonstrates that international consensus on human rights in the context of AI is achievable, yet further binding agreements will be necessary to address the distinct risks posed by AI in armed conflict and crisis settings. National legislations must adapt to cover AI systems used in military and humanitarian contexts, closing the gaps left by existing international conventions. In addition, further international treaties or agreements—e.g., addenda to the Rome Statute and the Geneva Conventions—may be needed to establish clear obligations and responsibilities for AI use in warfare and disaster relief, ensuring accountability and the protection of human rights.

In addition to legal measures, industry standards and self-commitments from user organizations will play a critical role in ensuring the ethical use of AI. Companies developing AI systems for healthcare and humanitarian aid must commit to high standards of transparency, accountability, and human oversight. Organizations such as the WHO, ICRC, and Médecins Sans Frontières (MSF) can lead by example,

[3] The ethics assessment framework for humanitarian drones developed by Wang et al. (2022) is an example of how academia can contribute to standard-setting regarding AI use in military and humanitarian healthcare.

establishing and publishing policies and standards for the responsible deployment of AI technologies.

Education and training are also vital to ensuring that ethical AI practices become ingrained in the professional culture of healthcare providers, military personnel, and humanitarian workers. Incorporating AI ethics into the curricula of military and humanitarian medical education programs will help prepare future leaders to navigate the ethical complexities of AI in conflict zones and crisis settings.

To operationalize these recommendations, we propose the following Action Plan to address the ethical and legal challenges of AI in military and humanitarian healthcare (Table 3.1).

Despite the progress made, it is clear that more work is needed to ensure that AI serves humanity, rather than exacerbating harm in the world's most vulnerable settings. As Albert Einstein famously noted, "It has become appallingly obvious that our technology has exceeded our humanity" (Szczerba 2022). This observation is particularly pertinent when considering the potential consequences of unregulated AI systems in warfare and healthcare. Without careful oversight, AI could lead to decisions that violate human rights or dehumanize critical aspects of military and humanitarian healthcare. As we continue to integrate AI into the most sensitive aspects of healthcare and conflict, we must remember another Einstein quote: "The human spirit must prevail over technology" (Szczerba 2022).

The challenge, therefore, is not simply to develop smarter, more powerful AI systems but to ensure that ethical principles, human oversight, and a commitment to humanity's well-being are at the heart of AI's development and deployment. Only then can we harness AI's potential for good in military and humanitarian healthcare, ensuring that technological progress serves to enhance, rather than diminish, our shared humanity.

Use of Generative Artificial Intelligence

We have used generative Artificial Intelligence following International Committee of Medical Journal Editors (ICMJE) and Springer Nature policies (see here: https://www.icmje.org/recommendations/browse/roles-and-responsibilities/defining-the-role-of-authors-and-contributors.html#four; https://www.springer.com/us/editorial-policies/artificial-intelligence%2D%2Dai-/25428500).

Based on literature, bullet points, and text fragments drafted and provided by the authors, we have used ChatGPT-4 to generate a first draft of each paragraph, which we have subsequently carefully reviewed and revised, finishing each paragraph and submitting it to ChatGPT-4 before starting drafting of the respective next paragraph. In addition, we have used ChatGPT-4 and Grammarly, Version 5.3.0, for proofreading and reference formatting of the full text. We have reviewed the final text with Similarity by Turnitin to ensure no copyright has been breached by ChatGPT-4 in generating text for this article, and to ensure that there is appropriate attribution of all quoted material, including full citations (which has also been checked manually by us). The authors take full responsibility for the content of the publication.

Table 3.1 Proposed Action Plan to Address Ethical and Legal Challenges of AI in Military and Humanitarian Healthcare

Action Area	Key Actions	Key Responsible Stakeholders	Key Issues to Address
Legal and regulatory frameworks	Develop legal and regulatory frameworks specific to AI in military and humanitarian contexts (at the supranational and national level)	Legal scholars, regulatory bodies	**Regulate dual-use AI systems** that cross military and civilian domains; **close regulatory gaps** created by exclusions of military uses in existing laws and regulations; clarify **scope of jurisdiction** for AI accountability across borders.
International law	Negotiate new treaties or extend existing ones (e.g., Rome statute, Geneva conventions) to address AI in conflict settings.	International organizations, national governments	Define **AI war crimes liability**; incorporate **AI-generated actions and decisions** into IHL compliance (e.g., distinction and proportionality); establish rules for **autonomous targeting, surveillance, and triage**; prevent **manipulation or destruction of evidence** via AI systems.
National law	Update national laws to include AI systems used in dual-use, military, and crisis-related healthcare contexts.	National governments, parliaments	Clarify **legal liability** (developer, deployer, commander); ensure **oversight mechanisms** for battlefield AI healthcare tools; set **standards for algorithmic transparency and explainability.**
Ethical guidance	Adapt existing guidance (e.g., WHO, UNESCO) to the specificities of military and humanitarian healthcare applications.	WHO, UNESCO, National Ethics Committees, ethics scholars	**Translate civilian AI ethics** into conflict and crisis settings; **establish ethics guidelines for AI-led medical prioritization** in military and humanitarian healthcare settings; **define standards for meaningful human oversight** in time-sensitive or remote environments where reliance on AI might increase; **address the risk of dehumanization** in military and humanitarian care due to automation; **develop ethics protocols for dual-use AI** (e.g., triage tools used in both battlefield and disaster zones).
Industry standards	Encourage companies to adopt self-regulatory standards focusing on transparency, accountability, and oversight.	AI developers, tech companies, standard-setting bodies, regulatory agencies	Promote **ethics-by-design** and **human-centered AI**; define **robust testing, validation, and documentation standards**; anticipate **malicious repurposing risks**; develop **clear protocols for data integrity, auditability, and safety** in high-risk contexts.

(continued)

Table 3.1 (continued)

Action Area	Key Actions	Key Responsible Stakeholders	Key Issues to Address
Education and training	Integrate AI ethics into military and humanitarian healthcare training and education programs.	Educational institutions, military training academies	Educate practitioners on **ethical and legal risks of AI in high-stakes environments**; provide **scenario-based training**; raise awareness about **bias detection**, **transparency**, and the **limits of automation** in life-and-death situations.
Ethical AI development	Ensure AI development prioritizes human oversight, rights protection, and humanitarian values.	AI developers, tech companies, ethics boards	**Embed ethics and human rights principles** in technical design; address "black box" problem and foster explainability and accountability; ensure respect for IHL in military and humanitarian contexts.

Conflict of Interest We are PIs of a project funded by the World Health Organization (WHO) entitled "Integrating ethics and governance into the design of artificial intelligence-based technologies for health" (WHO Registration 2023/1330509–0).

References

Asaro, P. 2020. Autonomous weapons and the ethics of artificial intelligence. In *Ethics of Artificial Intelligence*, ed. S. M. Liao, 212–236. Oxford: Oxford University Press.

Beduschi, A. 2022. Harnessing the potential of artificial intelligence for humanitarian action: Opportunities and risks. *International Review of the Red Cross* 104 (919): 1149–1169. https://doi.org/10.1017/S1816383122000261.

Bode, I. 2024 Falling Under the Radar: The Problem of Algorithmic Bias and Military Applications of AI. *ICRC Blog*, 14 March 2024. Available at: https://blogs.icrc.org/law-and-policy/2024/03/14/falling-under-the-radar-the-problem-of-algorithmic-bias-and-military-applications-of-ai/

Bode, I., and Bhila, I. 2024. The Problem of Algorithmic Bias in AI-Based Military Decision Support Systems. *ICRC Blog*, 3 September 2024. Available at: https://blogs.icrc.org/law-and-policy/2024/09/03/the-problem-of-algorithmic-bias-in-ai-based-military-decision-support-systems/

Bradford, A. (2020) The Brussels Effect: How the European Union Rules the World, Oxford: Oxford University Press.

Broughton, M. 2003. Humanitarian propaganda. *The Lancet* 361 (9372): 1480.

Brundage, M., S. Avin, J. Wang, H. Belfield, G. Krueger, G. Hadfield, et al. 2018. The Malicious Use of Artificial Intelligence: Forecasting, Prevention, and Mitigation. *arXiv preprint* arXiv:1802.07228.

Council of Europe. 2024. *Council of Europe Opens First Ever Global Treaty on AI for Signature*. https://www.coe.int/en/web/portal/-/council-of-europe-opens-first-ever-global-treaty-on-ai-for-signature

Crootof, R. 2016. War Torts: Accountability for Autonomous Systems. *University of Pennsylvania Law Review* 164 (6): 1347–1402.

Digital Switzerland Strategy. 2024. Swiss Approach To Regulating AI Systems. Available at: https://digital.swiss/en/strategy/focus-topics/swiss-approach-to-regulating-ai-systems

European Commission. 2020. *Assessment List for Trustworthy AI (ALTAI)*. https://digital-strategy.ec.europa.eu/en/library/assessment-list-trustworthy-artificial-intelligence-altai-self-assessment

European Commission. 2024. *'AI Act'*. Available at: https://digital-strategy.ec.europa.eu/en/policies/regulatory-framework-ai

European Medicines Agency (EMA). 2023. *Reflection Paper on the Use of Artificial Intelligence in the Lifecycle of Medicines*. Amsterdam: EMA.

European Parliament. 2024a. *Legislative Train Schedule–Artificial Intelligence Act*. https://www.europarl.europa.eu/legislative-train/theme-a-europe-fit-for-the-digital-age/file-regulation-on-artificial-intelligence

European Parliament. 2024b. *EU AI Act: First Regulation on Artificial Intelligence*. https://www.europarl.europa.eu/topics/en/article/20230601STO93804/eu-ai-act-first-regulation-on-artificial-intelligence.

Falconer Hall, T., S. Horne, and D. Ross. 2022. Comparison between Defence Healthcare Engagement and humanitarian assistance. *BMJ Military Health* 168 (6): 417–419.

Federal Office of Communications. 2025. *Artificial Intelligence and Switzerland's Regulatory Approach*. Available at: https://www.bakom.admin.ch/bakom/en/homepage/digital-switzerland-and-internet/strategie-digitale-schweiz/ai.html

Fernandez-Luque, L., and M. Imran. 2018. Humanitarian Health Computing Using Artificial Intelligence and Social Media: A Narrative Literature Review. *International Journal of Medical Informatics* 114:136–142. https://doi.org/10.1016/j.ijmedinf.2018.01.015.

International Committee of the Red Cross (ICRC). 2020. AI and Machine Learning in Armed Conflict: A Human-Centered Approach. *International Review of the Red Cross* 913:463–479.
OECD. 2019. *Recommendation of the Council on Artificial Intelligence*. Paris: OECD.
Schwab, K. 2016. *The Fourth Industrial Revolution*. Geneva: World Economic Forum.
Spitale, G., N. Biller-Andorno, and F. Germani. 2023. AI model GPT-3 (dis)informs us better than humans. *Science Advances* 9 (26): eadh1850. https://doi.org/10.1126/sciadv.adh1850.
Swiss National Science Foundation (SNSF). 2024. *Dual Use in the EU Framework Programme and SNSF Perspective*. https://www.snf.ch/media/de/YV0QMwYQjvlbcb3f/dual-use-in-the-eu-framework-programme-and-snsf-perspective-2024.pdf
Szczerba, Robert J. 2022. *20 Great Technology Quotes To Inspire, Amaze, And Amuse*. https://www.forbes.com/sites/robertszczerba/2015/02/09/20-great-technology-quotes-to-inspire-amaze-and-amuse/
Taddeo, M., and L. Floridi. 2018. Regulate Artificial Intelligence to Avert Cyber Arms Race. *Nature* 556 (7701): 296–298.
U.S. Congress. 2023. *Algorithmic Accountability Act*. Washington, D.C.: U.S. Congress.
U.S. Food and Drug Administration (FDA). 2021. *Artificial Intelligence/Machine Learning (AI/ML)-Based Software as a Medical Device (SaMD) Action Plan*, https://www.fda.gov/media/145022/download
UK Government. 2023. *Policy Paper: A Pro-Innovation Approach to AI Regulation*, https://www.gov.uk/government/publications/ai-regulation-a-pro-innovation-approach/white-paper
UK Government. 2025. *AI Opportunities Action Plan. Department for Science, Innovation and Technology*. Available at: https://www.gov.uk/government/publications/ai-opportunities-action-plan
UNESCO. 2021. *Recommendation on the Ethics of Artificial Intelligence*. Paris: UNESCO.
White House Office of Science and Technology Policy (OSTP). 2022. *Blueprint for an AI Bill of Rights*. https://www.whitehouse.gov/ostp/ai-bill-of-rights/
UN World Food Programme. 2019. *WFP Drones: Emergency Response in Mozambique*. World Food Programme. Available at: https://drones.wfp.org/activities/mozambique-emergency-response.
Wang, N., M. Christen, M. Hunt, and N. Biller-Andorno. 2022. Supporting Value Sensitivity in the Humanitarian Use of Drones Through an Ethics Assessment Framework. *International Review Of The Red Cross 919*: https://international-review.icrc.org/articles/supporting-value-sensitivity-in-the-humanitarian-use-of-drones-919.
World Health Organization. 2021. *Ethics and Governance of Artificial Intelligence for Health: WHO Guidance*. Geneva: WHO. Available at: https://www.who.int/publications/i/item/9789240029200.
World Health Organization. 2025. *Ethics and Governance of Large Multi-Modal Models (LMMs) for Health: Interim Guidance*. Geneva: WHO. Available at: https://www.who.int/publications/i/item/9789240084759.
Worsham, V., E. Gonzalez, M. Kucia, M. Matters, T. Hansen, D. Preczewski, M. Smallidge, and E. Michaud. 2024. Army Medicine and Artificial Intelligence: Transforming the Future Battlefield. *Military Review.*. Available at: https://www.armyupress.army.mil/Journals/Military-Review/English-Edition-Archives/May-June-2024/MJ-24-Army-Medicine-AI/.
Zhang, A. H. 2024. The Promise and Perils of China's Regulation of Artificial Intelligence. *Columbia Journal of Transnational Law* (forthcoming). Available at: https://papers.ssrn.com/sol3/papers.cfm?abstract_id=4708676

Dr. iur., Dr. med. et Dr. sc. med. Julian W. März studied medicine, law, and bioethics at the Universities of Zurich, Oxford, Munich, Regensburg, Passau, and the Institut d'Études Politiques (IEP) de Paris. Before joining the University of Zurich as a research fellow in 2022, he worked at the German Cancer Research Center (DKFZ) in Heidelberg, where he also wrote his doctoral thesis in medicine. Furthermore, he has worked as a trainee lawyer for the international law firms Cleary Gottlieb Steen & Hamilton LLP and Hogan Lovells LLP and as a trainee physician at the

General Hospital of Luxembourg. In October 2024, he was appointed to the World Health Organization's Research Ethics Review Committee (WHO-ERC) for a three-year term. From March 2024 to April 2025, he served as lead scientific advisor to the Swiss federal government for the review of the Federal Law on the Genetic Testing of Humans (GUMG).

Prof. Dr. med. Dr. phil. Nikola Biller-Andorno , MHBA, directs the Institute of Biomedical Ethics and History of Medicine, University of Zurich (UZH), Switzerland, a WHO Collaborating Centre for Bioethics. She leads the UZH Center for Medical Humanities as well as the PhD program "Biomedical Ethics and Law". Biller-Andorno is a member of both the Swiss Academy of Medical Sciences and the Swiss National Research Council and serves as Vice-President of the Clinical Ethics Committee of the University Hospital Zurich. A Past-President of the International Association of Bioethics, she is currently active as board member of the European Association of Centres of Medical Ethics and of DIPEx International. She held a Commonwealth Fund Harkness Fellowship and Visiting Professorship at Harvard University (2012-14) as well as a Fellowship at the Collegium Helveticum (2016-20), the joint Institute of Advance Studies of UZH, ETH Zurich and the Zurich University of the Arts. In 2018, she obtained a Master of Health Business Administration (MHBA). Since 2021 Nikola Biller-Andorno is Vice Dean Innovation and Digitalization of the UZH Medical Faculty.

Part II
Philosophical and Ethical Challenges of AI Usage in the Military Environment

In the second part, the present volume addresses examples of AI usage in the military environment and assesses the philosophical and ethical challenges.

Chapter 4
Given the Use of AI, Can There Still Be Good Military Medical Service or Only Bad One?

Bernhard Koch

4.1 AI as Technology and the Power(lessness) of Ethics

Investigating the use of Artificial Intelligence in military medicine is an exciting endeavor even for those ethicists who do not have a background in military medicine. This is because two areas collide in military medical ethics, which in themselves raise extremely exciting questions: In its escalation, ethics is about life and death, but military ethics is more often about the active *taking of life* and accordingly about legitimizing this, e.g. as out of self-protection or protection for others, while medical ethics is mostly about *saving lives* and, at best, allowing death. Added to this, however, is now the use of so-called "Artificial Intelligence" (AI), and there are AI-specific topics that cross all areas in which it is used.

"Artificial Intelligence" is a collective term and is not uniformly defined (cf. Emmert-Streib et al. 2020). AI can be used to address "different areas: a scientific research area, a technological method, concrete applications (such as in healthcare) or philosophical discussions on fundamental concepts and understandings." (Klein et al. 2024, 23; transl. Google). How clearly the definitions differ is shown by the various generic terms used for AI: For example, there can be talk of a "field of computer science" (Google: Aufbruch 2023, p. 4), a "scientific discipline" (EU High Level Expert Group 2019, 36), "the field devoted to building artificial animals (…) and, for many, artificial persons (…)" (Bringsjord and Govindarajulu 2024) and more. Many people understand AI colloquially as "an entity that simulates human intelligence processes such as analyzing and drawing conclusions using machines or computer systems" (Tucci and Laskowski 2025). Artificial intelligence is therefore often understood as a replica of human intelligence, but this merely shifts the

B. Koch (✉)
Institut für Wehrmedizinische Ethik der Bundeswehr, Munich, Germany
e-mail: bernhard.koch@theol.uni-freiburg.de

B. Koch, D. Winkler (eds.), *Artificial Intelligence Ethics in Military Medicine and Humanitarian Healthcare*, Military and Humanitarian Health Ethics,
https://doi.org/10.1007/978-3-032-11331-3_4

problem, as there is no clear definition of human intelligence either. "The lack of a universally accepted definition of intelligence in humans makes it difficult to define intelligence in computer systems." (Rubais 2024, 17). The other possible definition is to define AI in terms of its application goals. However, this moves away from AI as a science towards AI as a technology. "AI is therefore *part engineering, part science*." (Rubais 2024, 17). It is possible to distinguish between narrow Artificial Intelligence, where software is used to perform specific tasks, and broad Artificial Intelligence, in which cognitive tasks are generally addressed ("Artifical General Intelligence"). When we talk about the medical and military medical use of AI, we regularly mean Artificial Narrow Intelligence (ANI). Medical AI (MAI) "may therefore be understood as a subfield of ANI within the healthcare domain." (Rubais 2024, 19).

Artificial intelligence understood as a technology[1] can be used in many different devices, tools or data processing programs: for example, in electronic weather forecasts, in the control of robotics, in vehicles, capacity utilization calculations or lending systems. For military medicine, for example, developments in the field of "autonomous" evacuation drones or AI-allocation-of-resources-software are of particular interest[2] (cf. Pickell et al. 2019; Landgraf 2024; Schmidbauer et al. 2024).[3] However, such a new technology (or a cluster of technologies) also creates uncertainty—especially in terms of normative standards: What can it be used for? Which uses should be excluded? And—inspired by science fiction literature: Is it still a matter of utilizing a thing at all or is it not already a moral subject or at least an object subject to moral consideration, such as a highly developed animal? This uncertainty of action immediately brings ethics onto the scene. But ethics of technology is not really designed to eliminate all uncertainty of action. In the rarest of cases, it is able to definitively determine excluded or permissible uses of a technology. It also has a retroactive effect by analyzing the attitudes of those who develop or at least desire a technology. Armin Grunwald writes aptly about this:

[1] Emmert-Streib et al. 2020 reject speaking of AI as "*a technology*. No. AI is a methodology" (p. 3). But that's likely a minority opinion. Kornwachs (Kornwachs 2024) defines AI as a technology using the concept of convergence: "Two technologies converge when their operational shells remain the same, but their functional cores are exchanged.... The best-known convergence represents what is somewhat inaccurately called digitalization. From this perspective of the philosophy of technology, artificial intelligence is the offspring of a series of such convergence processes" (p. 800 f.; transl. Google).

[2] See e. g. the currently ongoing iMEDCAP project funded by the European Union: https://defence-industry-space.ec.europa.eu/system/files/2023-06/iMEDCAP-Factsheet_EDF22.pdf [20/11/2025].—The issue is loaded with military medical issues just like the questions whether data collected by a medical drone might be used for military purposes. How can medical and military data be separated, and should they be separated if they are beneficial?

[3] Schmidbauer et al. also envisage "AI-supported triage" (564). Autonomous Triage is ethically quite problematic because the individual and concrete judgement is replaced by a general value system that is embedded in general rules (as is the case with so-called 'autonomous vehicles').—According to Masood 2024 (315), triage, together with diagnosis, prediction, decision-making and operations, is one of the most important fields of emergency medicine that have so far been investigated for AI use.

> The task of technology ethics is to reconstruct the normative background of technology assessments and technology decisions according to the standards of rational argumentation in order to contribute to ethically reflected and responsible decisions. (Grunwald and Hillerbrand 2021, 5; trans. B.K. with support from DeepL)

And he goes on to warn against over-emphasizing the productivity of ethics of technology:

> Ethics of Technology *cannot* provide answers to the question of what should be done in cases of normative uncertainty. Society remains on its own when it comes to decisions about the future and setting the course for scientific and technological progress. Ethics does not relieve society of this responsibility, but merely provides conditional normative *advice* on such issues, e.g. in democratic decision-making processes. Ethical expertise in situations of normative uncertainty serves to inform, orient and enlighten the relevant debates and decision-making processes from a normative perspective, but does not determine their outcomes. Clarification of the moral background, not anticipation of decisions, is what follows from reflection in the field of ethics of technology. (Grunwald and Hillerbrand 2021, 8; trans. B.K. with support from DeepL)

Nevertheless, in many cases ethics of technology can and must make a contribution to regulating the use of a particular technology. In many cases, an openness may remain to the effect that other states or political communities regulate differently from one's own country. In principle, this should be tolerated. However, AI has become a kind of global technology that also represents a global problem due to the worldwide networks. Simply withdrawing into oneself is often no longer sufficient. The problem of autonomous weapons[4] systems makes this clear: Self-restriction in the use of AI, which other, possibly opposing, states do not undertake in this way, can jeopardize the basis from which one has undertaken one's own restriction, because it allows the potential opponent to gain technological superiority. If one party leads the way in a potential conflict, the others often have little choice but to follow suit. But then ethics is eliminated by realpolitik, and moral considerations give way to strategic necessity. The following considerations are written from an ethics of technology perspective, which assumes that AI is also a technology and thus AI ethics can be understood as a case of technology ethics (cf. e. g. Heinrichs et al. 2022; Funk 2023).

4.2 The Diversity of Ethical Approaches

While the call for ethics is welcome on the one hand, the appeal itself does not bring any clarity that guides action on the other, simply because it is first necessary to consider which ethical approaches are appropriate and worth considering when dealing with a technology. First of all, ethically considering the use of Artificial Intelligence also involves the usual tension between teleological/consequentialist

---

[4] On the issue of autonomous weapons cf. chap. 8 in this volume and „Short Afterword from a German Perspective"in: Koch 2022 and: Koch 2023, 455–479.

approaches and deontological approaches. The former are primarily present as utilitarian strategies, the latter as rights-based theories. Therefore, in the context of the ethics of AI, questions about risks (e. g. for employment; cf. Müller 2023) and questions about rights violations (e. g. privacy, bias) are raised above all. Technology is developed for the sake of certain advantages that are intended to increase benefits. If a technology generates more (overall) harm than benefit, it would not be justifiable to use it from a utilitarian perspective. In fact, AI promises to be enormously useful in medicine. Charles Davies et al. (2024)[5] mention the areas of "diagnostics and screening",[6] "therapeutics", "clinical care", "mental health and behavioural therapies", "health management systems", "hospital management systems" and "disease surveillance and prediction modelling". In July 2025, it was announced that an AI-controlled robot at Johns Hopkins University, trained with video recordings of gallbladder surgeries, was able to perform the first lifelike operation itself, marking a leap in the development of autonomous surgical robots (Rosen 2025). As Eric Topol writes in his foreword to Chayakrit Krittanawong's anthology on AI in clinical practice: "The cornerstone will be establishing incontrovertible evidence that health outcomes are significantly improved."[7] But even gains in benefits are for many people not sufficient a justification for its use if such a technology violates fundamental rights, such as the right to a certain degree of privacy. However, such fundamental antagonisms in pluralistic communities are often not particularly useful for applied ethical contexts, to which we also include technological and therefore AI-ethical considerations. It would be unusual, for example, if everyone in a moral community could agree on utilitarianism as the normative approach. But even in this case, agreement would still have to be reached on the more concrete form of utilitarianism, e.g. as rule or act utilitarianism, and in what the *utilitas* actually consists in.

Because it is implausible that action-guiding rules of behavior can be found when starting at the general normative level, applied ethics has long been proposing so-called "middle principles" (cf. Lutz-Bachmann 2013, 200–209), from which concrete criteria for a certain subject area are possible. The famous presentation of the "Principles of Biomedical Ethics" by James F. Childress and the late Tom L. Beauchamps is a prime example of this (Beauchamp and Childress 2019). The

[5] The essay is characteristic of a widespread techno-optimistic attitude toward artificial intelligence, especially in emerging countries like India and in Christian Theologies. But the core ethical question stems from the classic insight that ethical obligation presupposes the corresponding ability ("ultra posse nemo tenetur"): We are obligated to use AI responsibly as a tool. But can we continue to use AI responsibly as a tool in the long run? What does "use responsibly" mean when AI itself guides our criteria for reflection? Much remains mere empty phrases, without clarity about the conditions for fulfilling the requirement.

[6] The advantages of Generative Pretrained Transformer (GPT-)Models are available not only to physicians, but to medical laymen as well (cf. Mehnen et al. 2024).

[7] Eric Topol: Foreword. In: Krittanawong 2024, xxiii-xxv, here xxiv.—Topol distinguishes between "narrow" AI, as achieved through "unimodal tasks that capitalize on supervised learning" (xxiii) and has become important for diagnostics, and "wide" AI, which can ultimately take on tasks in clinical practice itself.

four criteria of "non-maleficence", "beneficence", "respect of autonomy" and "justice" are classic in medical and military medical ethics today. They are now also being adopted in other fields, and Luciano Floridi proposes them—supplemented by the further principle of "explicability"—for the ethics of AI as well (Floridi 2023, 57–66).[8]

4.3 Common Criteria in AI Ethics

Along with "responsibleness", "trustworthiness" and the avoidance of bias, "explainability" is now one of the classic criteria mentioned in connection with the ethics of AI (e. g. Schmid 2022). However, it is philosophically essential to scrutinize the factual content of these criteria if the ethics of AI are not to remain stuck in mere rhetoric or marketing language.[9]

(a) The criterion of responsibility ("responsible AI") is of course fundamental on the one hand, but on the other hand it is a formal criterion that leaves the content completely open. In its basic meaning, responsibility means that you have to justify an action by answering either the prospective or the retrospective question ("give a response"): "What are you going to do now?" or "Why did you do this?" (a question that you can and must also ask yourself). The answer is adequate if you state your *reasons* for the respective action. You may also adequately give your *motivations*, but which actions can be justified is determined by the reasons (not the motivations): Someone may argue against abortion because they believe that unborn life should not be killed. Someone may argue in favor of the permissibility of abortion because they do not yet regard embryos as human life worthy of protection. Both give an answer to the question of their actions, both give reasons, and both are therefore prepared to "take responsibility", but—as emphasized—this is a formal characteristic. In terms of content, the question of what is permitted or required to be done is decided by the reasons and justifications. Similarly, the assertion that the AI we have developed is "responsible AI" is not meaningful in terms of content. What it permits and what it excludes does not follow from responsibleness, but from the reasons given for permissibility and exclusion. For example, someone who harbors fun-

[8] "The principle of 'explicability' incorporates both the epistemological sense of 'intelligibility' and the ethical sense of 'accountability' (Floridi 2023, 63).—In a similar way, the High Level Expert Group of the European Commission introduces the four principles of (i) Respect for human autonomy, (ii) Prevention of harm, (iii) Fairness), and (iv) Explicability (2019, 12).

[9] Most of the time, the term "principle" itself remains undefined; can a single word even be a "principle", or does it require a normative preposition? Oniani, Hilsman, Peng et al. 2023 even name nine words (e. g. "equity", "traceability", "accountability") that they want to be understood as principles. Presumably, one should always add: "AI should have X (the principle)" or, in adjectival terms, "AI should be x" or, in adverbial terms, "AI should be used in x-way". But the language remains unclear.

damentally racist convictions may consider an AI that contains a corresponding racist bias to be the responsible AI and even regard it as superior to an AI without this bias. Whether "responsible AI" really represents an ethical quality feature can only be clarified once we know the content that has determined its development. Without such a substantive definition, "responsible AI" remains a buzzword that is more suitable for advertising than having any real ethical bite.

(b) The criterion of avoiding bias in fact draws attention to a serious and also substantive problem of AI. If learning data for an AI contains a bias, if it feeds one-sided prejudices, for example, the results of the processes that the AI operates ("AI decisions"[10]) will also be biased. This is not fundamentally different with human decisions. An employer in Hamburg who has had several bad experiences with employees from Bavaria may consider applicants from Bavaria to be a burden and treat them less favorably when filling another vacancy. However, truly comprehensive statistics do not confirm the theory that there are more difficulties with Bavarian employees. The bias was therefore unfounded. However, such a bias is usually dysfunctional: An entrepreneur who has such prejudices makes it more difficult to find suitable candidates for his company and may not hire the best people he could get. In a free and liberal society, there are therefore strong motivations to eliminate biases as far as possible.—Of course, there may be justified reservations: For example, a restaurant owner may harbor the prejudice, based on his experience, that serving staff with mathematical weaknesses are more likely to create problems in the cash register. In this respect, he will therefore look for employees whose maths skills are good. In this case, it could even be that the bias is "too small", so that overall he pays too little attention to the characteristic of maths ability. But even such an "under-bias" is dysfunctional in a liberal environment.—In the case of AI, for example, it is often pointed out that people with a certain ethnic background could have disadvantages in AI-based bank lending. Such a "racial bias" is indeed ethically unacceptable because racism is unacceptable. But there is also a motivational factor that should prompt every lender to eliminate such biases: She or he harms her- or himself. Not lending to creditworthy people means missing out on business opportunities. The question of biases therefore refers to the social environment: Is a community liberal enough to allow the truly objective criteria to apply? If

[10] Applying the term "decision"to AI processes is tricky. A human decision contains a moment of judgement and necessarily goes beyond an algorithmic process.—Human thinking should not be identified with the reconstructed heuristics of decision-making processes, as Sarah Spiekermann aptly points out. "The number of models that attempt to represent human thinking in the context of decision-making processes is large. But every reasonable scientist also knows that all these models, which break down human thinking regarding decisions into individual components and reassemble them in the dependent variable of action (or intended action), only represent crude heuristics of actual human thought and action. This does not make the models any less valuable. Heuristics are scientifically important for better understanding ourselves as a species. But they are not suitable for fully representing or reliably predicting human thought and action per se." (Spiekermann 2024, 844; transl. Google translate).

it can be shown in military medical ethics that certain biases are factually untenable, they should not guide decisions—neither human nor AI-based ones. However, it is not AI that is the problem here, but the question of what is considered "objectively tenable".

(c) The criterion of explainability is rooted in the justified concern that AI creates a kind of "black box" into which informational input is entered from the outside and informational output is handed out to the outside, but that what happens between input and output is not transparent. It is not clear what happens in the "black box". The problem is further exacerbated by the fact that learning algorithms are not only opaque but also plastic.[11] Here, too, an analogous situation can be observed with human decisions: Someone takes information and then decides in a certain way. However, the thought process cannot simply be observed objectively from the outside, but must basically be asked of the person processing the information (thinking): "Why did you decide this way?" The person who is asked to answer will usually answer by giving reasons. "I cancelled the mountain hike because the weather forecast wasn't good and I'm currently struggling with hip problems." Giving reasons is also ethically necessary because it fulfils the duty of justification that follows from responsibility (see a) above). The person who has asked for the reasons will be able to check the *plausibility* of the reasons given, but will have no definite certainty as to whether these reasons are or were the ones that actually led to the decision made. Perhaps the mountain tour was cancelled because the person wanted to meet up with his extramarital lover but did not want to admit this to the person asking the question. Yuval Harari also refers to the subconscious: "In fact our decisions are *subconsciously* influenced by thousands of additional data points. Being unaware of these subconscious processes, when we deliberate on our decisions or explain them, we often engage in post hoc single-point rationalizations for what really happens as billions of neurons interact inside our brain" (Harari 2024, 337; emphasis by the author). So we do not always deceive intentionally when we give false or simply incomplete explanations of our own behavior and actions.—We are in a similar situation with AI. If you ask AI to explain what led from input to output (an "AI decision"), it can make statements that *seem* plausible to the human recipient. But does this recipient also have the opportunity to check whether the explanation actually describes the processes in the black box? Or is it not rather the case that an AI can also learn to provide explanations that are considered as plausible as possible by human recipients? A serious problem arises here: What ensures the reference to facts or even truth

[11] Cf. Price 2018. Price suggests that the acceptable level of opacity depends on the importance of the algorithmic recommendation: "If, for instance, an algorithm suggests a hidden risk of lung cancer that calls for further testing or watchful waiting, even relatively low levels of validation might justify that recommendation. On the other hand, if an algorithm recommends forgoing a standard treatment, or treating an unknown indication with a powerful drug, provider experience could judge such a recommendation too risky in the absence of very strong validation." (476).

in connection with AI? Or is the very assumption of truth[12] and factuality a mistake? Must "AI decisions" be regarded as constructions without reference to reality and explanations of such decisions as constructions of explanations? Does an AI ethics that demands explainability actually demand something ontologically true or simply something psychologically plausible?[13]

It seems to me that a hasty anthropomorphic transference is leading us astray here. Rajpurkar et al. (2022) are confident that explainability will strengthen trust: "Moreover, when medical AI models achieve novel insights that go beyond current human knowledge, improved explainability may help researchers grasp those new insights and thus better understand the biological mechanisms behind desease" (35). But couldn't it be the other way around, that the methods of AI, which ultimately consist of recording correlations,[14] prevent us from gaining a "real" understanding of something? When we talk about "mechanisms", we are aiming at causality. In many natural and everyday processes, we assume that we have achieved insight when we have grasped the cause-effect relationships. But in this sense, AI does not link two events together. The insights of AI are therefore "beyond current human knowledge" in a stronger sense than these authors themselves probably think: not in the sense of an expansion of knowledge, but in the sense of a completely different kind of knowledge. Furthermore, Rajpurkar et al. (2022) think, "it may become easier to identify dangerous bias if model explainability improves, because human monitors will be able to double check the reasoning of AI systems and identify problematic elements" (36). That seems to me to be a very optimistic view of things. In certain cases, it may be that humans can correct misbehavior by imposing their own thought patterns on machines. But in other cases, human patterns may not be effective at all in explaining machine behavior.

In its statement on artificial intelligence, the German Ethics Council has rather scaled down the demand for explainability in the section on its use in medicine:

> Given the level of technology in modern medicine, it is neither possible nor necessary for those treating patients to always understand the internal processes of the technical aids they

[12] „Truth" is understood here simply as a property of propositions. A proposition is true if it represents a fact. (But perhaps it would be too strong to say that the proposition is true *only if* it represents a fact.—This does not need to be clarified here.)

[13] This point can be explored even further from a technological philosophical perspective, focusing on the relationship between AI and human intelligence as a whole. Explaining and understanding are forms of cognition. Successfully simulating a cognitive performance does not necessarily mean that we have understood that performance (cf. Kornwachs 2024, 805). We only know intuitively what we are performing when we understand or explain something. But do we understand understanding? After all, one can say that understanding already presupposes prior understanding: „Understanding integrates the new findings into the already existing knowledge"(Kornwachs 2024, 818; transl. Google).

[14] The 'optimistic' view is that "the age of causality is behind us, and we are already in the age of correlation, moving toward a future that, thanks to unlimited data, no longer needs to deal with errors, aberrations, and methodological limitations." Gerd Antes: Big Data und Personalisierte Medizin. Goldene Zukunft oder leere Versprechungen? Quoted from: Wiesing (2020), 615 (transl. B.K.).

> use in detail, as long as these processes can be sufficiently understood and thus verified at least by suitable bodies. (Deutscher Ethikrat 2023, 194; transl. B.K. with the help of Google translate).[15]

Tim Wiegand and Laura Velezmoro preface their book on artificial intelligence in medicine with five opinions. The third is as follows: "The results of AI systems should be explainable. This so-called explainability is crucial for building trust among practitioners and patients in the use of AI in medicine" (Wiegand and Velezmoro 2025, vii; transl. B.K. with DeepL). Explainability is therefore required here because it is seen as a prerequisite for trust. Trust, in turn, is a prerequisite for the use of a technology. If one assumes that the use of the technology is ethically preferable, one will probably also assume that explainability is ethically preferable. But strictly speaking, explainability is not an ethical criterion at all. It addresses an ability (explain-"ability") that can also be realized "technically". Like any ability it can be used for good or for bad. The criterion of trustworthiness is different. Here, reference is made to a value ("worthy"). The point is not that an AI is actually trusted, but that it actually *deserves* this trust. But what can be a criterion for determining whether something (or someone) deserves trust? A prime candidate in the case of technical devices is certainly how well they work: A hoover that does not work or only works very irregularly is not reliable. In this respect, it cannot be trusted. A dishwasher that works reliably will be trusted.

In that regard, you can also say of an AI: if it does what it is supposed to do, it is trustworthy. But the performance itself can be good or bad. An assault rifle can also function better or worse, but there is not always an ethical advantage in its functioning, e.g. if the rifle is used for a robbery. This becomes even clearer with humans: people who allow themselves to be used for bad purposes (e. g. hitmen) may be reliable in an extra-moral sense, but not trustworthy in a moral sense. We must therefore say that the AI-ethical criterion of trustworthiness does not answer the ethical question, but rather poses it itself. When is an AI good? When its work (Greek "ergon", Latin "opus") is good? If it reliably delivers this good work, it is trustworthy. In the case of artificial artefacts, e.g. the ropes attached to a via ferrata, the terms "reliable" and "trustworthy" can be used as synonyms to a certain extent, because the aim is to reliably achieve certain effects. But when applied to people, a differentiation seems possible. Similar to the criterion of explainability, we assume a reference to truth when we speak of "trustworthy": It is about the truth about a person's moral constitution, i.e. their character.

[15] However, according to German Ethics Council 2023, 195 this downgraded requirement for explainability affects the users (doctors and presumably also patients), but not the developers of the systems. For developers, „basic functions and work processes must be explainable and interpretable".

4.4 The Approach of the German Ethics Council

Statements on ethics in the field of Artificial Intelligence are currently springing up like mushrooms.[16] This is certainly a sign that there is a great deal of uncertainty or that it is assumed that there is a great deal of uncertainty that needs to be countered. With this in mind, the German Ethics Council also issued a comprehensive statement in 2023 (Deutscher Ethikrat 2023). I highlight this study in particular because it does not attempt to work with the vocabulary subjected to critical scrutiny above, but instead seeks to develop an alternative approach that is obviously inspired by the philosophy of Immanuel Kant. In contrast to other philosophical approaches to technology, this approach, which formulates AI ethics from a technical-ethical foundation, remains fundamentally anthropocentric and in this sense "classical" or "humanist" (cf. Nida-Rümelin and Weidenfeld 2022). The guiding principle is that ethical thinking should point the way to appropriate *human* behavior. In this "humanist(ic)" view, technology is understood as a human device that can fundamentally expand and improve human options for action, and a certain technology—such as AI applications in this case—is to be assessed according to whether it actually achieves this expansion of human authorship. For the authors of the statement, it is clearly recognizable that artificial intelligence can be a tool that supports and increases human agency:

> AI in particular opens up opportunities to improve human action, for example through pattern recognition in large amounts of data for medical or official purposes, through improved predictions based on this, for example on the spread of infectious diseases or for forecasts in police work (predictive policing), through new possibilities for individualized information and advertising, but also through applications in the field of education. (section 4.4. p. 177; transl. B.K.).

In this view, the vanishing point for successful human action is that further successful human action is made possible. Or to put it another way—in more modern terms—free action is about ensuring that free action remains possible and that the scope for freedom continues to expand. Armin Grunwald speaks of the "technological ethical imperative to preserve the conditions for the possibility of technological design" (Grunwald 2024, 881), which is more of a minimum requirement[17] and falls short of the demand to expand people's freedom of action. However, there is a problematic ambivalence here, particularly in the case of AI applications. Washing machines and hoovers have made life easier and significantly improved the ability to keep laundry and the home clean without significantly restricting freedom of action. But will this be the same with AI? The opinion of the German Ethics Council identifies the following dangers: (1) emerging dependencies, (2) pressure to conform and (3) closure of options. The opinion then goes on to apply this fundamental criterion to selected social areas: a) medicine, b) education, c) public communication

[16] Cf. chap. 2 in this volume.

[17] Grunwald speaks against the background of the thesis (e.g. by Ray Kurzweil) that sooner or later technology itself will or even should take over the development of technology („singularity“).

and opinion-forming and d) public administration. Only one example from the medical field will be given here, which is also relevant to military medicine because military service is often associated with great psychological stress:

> In recent years, a wealth of tools for the (partial) diagnosis and treatment of various mental health problems has emerged, mostly in the form of freely available screen-based apps, such as chatbots, with which a kind of therapy ... takes place with those affected on an algorithmic basis." (p. 210f.) "However, there are important concerns and problems from an ethical perspective, particularly in the case of replacing therapeutic professionals with machines. There are obvious problems such as the lack of quality control of the bots (...), questions about data collection and further use, questions about the protection of privacy and the ... lack of a warning function, for example in the case of clear suicidal behavior. (p. 213).

Feelings of attachment to the chatbot or feelings of only receiving second-class treatment are also addressed. However, it would also be particularly serious if the chatbots were so powerful that the human psychotherapists had to recognize their inferiority and recommend replacing their work with that of the chatbot. This is where the aspect of limiting the ability to act through the use of technology comes fully into play: The more powerful the AI becomes, the more superfluous human expertise and action becomes—at least to all appearances—so that one must honestly suggest replacing oneself with the algorithmic execution. This circumstance can also be relevant in diagnosis at present: AI may recognize certain diseases better than human doctors, so it is only natural that AI should take on this task. ("Automation bias" may be reasonable in many cases.) In this case, however, AI has not strengthened the ability of humans to act, but rather weakened it. As Rosalind McDougall has pointed out, the use of AI is putting the concept of shared decision making between doctor and patient under pressure. AI seems to provide both doctor and patient with a solution that is no longer contestable, thus bringing paternalism back into medicine. The values of doctor and patient are no longer adequately taken into account. However, McDougall hopes to remedy this through "value sensitive design" (McDougall 2019, 156–160).

Anyway, AI ethics is often concerned with criteria that affect the "recipients" of AI actions, such as data protection or bias; sometimes AI ethics is also concerned with criteria that affect the AI itself, e.g. in the question of whether AI-controlled robotics itself can be a subject or object of ethical concern—e.g. in the question of whether there can be robots that may not simply be switched off any more than humans can be killed; but AI can also be viewed ethically from the perspective of its "users", i.e. those who use AI in a certain function because they want to achieve certain goals with its help. They embed the technology in their actions or expand their cognitive and behavioral abilities with the help of the technology.[18] This is the perspective that will be taken on AI in the context of military medicine in the following.

[18] Cf. chap. 10 in this volume.

4.5 The Basis of Morality

What is ethical about AI ethical considerations anyway? The answer depends on what one understands by "ethics". But there is doubtlessly a certain basic philosophical understanding that has a common core and then recognizes differences at the edges. I consider this core to include the thesis that there is a fundamental separation between descriptive and normative considerations and that theoretical and practical reason should also be distinguished in this sense. The exact extent of the separation is certainly controversial, but it is generally accepted that no conclusions about what ought to be can be drawn from descriptions of a being (what is the case; "is-ought-problem"). It is therefore not ethically sufficient to refer to risks or negative consequences associated with the use of a technology. Risks can be countered by opportunities, and if opportunities and risks are to be weighed up, a normative principle of balancing is required. Utilitarians also struggle with this difficulty because the respective principles of weighing up cannot simply be justified in utilitarian terms if one has not simply *set* a certain descriptive goal; a "setting" that could itself be justified normatively. Ethical reasoning therefore has a different basis than simple empirical observation. The thesis, which cannot be substantiated here, is that ethical deliberation rests on a practice of moral judgement that is simply fundamental to human practice (cf. Ricken 2013, 91 f.). As Peter Strawson has shown in "Freedom and Resentment" (Strawson 1962), there are basic moral reactions that cannot simply be traced back to empirical facts. Someone who is willfully kicked in the shin on a tram reacts with indignation, and this indignation is not only a psychological but also a moral reaction. If it turns out that the kick was not willful but unintentional, the moral reaction changes immediately, although the "empirical" pain does not change. As human beings, we therefore relate to each other directly in moral terms. However, these basic reactions include not only moral reproaches, but also attributions of moral merit, as they can underlie the attitude of gratitude. Anyone who rescues me from a precarious situation that I have caused myself will—at least with a healthy moral attitude—be able to expect a reaction of gratitude from me. Now there do indeed seem to be people who react somewhat insensitively in situations that usually suggest gratitude or praise. In situations, however, in which actions or behavior occur that are morally reproachable, even people who usually find it difficult to praise react with a feeling or rather an attitude of resentment. As a psychological fact, praise/gratitude and reproach/grief may be distributed asymmetrically, but from a moral point of view we usually claim symmetry: if someone is given something that they urgently need, we expect them to be grateful; if someone is deprived of something that they urgently need, we expect moral reproach. Mind you, this is only about an *attitude*; it does not determine which specific *actions* should follow from this attitude. Of course, the difference between action and omission plays a role here: we often demand obligations to refrain with greater stringency than a corresponding duty to act. The most drastic example concerns the life of our fellow human beings as such: We demand the strictest omission of actions that take life; but we by no means demand a duty to produce life. This is why gratitude towards parents is often not symmetrical to the reproach we level at a murderer or manslayer. At this level of the organization of our moral coexistence, asymmetries are not strange.

4.6 The Credit-Blame Asymmetry

Now, however, the AI ethicist Sven Nyholm and others (cf. eg. Danaher & Nyholm 2020) have introduced a point of view in connection with generative Artificial Intelligence that does not locate asymmetrization at the level of already existing asymmetries in the moral evaluation of actions, but rather states an asymmetrization effect due to the actual use of AI. We can take the example of an AI-generated text for politics or pastoral care: If a politician gives a speech or a priest gives a sermon, it can be good or bad according to the respective criteria for political speeches or priestly sermons. Aspects such as their ability to motivate certain actions will be among the criteria. Depending on the quality of the speech or sermon, the politician or priest will be praised or criticized. Insofar as such a speech or sermon is also morally required or preferable, the praise or censure also contains a moral aspect. Now, as Nyholm points out, the politician can be reprimanded if the AI-generated speech is bad, but the priest cannot be praised if the AI-generated sermon is good. This is because the successful sermon is not the work of the priest, and in this respect it is not attributable to the priest when he delivers it. But the politician should not have given the bad speech, so that the speech is still attributed to her if she gives it. She has at least neglected her duty of care if she delivers the speech unchecked. Nyholm locates the factual problem in the context of the debate about responsibility gaps arising from the use of AI:

> Positive and negative responsibility gaps are asymmetrical.—Traditional theories of blame, reflected in many legal standards, suggest that if we are reckless or negligent with respect to bringing about a negative outcome, even if we did not intend to do so, we can still be held responsible for it. By contrast, to deserve credit for a positive outcome, we must exert some effort, or display some form of talent, or make some sacrifice to bring it about. (Mann, Earp, Nyholm et al. 2023, 472)

It is not necessarily only generated texts that are affected by this problem. Generated images or other artefacts are also subject to it. If they succeed, they are the work of anonymous technology; if they fail, they are attributable to the person who uses them in any further use:

> The use of generative AI elevates the bar for earning credit, but standards for assigning blame remain the same. (Mann, Earp, Nyholm et al. 2023, 472)

Perhaps the standard for blame will even be lowered because one can now accuse someone of having better technical tools available. In any case, this observation can also be made in the context of military medical services, even if there were still no powerful examples of the use of generative AI. But it's enough to imagine the use of AI presented by Patty Nieberg for military medicine (Nieberg 2025): To compensate for the shortage of specialists, AI is intended to enable even soldiers who are not fully trained in the field to administer the correct anesthesia. Here, too, the credit-blame asymmetry can come into play. If you do it wrong, you are responsible and possibly even liable. If you do it right, you still don't get praise. With the advent of generative AI, this is becoming even more acute. The increasing use of generative AI raises the serious question of whether there can still be good military doctors at all, or whether there are only bad ones left.

4.7 Liability Culture

Although the problem seems particularly relevant to generative AI, it is perhaps a problem of technology utilization in general and in any case already relevant in the field of pattern recognition, e.g. in medical diagnostics. If we know or assume that an AI system is capable of significantly superior diagnostics, there is not only psychological pressure to use the diagnostics and consider its results to be the most authoritative ("automation bias"), but also a moral obligation to favor AI diagnostics. However, the expectation of competence on the part of doctors when making diagnoses is not off the table. If the AI-based diagnosis is correct, the doctor who has used AI (for good reasons) cannot expect praise or recognition. However, if she adopts an AI diagnosis that is flawed, she will not be completely exempt from (moral) reproach. After all, it was her decision to orientate herself on the AI's diagnosis. So here, too, we find a credit-blame asymmetry. The consequences of this asymmetry obviously lie in the fact that hardly any doctors still excel in diagnostics, but can continue to fail in diagnostics. Of course, this also applies to military medicine when AI is used. When it comes to the question of whether there can still be good military physicians, "good" is understood not only as "technically good" but also morally. The problem leads into the field of virtue ethics.[19] Can there still be virtues of the doctor or the military physician at all—or only more or less incompetence and vice? Or does virtue itself generally only lie in the avoidance of mistakes?

[19] However, "virtue ethics" can mean different things. One of the questions that is repeatedly asked in connection with digital technology is whether the technical artifacts themselves can be virtuous. E. g. Hindocha and Badea 2022 affirm the idea that medical AI based on machine learning should simply 'copy' many examples of good or virtuous human role models. Such an AI would then become virtuous itself. However, we find two flaws: Virtue also requires a standard. Whether someone is a good role model is not easily determined. And virtues are attitudes. Mere external replication says nothing about whether the attitude is the same or whether an attitude exists at all. So speaking of machine virtue is at best anthropomorphizing. As Constantinescu and Crisp point out: AI systems may be able "to mimic human virtuous actions and even to function behaviourally in ways equivalent to human beings", but they "cannot perform virtuous actions in accordance with virtues, that is, rightly or virtuously" (Constantinescu/Crisp 2022: 1555). Virtue ethics aims at the virtues of people as people: "The central goal of every technical development must be that the promotion of the artificial 'virtues' of a system does not come at the expense of the natural virtues of the system users." (Beier et al. 2024, 57; transl. B.K.).

Can one still maintain a "good attitude" towards correct action if one leaves the action (or a functional substitute for it) to technology?

So, a doctor's technical goodness (which could also be called "virtue", "arete") must of course be distinguished from his ethical goodness, but it is probably not the case, especially in medicine, that one can objectively separate the two completely. Medicine is caring, and caring is not simply a technical process with success and failure rates. Therefore it is important to see that so-called "de-skilling" as such is not the crucial moral problem.[20] De-skilling occurs in the area of skills, and recent studies on cognitive performance in users of Large Language Models such as ChatGPT are very worrying (Kosmyna et al. 2025), but this is not always morally problematic. Virtue, however, consists in an attitude (*hexis*); with a good attitude to de-skilling, skills would be lost, but not virtue. Shannon Vallor has argued (also drawing on Julia Annas) that attitudes should not simply be viewed as relevant to virtue without recourse to practices. But practices require practical skills. She names the relevant skill as "an acquired quasi-perceptual sensitivity to the morally salient features of particular circumstances, or to put it another way, to the moral reasons that such circumstances generate".[21] Generative AI, one could say, makes us lose certain practices, e. g. a) writing a good sermon, and b) attributing praise—which also impairs our ability to praise or be grateful, which brings us into the area of attitudes that constitute virtues in the true sense.[22]

If a culture of gratitude declines because there are no more occasions for gratitude, but a culture of moral reproach persists because there are still faulty actions that are morally reproachable and have led to bad results, this will presumably also lead to a culture of liability and recourse claims. The WHO's new guidelines on generative AI also focus on liability.[23] This is, it says, a task for governments in particular and even goes so far as to demand "strict liability", which means that there are no longer any human intent or negligence that create a connection between the person who is liable—or is considered/constructed as liable—and the damage itself. The WHO statement then also worries about discouragement, but not in the

[20] The fact that good translation tools are available today also compels the author of this text to use them. This undoubtedly does not strengthen his ability to master the foreign language. This de-skilling is worrying, but probably not yet morally worrying.—On the loss of competence due to AI, see briefly: BBAW 2021, 48–51.

[21] Cf. Vallor 2015: "If new technological practices disrupt the cultivation of moral skills on a large enough scale, the future of human character may be profoundly affected" (111). In the context of the discussion of autonomous weapons systems, Vallor aptly emphasizes that moral deskilling does not only mean losing certain moral abilities, but also the ability to judge machines in this regard at all (115).

[22] On gratitude cf. Darwall 2024, 135–150.—Darwall makes a strict distinction between reactive attitudes of the will and reactive attitudes of the heart. The former ("deontic reactive attitudes") are moral reactions that respond to compliance with norms or violations of norms. He places gratitude entirely on the side of attitudes of the heart. This can probably be questioned. One can also be grateful for morally correct actions (as an attitude). Maybe what Darwall really wants to say is: Gratitude cannot be represented as a 'technocratic' response with a stimulus-response-model.

[23] E. g. WHO 2024, xiv.

sense of human creativity, but rather that the use of "sophisticated LLMs" is discouraged. The concern is that the advantageous technology is not used enough, but not to the extent that people in this technical context experience a kind of moral overload, which consists in being held responsible for processes that they were no longer able to shape or influence. (To me this seems to be a true source of so-called "moral injury".) In order to ward off liability claims, technical means could then be resorted to. To protect against such claims, there will probably be an attempt to interpose technical instances—including AI. A second-instance technology will then check whether the first-instance technology has worked as error-free as possible. In this way, technology will gradually force humans out of (still) basic moral reactions.

This "culture of liability" is itself a technocratic construct on the outside. "If X performs the action f, then X is liable to Y"—with universal regularity. What constitutes the moral behavior of people among and in connection to people no longer applies: Their awareness of their singularity and the recognition of the singularity of the other. The individual person is not an abstract X with the characteristics a, b, c, but "this" or "that". The military doctor also wants to be recognized as herself and—if her actions are good—receive moral praise (i.e. praise based on her integrity). The praise may flatter her, but she probably does not (only) want the praise because it is flattering, but because it is based on her actions. If she consistently and reliably performs such good acts of military medicine, she is a good military doctor. However, if there is no longer any opportunity for (good) action because such actions are left to the machines in terms of their external form (not their moral quality), the morally recognizable motivation for good action also ceases to exist: namely, her being motivated by good action itself (and not by its effects). Ex negativo, however, bad behavior remains possible, namely as a failure to control and supervise the technology. The fear of liability then becomes a motivational factor, but it is not focussed on an ethical good, but rather on the loss of material and external goods. In fact, such a loss of our basic moral reactions is not unlikely. There are no moral grounds for praise, and the moral grounds for blame are merely transformed into liability considerations, which themselves require technical solutions to prevent or contain a loss. Applied to military medicine, this means that there are no longer any good military doctors, and the badness of the bad ones has no moral quality, but merely a structural one. It seems to require a technical remedy.

4.8 Conclusion

AI is associated with a multitude of real risks of incapacitation (cf. Koska 2023, 130–133). Many of these relate to non-moral contexts. For example, medical expertise may be lost because it is taken over by a powerful AI and thus no longer practiced. The intriguing question for ethics is whether a kind of moral incapacitation could also occur. It was the task of the above considerations to show how the use of generative AI can actually lead to an erosion of basic moral awareness. Of course, not all argumentative transitions are logically compelling, but rather often psychologically plausible. If we take the approach of the German Ethics Council seriously and demand that the use of AI should broaden and not constrict human action scopes, then we must come up with creative solutions with regard to the use of AI as to how logics and technical dynamics can be broken in such a way that they do not take all moral awareness with them, but instead create a "pause" that also allows judgement and prudence to come into play again. This is perhaps where a military medical situation offers an opportunity that sets it apart even from civilian medicine and other fields of AI application: By embedding it in a "combat situation", which also evokes role conflicts, for example, there may be such a refraction. In recent decades, there has been intense philosophical debate about the plausibility or implausibility of the thesis of the equality of combatants (cf. Koch 2023). The moral implausibility of the legal equality of combatants—which equality is provided for in International Humanitarian Law—thus might evoke a "pause". Although the norm of International Law initially has a restrictive effect, it brings reflection and consideration and thus freedom back into the action—especially in the context of a technicist dynamic. For now, judgement is once again required, which cannot simply be produced technically. But this aspect needs to be examined in more detail.

References

BBAW Berlin-Brandenburgische Akademie der Wissenschaften: 2021. *Verantwortungsvoller Einsatz von KI? Mit menschlicher Kompetenz!, Berlin 2021.* Online Available: https://www.bbaw.de/files-bbaw/user_upload/publikationen/BBAW_Verantwortung-KI-4_A5_Broschuere_2020_online-version.pdf

Beauchamp, Tom L. and James F. Childress: Principles of Biomedical Ethics. Eight Edition, Oxford (Oxford University Press) 2019.

Beier, Kathi, Dagmar Borchers, H.-H. Dassow, Martin Hähnel, Björn Haferkamp, Antonia Kempkens, and Regina Müller. 2024. Tugendethische Ansätze. In *Digitale Ethik*, ed. Petra Grimm, Kai Erik Trost, and Oliver Zöllner, 49–61. Baden-Baden: Nomos.

Bringsjord, Selmer, and Naveen Sundar Govindarajulu, 2024. Artificial Intelligence, *The Stanford Encyclopedia of Philosophy* (Fall 2024 Edition), Edward N. Zalta & Uri Nodelman (eds.), URL = https://plato.stanford.edu/archives/fall2024/entries/artificial-intelligence/

Constantinescu, Mihaela, and Roger Crisp. 2022. Can Robotic AI Systems Be Virtuous and Why Does This Matter? *International Journal of Social Robotics* 14:1547–1557.

Danaher, John, and Sven Nyholm. 2020. Automation, Work and the Achievement Gap. *AI and Ethics* 1:227–237.

Darwall, Stephen: The Heart and its Attitudes, Oxford (Oxford University Press) 2024.

Davies, J. Charles, Maria Frances Bukelo, and Manjulika Vaz. 2024. Artificial Intelligence in Healthcare: A Theological Standpoint. *Vidya Deep Journal* 12 (2):

Deutscher Ethikrat: 2023. Mensch und Maschine–Herausforderungen durch Künstliche Intelligenz. Stellungnahme, Berlin, 20th march 2023 (Executive summary in English: German Ethics Council: Humans and Machines, Opinion. Executive summary and recommendation, Berlin, 20th march 2023). Online available: https://www.ethikrat.org/publikationen/stellungnahmen/mensch-und-maschine/

Emmert-Streib, Frank, Olli Yli-Harja, and Matthias Dehmer. 2020. Artificial Intelligence. A Clarification of Misconceptions, Myths and Desired Status. *Frontiers in Artificial Intelligence* 3:524339. https://doi.org/10.3389/frai.2020.524339.

Floridi, Luciano: The Ethics of Artificial Intelligence, Oxford (Oxford University Press) 2023.

Funk, Michael: Ethik künstlicher Intelligenz. Eine Topographie zur praktischen Orientierung, Wiesbaden (Springer Vieweg) 2023.

Google: Aufbruch. 2023. Mensch und Gesellschaft im digitalen Wandel, Nr. 30/2, 2023. Online available: https://issuu.com/google_2021/docs/aufbruch-ki-2023-de [2/7/2025; not available 20/11/2025]

Grunwald, Armin, and Rafaela Hillerbrand. 2021. *Handbuch Technikethik*. 2nd ed. Berlin: J. B. Metzler; Springer.

Grunwald, Armin. 2024. Technikgestaltung: KI als Dienstleistung. In *Philosophisches Handbuch Künstliche Intelligenz*, ed. Klaus Mainzer, 865–883. Wiesbaden: Springer VS.

Harari, Yuval Noah: Nexus. A Brief History of Information Networks from the Stone Age to AI, New York (Random House Fern Press) 2024.

Heinrichs, Bert, Jan-Hendrik Heinrichs, and Markus Rüther. 2022. *Künstliche Intelligenz*. Berlin/Boston: de Gruyter.

High Level Expert Group on Artificial Intelligence. 2019. *set up by the European Commission: Ethics Guidelines for Trustworthy AI*. Vol. 8. Brussels.

Hindocha, Sumeet, and Cosmin Badea. 2022. Moral exemplars for the virtuous machine. The clinician's role in ethical artificial intelligence for healthcare. *AI and Ethics* 2:167–175.

Klein, Andreas, Sebastian Dennerlein, and Helmut Ritschl. 2024. Einleitung. In *Healthcare und Künstliche Intelligenz. Ethische Aspekte verstehen—Entwicklungen gestalten*, ed. Andreas Klein, Sebastian Dennerlein, and Helmut Ritschl, 19–47. Tübingen: Narr Francke Attempto.

Koch, Bernhard: Short Afterword from a German Perspective. In: Bernhard Koch/Richard Schoonhoven (eds.): Emerging Military Technologies. Ethical and Legal Perspectives, Leiden (Brill) 2022, 258–264.

Koch, Bernhard: Der Gegner als Mitmensch. Michael Walzer, Jeff McMahan und die moralphilosophische Kritik am Humanitären Völkerrecht, Münster (Aschendorff) 2023.

Kornwachs, Klaus. 2024. Positionen der Technikphilosophie. In *Philosophisches Handbuch Künstliche Intelligenz*, ed. Klaus Mainzer, 793–835. Wiesbaden: Springer VS.

Koska, Christopher: Ethik der Algorithmen. Auf der Suche nach Zahlen und Werten, Berlin: J.B. Metzler bei Springer Nature 2023.

Kosmyna, Natalia, Eugene Hauptmann, Ye Tong Yuan, Jessica Situ, Xian-Hao Liao, Ashly Vivian Beresnitzky, and Iris Braunstein. 2025. Pattie Maes: Your Brain on ChatGPT: Accumulation of Cognitive Debt when Using an AI Assistant for Essay Writing Task. *MIT*. Online available: https://www.media.mit.edu/publications/your-brain-on-chatgpt/.

Krittanawong, Chaykrit. 2024. *Artificial Intelligence in Clinical Practice. How AI Technologies Impact Medical Research and Clinics*. London/San Diego: Academic Press.

Landgraf, Susann. 2024. Deutlich mehr als nur eine fliegende Patiententrage. *Europäische Sicherheit & Technik*60–62.

Lutz-Bachmann, Matthias. 2013. *Grundkurs Philosophie. Band 7: Ethik*. Stuttgart.

Mann, Sebastian Porsdam, Brian D. Earp, Sven Nyholm, et al. 2023. Generative AI Entails a Credit-Blame Asymmetry. *Nature Machine Intelligence* 5:472–475.

Masood, Sameer. 2024. Artificial intelligence in emergency medicine. In *Artificial Intelligence in Clinical Practice. How AI Technologies Impact Medical Research and Clinics*, ed. Chaykrit Krittanawong, 315–317. London/San Diego: Academic Press.

McDougall, Rosalind J. 2019. Computer Knows Best? The Need for Value-Flexibility in Medical AI. *Journal of Medical Ethics* 45:156–160.

Mehnen, Lars, Stefanie Gruarin, Mina Vasileva, and Bernhard Knapp. 2024. ChatGPT als Arzt? Eine experimentelle Studie zur diagnostischen Genauigkeit bei häufigen und seltenen Krankheiten—ein Forschungsbericht. In *Healthcare und Künstliche Intelligenz. Ethische Aspekte verstehen—Entwicklungen gestalten*, ed. Andreas Klein, Sebastian Dennerlein, and

Helmut Ritschl, 143–151. Tübingen: Narr Francke Attempto. English preprint available: ChatGPT as a medical doctor? A diagnostic accuracy study on common and rare diseases | medRxiv.

Müller, Vincent C., 2023. Ethics of Artificial Intelligence and Robotics, *The Stanford Encyclopedia of Philosophy* (Fall 2023 Edition), Edward N. Zalta & Uri Nodelman (eds.), URL = https://plato.stanford.edu/archives/fall2023/entries/ethics-ai/

Nida-Rümelin, Julian, and Natalie Weidenfeld. 2022. *Digital Humanism. For a Humane Transformation of Democracy, Economy and Culture in the Digital Age*. Cham: Springer.

Nieberg, Patty: 2025. *Army Researchers Want AI to Help Soldiers Deliver Anesthetics in Battle*. Task Purpose 10/3/2025. Online available: https://taskandpurpose.com/news/army-tool-ai-anesthetics/

Oniani, David, Jordan Hilsman, Yifan Peng, et al. 2023. Adopting and Expanding Ethical Principles for Generative Artificial Intelligence from Military to Healthcare. *Npj Digital Medicine* 6:225.

Pickell, W., A. Kopeikin, E. Bristow, and J. Bluman. 2019. Feasibility Study for a MEDEVAC Electric UAS Capability. In *2019 International Conference on Unmanned Aircraft Systems (ICUAS)*, 630–635. Atlanta, GA, USA. https://doi.org/10.1109/ICUAS.2019.8797946.

Price, W. Nicholson, II. 2018. Big Data and Black-Box Medical Algorithms. *Science Translational Medicine* 10:471–476.

Rajpurkar, Pranav, Emma Chen, Oishi Banerjee, and Eric J. Topol. 2022. AI in Health and Medicine. *Nature Medicine* 28:31–38.

Ricken, Friedo: Allgemeine Ethik, 5th, Stuttgart (W. Kohlhammer) 2013.

Rosen, Jill: 2025. Robot Performs First Realistic Surgery without Human Help. System Trained on Videos of Surgeries Performs like an Expert Surgeon. Online: https://hub.jhu.edu/2025/07/09/robot-performs-first-realistic-surgery-without-human-help/. With reference to: Axel Krieger et al.: SRT-H: A Hierarchical Framework for Autonomous Surgery via Language-Conditioned Imitation Learning. *Science Robotics* 10 (104).

Rubais, Giovanni: Ethics of Medical AI, Cham (Springer Nature) 2024.

Schmid, Stefka. 2022. Trustworthy and Explainable: A European Vision of (Weaponised) Artificial Intelligence. *Die Friedens-Warte* 95 (3–4): 290–315.

Schmidbauer, W., C. Jänig, E. Vits, T. Gruebl, S. Sauer, N. Weller, K. Kehe, F. Holzapfel, T. Lüth, K. G. Kanz, E. Rittinghaus, and P. Biberthaler. 2024. Ein neues Rettungskonzept für Schwerstverletzte in militärischen und zivilen Großschadenslagen: DRONEVAC. *Notfall + Rettungsmedizin* 27 (7): 560–567.

Spiekermann, Sarah. 2024. Zum Unterschied zwischen künstlicher und menschlicher Intelligenz und den ethischen Implikationen der Verwechslung. In *Philosophisches Handbuch Künstliche Intelligenz*, ed. Klaus Mainzer, 837–852. Wiesbaden: Springer VS.

Strawson, Peter F. 1962. Freedom and Resentment. *Proceedings of the British Academy* 48:187–211.

Tucci, Linda, and Nicole Laskowski: 2025. Definition Künstliche Intelligenz (KI). ComputerWeekly.de. Online available: https://www.computerweekly.com/de/definition/Kuenstliche-Intelligenz-KI (updated May 2024) [28/7/2025].

Vallor, Shannon. 2015. Moral Deskilling and Upskilling in a New Machine Age. Reflections on the Ambiguous Future of Character. *Philosophy & Technology* 28 (1): 107–124.

WHO. 2024. *World Health Organization: Ethics and Governance of Artificial Intelligence for Health. Guidance on Large Multi-Modal Models*. Geneva: World Health Organization. Online available: https://www.who.int/publications/i/item/9789240084759.

Wiegand, Tim, and Laura Velezmoro: Künstliche Intelligenz in der Medizin. Anwendungen, Algorithmen und Programmierung, München (Elsevier) 2025.

Wiesing, Urban. 2020. *Ethik in der Medizin. Ein Studienbuch*. Stuttgart: Reclam.

Bernhard Koch is a research associate at the Institut für Wehrmedizinische Ethik der Bundeswehr in Munich and adjunct professor of moral theology at the University of Freiburg. He worked at the Institute for Theology and Peace in Hamburg for more than 17 years, most recently as acting director. His research focuses on the ethics of (military) violence, International Humanitarian Law and new military technologies. He has been co-teacher ethics at the ICMM Courses on Military Medical Ethics for more than a decade.

Chapter 5
Ethical Analysis of Emerging Health-Monitoring Technologies in Military Settings

Sheena M. Eagan

5.1 Introduction

Whether in the form of a watch, a ring, or even sewn into the fabric of clothing, continuous health monitoring technologies are rapidly advancing and becoming a part of everyday life. These new technologies have proven useful in various health-related capacities, ranging from personalized medicine and research to public health monitoring, contact tracing, and infectious disease prevention (Dignam and Vandebilt 2024, Smith 2024). The use of this technology has also become widespread in the training of high-performance athletes for injury prevention, training optimization, and team management (Bourdon et al. 2017). With this increasingly widespread use, it is worth considering how military organizations may integrate health-monitoring technology (Friedl 2018).

Military organizations may use these new technologies to monitor vital signs, sleep patterns, and overall well-being among service members. Much like its use in athletics, this technology could improve training, prevent injury, and promote general force readiness (A2 Global Electronics, DEVCOM 2021, South 2023, Vergun 2023). While continuous health monitoring technologies seem to offer promise with regard to population health management, ethical concerns related to privacy, autonomy, and data misuse must be addressed. The chapter provides speculative analysis based on how health-monitoring technologies are currently being used and argues a basic framework for the ethical application of these technologies within the military context. The chapter examines how considerations evolve based on key features, including: the invasiveness of the technology (wearable vs. implantable), the

S. M. Eagan (✉)
Brody School of Medicine at East Carolina University, Greenville, NC, USA
e-mail: eagansh17@ecu.edu

B. Koch, D. Winkler (eds.), *Artificial Intelligence Ethics in Military Medicine and Humanitarian Healthcare*, Military and Humanitarian Health Ethics,
https://doi.org/10.1007/978-3-032-11331-3_5

autonomy of the service-member (whether participation is mandated or voluntary), and the nature of the military activity (in-garrison, during training, pre/post/deployment).

5.2 What Is Continuous Health Monitoring?

Continuous health monitoring technologies refer to devices and systems that track and record various physiological metrics in real-time, allowing for continuous and constant monitoring of an individual's health.

5.2.1 Wearable Technology

These technologies typically come in the form of wearables, such as smartwatches, fitness trackers, and smart rings. Due to the constant data collection and internet connectivity, these wearables offer real-time tracking of various physiological metrics. The Apple Watch, for example, incorporates sensors that monitor heart rate and can detect irregular rhythms such as atrial fibrillation. Another example is the Oura Ring, which measures sleep patterns and heart rate variability to inform users about their recovery and readiness for daily activities. The data collected is then stored, analyzed, and even transmitted. These technologies are designed to provide users with immediate feedback on their health to promote proactive self-care and/or facilitate early detection of potential issues. The wearable devices are equipped with sensors that measure key health metrics like heart rate, physical activity, sleep patterns, blood oxygen levels (SpO2), and sometimes more specialized indicators such as glucose levels or electrocardiogram (ECG) readings. Beyond consumer wearables, a growing array of devices are designed for more advanced health monitoring. Continuous glucose monitors (CGMs) offer real-time blood glucose monitoring for individuals with diabetes to improve disease management. For healthcare providers, continuous health monitoring allows tracking patients remotely, enabling more personalized care and data-driven decision-making. In some cases, these devices can alert individuals or medical professionals to abnormal readings, helping to prevent more serious health events.

In addition to individual and clinical use, wearable technologies are increasingly used across research and athletic/training contexts. In biomedical and behavioral research, wearables provide a powerful means of collecting continuous physiological and behavioral data in real-world settings, supporting studies on physical activity, sleep quality, stress responses, cardiovascular health, and chronic disease management (Piwek et al. 2016). Their ability to capture longitudinal, ecologically valid data has expanded the scope of health research beyond traditional laboratory settings. In athletics, wearable technologies are now a common component of elite and amateur sports training. Athletes and coaches use wearables to monitor workload, optimize training regimens, and reduce injury risk through better recovery and fatigue management (Bourdon et al. 2017).

5.2.2 Implantable Technology

While wearable technologies are becoming increasingly prevalent, there are also more invasive implantable (permanent or semi-permanent) technologies. Implantable continuous health monitoring technologies are advanced medical devices that are surgically implanted into the body to provide real-time, long-term data collection. Unlike wearable devices, which are worn externally, these implantable devices are designed to continuously monitor critical health metrics from *within* the body. They are used in patients who require ongoing health surveillance, such as those with chronic conditions like heart disease or diabetes. Examples of implantable technologies include continuous glucose monitors (CGMs), which are implanted under the skin to monitor blood sugar levels in real time for individuals with diabetes. Another example is the implantable cardiac monitor (ICM), also known as a loop recorder, which detects abnormal heart rhythms over an extended period, providing early detection and warning of cardiac events.

Emerging military research is exploring the potential of implantable biosensors that can track multiple physiological markers, such as hydration, electrolyte balance, and core body temperature (DARPA 2020). This technology could be used to monitor soldier readiness in real-time and offer the possibility of wireless communication with command centers or medical personnel (Khalili 2023). One notable example is the research conducted under the Defense Advanced Research Projects Agency (DARPA), which has been developing implantable biosensors through programs like The Next-Generation Nonsurgical Neurotechnology (N3) Program and other health-monitoring projects aimed at enhancing soldier performance and safety in extreme environments. These efforts are focused on advancing wearable and implantable sensor technologies to monitor vital signs and overall health in real time, with the goal of improving operational readiness and medical response in the field (DARPA 2020).

5.3 Review of Literature/Programs

A growing number of studies highlight the impact of enhanced health monitoring on pre-symptomatic diagnosis and chronic disease management (Vergun 2023; Hoy 2017). These studies demonstrate the utility of wearable sensors in providing continuous, real-time monitoring of vital signs. According to Dhillon et al., the application of remote monitoring technologies will enhance the combat readiness of U.S. military service members (Dhillon et al. 2022).

The value of this technology was also demonstrated during the 2023 U.S. Army Best Squad Competition (Smith 2024). The U.S. Army Medical Materiel Development Activity (USAMMDA) deployed the Health Readiness and Performance System (HRAPS) to monitor soldiers' physiological data in real time. This wearable device, consisting of a lightweight chest-mounted transmitter, provided commanders and medical personnel with minute-by-minute updates on vital signs and locations of the 60 competitors from 12 Army commands (US Army 2023). The data collected through continuous health monitoring provided real-time health data that enhanced both individual and squad performance (Smith 2024). According to participants, the availability of individualized real-time feedback allowed them to optimize performance, ensuring safety and effectiveness during physically demanding tasks.

Wearables are already being used in military training. At Edwards Air Force Base's Ellington Airman Leadership School, instructors introduced smartwatches into their leadership training program in July 2021 (Hatch 2021). Cadets used these wearables to track real-time bio-metrics like sleep, stress, heart-rate variability, and physical activity. Through a "body battery" metric (a 1–100 scale estimating energy reserves), trainees reported the ability to time their tasks better, optimize recovery, and elevate performance in both personal and professional domains (Hatch 2021).

At Joint Base San Antonio–Randolph, Air Force and Army pilots have been equipped with smartwatches, smart water bottles, and smart rings to monitor hydration, fatigue, sleep quality, and stress (McQuiston 2021). These wearables provide real-time data that informs both personal readiness and operational risk management, helping optimize performance during flight and training missions (McQuiston 2021).

The U.S. Army War College piloted a wearable program involving more than 200 senior officers, who used smartwatches and rings to track their sleep, stress, and activity levels. This initiative, part of the "Optimizing the Human Weapon System" effort, not only helped officers enhance their performance but also modeled the importance of wearable biofeedback to improve health and resilience across command structures (Lagasse 2024).

The military's adoption of wearable devices could expand with the introduction of new technologies under programs like the Measuring and Advancing Soldier Tactical Readiness and Effectiveness (MASTR-E) (U.S. Army Medical Research and Development Command 2023). These initiatives pair wearable technology with comprehensive health, fitness, and performance data to assess and enhance soldier readiness (A2 Global Electronics 2024). The inclusion of wearables as part of the broader Optimizing the Human Weapon System (OHWS) initiative further demonstrates the military's movement towards health-monitoring technology as part of programs to improve soldier readiness and performance (U.S. Army Medical Research and Development Command 2023).

Moving beyond training, fitness, and performance data, the Department of Defense (DOD) has also recognized the potential therapeutic benefit of this technology. The Rapid Assessment of Threat Exposure (RATE) was initiated during the COVID-19 pandemic and demonstrated the effectiveness of AI algorithms in early disease detection using biometric data from wearable devices. RATE was able to predict COVID-19 infections up to 48 h before symptoms appeared (Vergun 2023).

This example highlights the role of artificial intelligence (AI). AI will likely be critical in managing and analyzing the vast amount of data generated by continuous health monitoring technologies, identifying trends and anomalies that may otherwise go unnoticed. According to the 2020 Data Strategy published by the DoD's Chief of Digital and Artificial Intelligence Office, the DoD envisions itself as a data-centric organization that can employ data-supporting advanced capabilities for operational advantage and increased efficiency (Chief Digital and Artificial Intelligence Office 2024). However, the reality of ever-increasing technology use, or even reliance, also raises critical ethical concerns, particularly in terms of privacy, informed consent, and data security. These issues are even more pronounced in military settings, where the protection and appropriate use of soldiers' health data are more nuanced than in the civilian world. The U.S. DoD has published a list of ethical principles for the use of AI with five core ethical principles. These are *Responsible, Equitable, Traceable, Reliable, and Governable* (DoD 2020).

5.4 Internet of Things

On today's battlefield, things are increasingly connected, and vast amounts of data are continuously collected. As part of this analysis, we must consider the broader web within which continuous health monitoring technologies will collect data. The modern battlefield has evolved into a highly technological arena with the introduction of drones, cyber warfare capabilities, artificial intelligence, and autonomous systems. Additionally, real-time data analytics and satellite communications have created network-centric military forces with unprecedented situational awareness. The modern battlespace is a place where connected technologies proliferate, creating the Internet of Battlefield Things (Amyx 2014).

The Internet of Things (IoT) is a network of interconnected devices that communicate and exchange data with each other via the Internet (Amyx 2014). The Internet of Battlefield Things (IoBT) is a specialized subset of the IoT (Devcom n.d.). IoBT integrates sensors, drones, autonomous vehicles, and wearable technology to provide real-time situational awareness, improve communication, and optimize decision-making processes for soldiers and commanders. Dhillon et al. (2022) discuss embedding health sensors in military uniforms to monitor physiological parameters such as heart rate, temperature, and hydration levels, enhancing overall readiness and prompt medical intervention. Thus, the service-member themselves may become a part of the IoBT (Amyx 2014).

5.5 Key Features Influencing Ethical Considerations

On its face, it appears that the benefits of continuous health monitoring align with the goals of military medicine—when conceptualized as promoting health and force readiness. The remainder of this chapter will explore ethical considerations related to this technology's use in military settings. This section focuses on ethical considerations, including the invasiveness of the technology (wearable vs. implantable), the autonomy of the service member (whether participation is mandated or voluntary), and data management/privacy. A basic framework is then offered, grounded in contextual differences and the nature of the military activity (in garrison, during training, pre/post/deployment). Ultimately, the use of these technologies in military settings should be limited to specific types of military activities where the stakes are higher—altering the risk/benefit analysis and increasing the ability to restrict individual service-member autonomy for the benefit of the group. This framework aims to be responsive to military necessity while maximizing the autonomy of the service member.

5.5.1 Invasiveness of the Technology

The degree of invasiveness is critical to ethical implementation and practice in the military setting. Wearable devices provide a less intrusive means of data collection, allowing soldiers to engage with health monitoring technologies without significant discomfort or concern. These devices can be easily removed or turned off, giving users control over their participation in health surveillance—an ethical advantage noted in discussions of proportionality and invasiveness in the enhancement ethics literature (Emanuel and Verdun 2021). However, implantable technologies present significantly more ethical challenges than wearable devices due to their inherent invasiveness. Unlike wearables that can be easily removed, implantable devices are embedded within the body, leading to more severe privacy violations, potential physical harm, and possible psychological impacts (Henschke 2021).

The permanence of implantable devices also raises concerns about autonomy and bodily integrity, as they involve continuous, intrusive monitoring from which individuals cannot simply opt out. This lack of agency is particularly problematic in the military context, where the balance between service requirements and individual rights is nuanced and complex (discussed in the next section). Ethical concerns also arise around the long-term implications of implantable devices, including questions about human enhancement: who controls or owns these enhancements once they are implanted? Are these devices considered part of the soldier's body, or does the government retain ownership over the technology, given that it may have been funded or developed through military resources? Moreover, the requirement for removing such enhancements upon separation from service raises questions about whether soldiers might face compulsory medical procedures, further complicating the ethics of their use (Eagan 2020).

While implantable technologies are still primarily in the developmental phase, the future use of wearable devices and embedded sensors in military operations could contribute to the normalization of constant monitoring, necessitating careful ethical scrutiny. As these technologies become more prevalent, they set a precedent for continuous surveillance that could be extended to more invasive methods, including implantables. The shift towards ubiquitous health monitoring also raises significant concerns about privacy, data security, and the potential misuse of personal health information. The military must carefully navigate these concerns to prevent overreach, ensuring that these technologies enhance soldier welfare without unnecessarily compromising individual autonomy.

5.5.2 Autonomy & Informed Consent

Autonomy is a cornerstone of medical ethics (Beauchamp and Childress 2019). However, it is well established that the military setting impacts an individual's ability to exercise autonomy. Military service members operate within a framework that restricts their autonomy and self-governance. This population is governed by a rigid hierarchy and stringent regulations designed to maintain discipline, promote cohesion, and support operational effectiveness (Gross 2006). The demands of military life necessitate adherence to a structured chain of command, where (legal) orders must be followed without question to ensure vertical cohesion. Furthermore, the nature of military duties, which can include deployments, relocations, and prolonged separations from family, imposes additional constraints on their personal lives and choices.

Within the civilian context, many argue that the responsible use of these wearable technologies depends on the user's ability to autonomously consent to this type of continuous health monitoring, as well as the user's ability to revoke consent or opt out of data collection (Li and Cheng 2020). However, the moral reality of military service-members is one of compulsion rather than autonomy. Accordingly, the extent to which service members can exercise autonomy depends significantly on whether their participation in monitoring programs will be mandated or voluntary. Within the American military context, there are many mandatory activities, including various aspects of health care. The nature of the military activity will impact the level of voluntariness allowable while still maximizing benefit.

Service-member autonomy is significantly impacted by the military's ability to mandate participation in service-related activities (Howe 2003). The ethical considerations related to mandated versus voluntary monitoring are even more complex (Mehlman and Li 2014). Mandating health monitoring may be justified in high-risk environments, such as deployments, where the health and readiness of the entire unit depend on each member's well-being (Coker 2007). However, this approach must be balanced against the risk of infringing on personal autonomy and the potential for perceived coercion (Coker 2007; Mehlman and Li 2014). From a force-readiness perspective, mandated participation may be more useful than voluntary participation; although it respects individual autonomy, not mandating participation in health monitoring may result in incomplete data and failure to accomplish the goals of the military (Mehlman et al. 2013).

Ultimately, securing informed consent is critical. However, standard consent procedures may fall short in addressing the novel and extensive nature of data collection involved in wearable technologies. The reviewed literature on the topic noted that many participants may not fully understand the implications of their consent (Segura Anaya et al. 2018). Enhanced consent procedures should include ongoing education about the technology, clear communication about data usage, and options for revoking consent. Since autonomy in the military is inherently limited, consent procedures must be clear, comprehensive, and designed to mitigate the power dynamics inherent in military settings. Special protocols should be established for research and piloting stages, ensuring service members understand their rights and can opt out without repercussions.

5.5.3 Data Management & Privacy

The extensive data harvested by wearable technologies presents significant privacy risks that may undermine autonomy and agency in this population (Mehlman 2013). The sheer volume of sensitive health information necessitates robust measures to protect confidentiality and prevent unauthorized access (Mone 2023). Beyond that, there is potential for the misuse of or unauthorized access to collected data in the military context (Giordano 2014). Since the military is a total organization, the health data collected could be used in ways that extend far beyond the original purpose. For instance, health data could be leveraged for disciplinary actions if deviations from expected health standards are interpreted as non-compliance or lack of fitness for duty (Giordano 2014). Additionally, there is the potential for using this data in criminal investigations, where personal health records could potentially incriminate service members or be used as evidence in legal proceedings (Giordano 2014). Such uses of health data raise significant ethical concerns about privacy, consent, and the potential for abuse of power within the military hierarchy.

Given the military context, there may also be an increased risk that health information could be leveraged in cyber warfare. This includes the potential that the enemy could access this data and thereby gain unprecedented insight and situational awareness related to the location and status of troops. In a cyber warfare context, health data could be exploited to disrupt military operations or to gain a strategic advantage. Additionally, the interception of location data linked to health monitoring devices could reveal troop movements, compromising operational security and endangering lives.

An illustrative example is the Strava fitness tracking app, which inadvertently revealed military base locations through its publicly available "heat map" (Schmidt and Rosenberg 2018). Strava is used widely for exercise and fitness tracking and produces a global map where it is being used. The outlines of known military bases worldwide were visible on the map, clearly showing both training and patrol routes due to individual user activity. The heat map was especially significant in countries like Afghanistan, Iraq, and Syria, where few locals own exercise tracking devices, meaning that the heat signatures of American bases are set against vast dark spaces (Schmidt and Rosenberg 2018).

5.6 A Basic Framework: Grounded in Autonomy and Context

Health-monitoring technology should be used to appropriately balance military necessity with individual service-member autonomy. As noted in the previous section, the military is a setting of compulsion that challenges the very concept of autonomy. Still, fully-informed consent is critical and must be free of coercion.

That being said, service-member autonomy varies across the different environments inherent to military service. Each environment—ranging from in-garrison to deployment—presents unique ethical challenges related to balancing individual rights with collective military needs. Therefore, the nature of the military activity wherein these technologies will be used can help guide us in developing a framework for their ethical application. Each context presents differing levels of military necessity, differing expectations of service-members, and distinctive ways to benefit from health monitoring. This section will review each setting to show how the nature of military activity or the context of use is critical to the risk/benefit analysis.

5.6.1 In-Garrison

This military context is most similar to the civilian world. While in-garrison, service-members are in their home country and generally enjoy greater autonomy than in other military settings. Within the realm of health care, this is most similar to civilian medicine, where the individual patient is the priority and aggregate military concerns are less pressing. Within this setting, health-monitoring technologies would likely be used as with most other populations—in chronic disease management and overall health promotion. In this setting, service-members should be able to consent or opt-out of such technological monitoring in conversation with their healthcare providers. Given the low-risk nature of the environment, service members should have the right to consent or opt out of such monitoring. The military's claim to service-member health data is still greater than their claim to civilians but less than in the other military contexts to be discussed.

5.6.2 Training

During training, service-members experience a more structured and regimented environment where the emphasis is on physical and tactical preparation for deployment. Autonomy is further restricted as the emphasis shifts to optimizing physical performance and ensuring readiness. While there is more justification for the use of health monitoring technologies, such monitoring should still be limited to training activities. Consent should still be sought, especially in pilot programs, but it might be more implicit or unit-based, with service-members expected to participate as part of their training regimen. The military's claim to health data in this setting is stronger, as ensuring the preparedness and safety of trainees is paramount to military planning and mission success. Within this context, it would be ethically preferable to limit data-collection to training activity. If sleep data and general health data is requested, service-members should be able to opt-out of constant monitoring.

5.6.3 Pre-Deployment

Pre-deployment involves intense preparation and logistical coordination, with service-members undergoing mandated medical evaluations and training to ensure they are fit for deployment. Autonomy is significantly curtailed as the mission's success and the safety of the unit take precedence, representing a greater shift from the individual to the aggregate. Health-monitoring technologies are crucial in this phase to assess readiness, manage any existing health conditions, and mitigate potential health risks. Service-members will likely have limited ability to opt-out of monitoring. The military's claim to health data is more robust, driven by the need to ensure that all personnel are fully prepared for the demands of deployment.

5.6.4 Deployment

During deployment, service-members face the most restricted autonomy, operating in high-stress and potentially dangerous environments where adherence to orders and protocols is vital for survival and mission success. Health-monitoring technologies are likely to be mandated and (when fully vetted) seen as indispensable for real-time tracking of vital signs, detecting injuries or illnesses, and ensuring immediate medical intervention if needed. The ability to consent or opt-out of any activity, including monitoring, is minimal, as the operational needs and safety of the unit override individual preferences. The military's claim to health data is at its strongest in this context, prioritizing the overall effectiveness and safety of the mission. Within this context, it is also likely that service members would want such monitoring as it will likely improve the survivability and chances of mission success.

5.6.5 *Post-Deployment*

Post-deployment (sometimes called "re-deployment") is the period wherein service-members transition back to a less restrictive environment. However, they still undergo extensive health assessments and monitoring to address any physical or psychological issues arising from their deployment. Autonomy arguably increases as the immediate operational pressures diminish. However, an important aspect of this period is to assess suitability for further deployment, while addressing health needs. Thus, health-monitoring technologies will continue to play a role in managing post-deployment health concerns. Although, service-members should have greater autonomy related to their health care and the use of monitoring technologies, the military retains a vested interest in their long-term health outcomes. The claim to health data is strong but gradually recedes as service-members reintegrate into civilian life or in-garrison status. On a particularly American note, the post/re-deployment period also logs service-related injuries and disabilities that will shape service-member access and coverage within the Veteran-specific healthcare system (Veteran Affairs know as the "VA").

5.6.6 *Overview*

In sum, the ethical application of continuous health-monitoring technologies in the military must be grounded in both respect for service-member autonomy and responsiveness to the contextual demands of military service. As service-members move through different operational settings—from garrison to deployment—the balance between individual rights and military necessity appropriately shifts. However, this shift must always be proportional and justified by both clear operational needs and attention to the implications service-members as individuals. Participation in health monitoring should be voluntary whenever possible, with informed consent processes that meaningfully account for the coercive dynamics of military hierarchy. Where monitoring might be mandated, as in deployment, strong procedural protections should be established to limit data misuse and preserve trust between service-members and the institution.

5.7 Conclusion

Ultimately, the integration of wearable and implantable health-monitoring technologies offers the potential to promote force readiness, improve safety, and enhance medical care across the continuum of military service. In the future, military leaders, ethicists, and policymakers should work collaboratively to establish clear ethical guidelines, context-sensitive protocols, and ongoing oversight to ensure that these powerful tools serve both the mission and the rights of those who serve.

References

A2 Global Electronics. 2024. *The Rollout of Wearable Devices for Military Use*. A2 Global Electronics, 2024. https://a2globalelectronics.com/defense-aerospace/the-rollout-of-wearable-devices-for-military-use. Accessed: July 2024.

Amyx, Scott. 2014. *Wearing Your Intelligence: How to Apply Artificial Intelligence in Wearables and IoT*. Medium. https://medium.com/@ScottAmyx/wearing-your-intelligence-how-to-apply-artificial-intelligence-in-wearables-and-iot-51ae7710385. Accessed: July 2025.

Beauchamp, T. L., and J. F. Childress. 2019. *Principles of Biomedical Ethics*. 8th ed. Oxford: Oxford University Press.

Bourdon, P. C., M. Cardinale, A. Murray, P. Gastin, M. Kellman, M. C. Varley, T. J. Gabbett, A. J. Coutts, D. J. Burgess, W. Gregson, and N. T. Cable. 2017. Monitoring Athlete Training Loads: Consensus Statement. *International Journal of Sports Physiology and Performance* 12 (s2). Accessed: June 2025.

Chief Digital and Artificial Intelligence Office (CDAO). 2024. *Responsible AI Toolkit*. https://rai.tradewindai.com/executive-summary. Accessed: August 2024.

Coker, W. J. 2007. Human Enhancement and Soldier Performance: Ethical Considerations. *Journal of the Royal Army Medical Corps* 153 (2): 112–116.

DARPA. 2020. *Next Generation Non-Surgical Neurotechnology*. https://www.darpa.mil/program/next-generation-nonsurgical-neurotechnology. Accessed: July 2024.

DEVCOM. Army Research Laboratory Public Affairs. 2021. *Uniforms with Programmable Fiber Could Transmit Data and More*. The United States Army. https://www.army.mil/article/247472/uniforms_with_programmable_fiber_could_transmit_data_and_more. Accessed: July 2024.

Devcom. n.d. *Internet of Battle Things*. https://arl.devcom.army.mil/cras/iobt-cra/. Accessed: June 2025.

Dhillon, Paul, Kristian Tam, and Eric Juneau. 2022. Dress for Success: Embedded Health Sensors in the Future Soldier. *Journal of Military, Veteran and Family Health* 8 (2): 109–115.

Dignam, Timothy, and Katherine Vandebelt. "Use of a Health Monitoring System During a US Military Exercise During the COVID-19 Pandemic (April 2021): Participant Characteristics, Demographics and Differences in Participation." Journal of military and veterans' health vol. 32,1 (2024): 6-17.

DoD. 2020. *Ethical Principles for Artificial Intelligence. U.S. Department of Defense*. https://www.defense.gov/Newsroom/Releases/Release/Article/2091996/dod-adopts-ethical-principles-for-artificial-intelligence/. Accessed: July 2024.

Eagan, Sheena M. 2020. Genetic Manipulation and the Future of American Warfighters. In *Ethics of Military Medical Innovation, Experimentation, and Enhancement*, ed. Daniel Messelken and David Winkler, 159–173. Cham: Springer.

Emanuel, R., and E. Verdun. 2021. *Military Human Enhancement: Ethical, Legal and Policy Perspectives*. In *The Routledge Handbook of War, Law and Technology*, ed. James Gow, Ernst Dijxhoorn, Rachel Kerr, and Guglielmo Verdirame, 269–282. Routledge.

Friedl, K. E. 2018. Military Applications of Soldier Physiological Monitoring. *Journal of Science and Medicine in Sport* 21 (11): 1147–1153.

Giordano, James. 2014. *Neurotechnology in National Security and Defense: Practical Considerations, Neuroethical Concerns*. CRC Press.

Gross, M. 2006. *Bioethics and Armed Conflict: Moral Dilemmas of Medicine and War*. Cambridge, MA: MIT Press.

Hatch, Gary. 2021. *Edwards Pioneers Smart Watch Effort to Help Future Leaders Be Better, Faster*. Air Force Materiel Command. https://www.afmc.af.mil/News/Article-Display/Article/2707815/edwards-pioneers-smart-watch-effort-to-help-future-leaders-be-better-faster. Accessed May 2025.

Henschke, A. 2021. When Enhancements Need Therapy: Disenhancements, Iatrogenesis, And The Responsibility Of Military Institutions. *Monash Bioethics Review* 41:6–21.

Howe, E. G. 2003. Mixed Agency in Military Medicine: Ethical Roles in Conflict. *Cambridge Quarterly of Healthcare Ethics* 12 (4): 457–465.

Hoy, Matthew B. 2017. *Health at Hand (or Wrist): Ethical Considerations for Wearable Fitness Trackers in Clinical Medicine*. Health Ethics Blog. https://www.healthethicsblog.com/single-post/2017/11/14/health-at-hand. Accessed: July 2024.

Khalili, Ramin A. 2023. *With OWHS, USAMRDC Fusing Soldier Care, Technology for Future Fight*. U.S. Army Medical Research and Development Command. https://mrdc.health.mil/index.cfm/media/articles/2022/USAMRDC_fusing_soldier_care_technology_for_future_fight. Accessed: July 2024.

Lagasse, Paul. MOMRP, Army War College team up for wearables pilot. U.S. Army News. Oct. 15 2024. Accessed July 2025.

Li, J., & Cheng, T. (2020). A Review on the Privacy and Security of Wearable Health Systems: Requirements, Solutions, and Challenges. IEEE Access, 8, 188754-188766.

McQuiston, Tyler. 435th FTS pilots test new wearable technology. 12th Flying Training Wing Public Affairs. July 28, 2021. https://www.12ftw.af.mil/News/Article-Display/Article/2711506/435th-fts-pilots-test-new-wearable-technology/

Mehlman, M. J., and T. M. Li. 2014. Ethical, Legal, Social, and Policy Issues in the Use of Genomic Technology by the U.S. *Military. Journal of Law, Medicine & Ethics* 42 (4): 546–564.

Mehlman, Maxwell J. 2013. *Military Medical Ethics: Issues Regarding the Use of Emerging Technologies*. In *Military Medical Ethics for the 21st Century*. Ashgate.

Mehlman, Maxwell and Lin, Patrick and Abney, Keith, Enhanced Warfighters: Risk, Ethics, and Policy (January 18, 2013). Case Legal Studies Research Paper No. 2013-2. http://dx.doi.org/10.2139/ssrn.2202982

Mone V, and F. Shakhlo. 2023. Health Data on the Go: Navigating Privacy Concerns with Wearable Technologies. *Legal Information Management* 23 (3): 179–188.

Piwek, L., D. A. Ellis, S. Andrews, and A. Joinson. 2016. The Rise of Consumer Health Wearables: Promises and Barriers. *PLOS Medicine* 13 (2): e1001953.

Schmidt, M. S., and M. Rosenberg. 2018. Fitness Tracking App Strava Gives Away Location of Secret U.S. Army Bases. *The New York Times*, January 29. https://www.nytimes.com/2018/01/29/world/middleeast/strava-heat-map.html

Segura Anaya, L. H., A. Alsadoon, N. Costadopoulos, et al. 2018. Ethical Implications of User Perceptions of Wearable Devices. *Science and Engineering Ethics* 24:1–28.

Smith, Katie. 2024. *The Transformative Power of Wearable Health and Performance Devices*. The U.S. Army. https://www.army.mil/article/272846/the_transformative_power_of_wearable_health_and_performance_devices. Accessed: July 2024.

South, Todd. 2023. *These Are the New Pieces of Wearable Tech Coming to the Army in 2024*. Army Times. https://www.armytimes.com/news/your-army/2023/12/25/these-are-the-new-pieces-of-wearable-tech-coming-to-the-army-in-2024. Accessed: July 2024.

U.S. Army. 2023. *System Provides Critical, Real-Time Health Data at Best Squad Competition.*https://www.army.mil/article/270395/system_provides_critical_real_time_health_data_at_best_squad_competition. Accessed June 2025.

Vergun, David. 2023. *DOD Investing in Wearable Technology That Could Rapidly Predict Disease*. U.S. Department of Defense News. https://www.defense.gov/News/News-Stories/Article/Article/3377624/dod-investing-in-wearable-technology-that-could-rapidly-predict-disease. Accessed: July 2024.

Sheena M. Eagan is an Associate Professor with the Department of Bioethics and Interdisciplinary Studies in the Brody School of Medicine at East Carolina University (North Carolina, USA). Dr. Eagan's research and teaching focus on medical ethics and the history of medicine, with a subspecialized focus on military medicine. She holds a PhD in the medical humanities from the Institute for the Medical Humanities at the University of Texas Medical Branch as well as a Master of Public Health from the Uniformed Services University. Dr. Eagan is co-director of ECU's Veteran to Scholar Boot Camp, and faculty advisor to the Military Medicine Student Interest Group. Sheena serves as Head of the North Carolina Unit for the International Chair of Bioethics/WMA Cooperating Centre and is also the creator/founding president of the American Society of Bioethics and Humanities group for Military, Humanitarian, and Disaster Medicine.

Chapter 6
Ethical, Legal, and Societal Implications of the DARPA *in the Moment* Program

Daniel Trusilo, Lauren Diaz, and Ellie Tyler

6.1 Introduction

In 2022, the United States Defense Advanced Research Projects Agency, known as DARPA, initiated a multi-phase, basic research program called "In The Moment" (ITM) with the objective of enabling human-off-the-loop delegation to tactical algorithmic decision-making (ADM) systems in high-stakes domains where there is no agreed upon right answer, such as battlefield triage (DARPA 2024a). In line with DARPA's mission, "To make pivotal investments in breakthrough technologies for national security," ITM is supporting the development of ADMs that are trusted by humans to independently make human-off-the-loop decisions when human lives are at stake. Dr. Patrick Shafto, DARPA's ITM Program Manager, explains, "[ITM] addresses, in the broadest sense, a key question about how we should think about humans and AIs working together in the future" (Voices from DARPA 2024). Specifically, the program is exploring if autonomous algorithmic systems that are aligned to human attributes will be more trusted by their human operators than unaligned systems. Shafto describes this work as a "bit more forward leaning than many DARPA programs. At some sense, we're anticipating technology that will come soon, as opposed to trying to develop that technology right away…If we can come away from the program with a clear statement of what we mean by alignment and why it matters, then I think we will have made a great contribution to society broadly" (Voices from DARPA 2024). Since its inception, the ITM program has included an ethical, legal, and societal implications (ELSI) component, which is the

D. Trusilo (✉) · L. Diaz · E. Tyler
University of St. Gallen, St. Gallen, Switzerland

Applied Research Laboratory for Intelligence and Security (ARLIS), University of Maryland, Rockville, MD, USA
e-mail: daniel.trusilo@unisg.ch

B. Koch, D. Winkler (eds.), *Artificial Intelligence Ethics in Military Medicine and Humanitarian Healthcare*, Military and Humanitarian Health Ethics,
https://doi.org/10.1007/978-3-032-11331-3_6

focus of this chapter. Shafto explains why considering ELSI is essential, stating, “The question of alignment and whether it matters for delegation is one that could have much broader implications than any specific technology that we could develop. And the social and legal regimes in which we think about that also could have extremely broad implications” (Voices from DARPA 2024).

Before discussing the ELSI aspects of ITM, in Sect. 2 we will give an overview of the ITM program including its underlying motivations, structure, and the metrics that are being used to measure success. Next, in Sect. 3, we will discuss the ELSI work being done as an integral part of the ITM program. This discussion will present the findings of a March 2024 event that was designed to share ITM with external experts; build a community of interest; and foster collaboration and debate on operational, as well as ELSI aspects of the program. Section 4 will then present an overview of challenges that have emerged and discuss future directions of this research. Finally, Section 5, will offer a brief conclusion.

6.2 ITM Overview

DARPA seeks to be disruptive. Classic examples of technology that has emerged from DARPA’s storied history include stealth and GPS capabilities (DARPA 2024b; Alexandrow 2008). Dr. Matt Turek, Deputy Director for the Information Innovation Office at DARPA, explains that in order to achieve breakthroughs, DARPA invests in research that falls along a continuum. On one end of the continuum, DARPA invests in research communities in a particular problem-space that’s relevant to the Department of Defense (DoD). This focus is intended to address perceived gaps in DoD’s technical capabilities. On the other end of the continuum, DARPA invests in building transformative capabilities that can be rapidly deployed to meet pressing needs of the warfighter (Center for Strategic and International Studies 2024).

The ITM program is a basic research program that is designed to support the research and development of algorithms that are trusted to autonomously make decisions in difficult domains, such as battlefield triage and disaster relief. ITM instantiates “trust” as “the willingness of a party to be vulnerable to the actions of another party based on the expectation that the other will perform a particular action important to the trustor, irrespective of the ability to monitor or control that other party” (Mayer et al. 1995). The ITM program hypothesizes that humans will be more likely to trust an ADM that aligns with, and demonstrates human decision-making styles. ITM’s approach to developing such a capability is focused on the possibility of identifying human values and attributes that underline decision-making and encoding them to be represented in an ADM. Additionally, battlefield triage presents an objectively complex and highly consequential setting for researching humans’ willingness to delegate decision-making authority to an algorithmic system that is intended to operate without human input or oversight. Although military medicine is the primary use case, an alignment framework for a trusted human decision-maker and an autonomous algorithm can be applied to other domains.

Addressing the fundamental questions related to human decision-making, conditions for delegation, and human-AI alignment will inform future development and adoption of autonomous systems.

6.2.1 Motivations for ITM

ITM conceptualizes how humans and autonomous algorithms can work together in the future and is motivated by scenarios specifically related to triage and mass casualty events. Real-world events indicate that a human-off-the-loop ADM for triage may be needed by modern militaries to a) improve triage decision-making in scenarios in which human capacity is overwhelmed, and b) operate beyond current capabilities during peer and near-peer conflicts. A key question emerges when considering events that overwhelm hospitals and medical personnel. Dr. Patrick Shafto asks, "under what condition would a human delegate life or death decision to an AI system?" (Voices from DARPA 2024). For example, a 2017 Las Vegas concert shooting resulted in 215 gunshot wounds, straining the local emergency care facilities and challenging human-run triage operations (Menes et al. 2017). Could an ADM, developed to conduct triage in alignment with trusted human counterparts, help in such a situation? In addressing this question about alignment, Shafto asks, "Does it matter to humans that the AI system reflects our decision-making preferences, our morals, ethics, and so on? And would that increase the chances of us delegating in a particular situation?" (Voices from DARPA 2024). Perhaps, but such an ADM will have to be able to operate with limited data, making decisions that humans trust, when there is no clear right or wrong answer.

The challenge of developing an algorithmic system that can operate when there is no clear right or wrong answer is exemplified by three categories of conflicts that were evident in the Las Vegas triage operations. These three conflicts are: (1) rule conflicts, (2) policy conflicts, and (3) resource conflicts. First, the Las Vegas mass casualty event highlights the challenge of abiding by standard rules in a dynamic, high-consequence situation. Dr. Kevin Menes, the triage surgeon leading the effort, discussed the way in which he categorized incoming patients, reporting: "By textbook standards, some of these first arrivals should have been black tags, but I sent them to the red tag area anyway. I didn't black tag a single one" (Menes et al. 2017). Menes's statement means multiple patients should have been labeled as non-recoverable according to modern medical standards, but Menes, the human decision-maker, chose to prioritize emergency medical care for these patients to accelerate initial patient processing. This is an example of a conflict with existing rules, which an operational ADM must take into account.

Second, the Las Vegas mass casualty event resulted in a conflict with policy rules as Menes chose to delegate triage responsibilities to a nurse who had been assisting him, despite policy stating triage should be run by the most experienced doctor (Menes et al. 2017). This raises the question, could an aligned ADM serve as a viable, even necessary, alternative to a human decision-maker should the situation require non-standard solutions, potentially conflicting with existing policy?

Third, during the Las Vegas mass casualty event, medical resources were strained. With twenty-eight damage control surgeries happening in the first six hours after the event and every single ventilator being used, the Las Vegas hospital network had exceeded its capacity (Menes et al. 2017). If we look beyond ITM and consider an operational ADM, we can hypothesize that an ideal system will account for a constantly changing resource environment, in which non-standard uses of resources may be required to maximize life-saving potential. With the Las Vegas mass-casualty event serving as a compelling example, the ITM program is driven to address high-consequence decision-making challenges related to standard rules and policy, as well as resource constraints, when there is no clear right answer, and alternative outcomes cannot possibly be known.

A second real-world case that exemplifies the motivation behind ITM is related to battlefield casualties. Namely, combat casualty medical care in the ongoing conflict in Ukraine indicates that human-off-the-loop automation may be required in future conflicts. Specifically, there is evidence that Russia incurred between 1000 and 1200 casualties per day during the peak of the Battle of Bakhmut (Axe 2023) resulting in potentially 66,000 to 88,000 deaths in the span of 9 months (The Economist 2024). The triage personnel of any military, no matter how well trained, will be overwhelmed given similar numbers. Further, there may be limited human capacity to perform triage operations in the event that forward operating medical personnel are wounded or killed. ITM is motivated to address this gap by exploring how to build trusted systems that can improve decision-making in such a scenario, aiding medical operations, and possibly reducing the number of deaths.

Underlying these motivations are a series of technical challenges that raise explicit and implicit questions related to ELSI. For example, when a human decision-maker is faced with multiple casualties, how do they decide, under extreme time constraints with limited data points, who to treat first? Such triage decisions can impact who lives and who dies, and there is no way to check the outcomes of a different choice after the fact. Do human decision-makers performing triage automatically act in compliance with the law of armed conflict; treating enemy combatants, civilians, and friendly force causalities the same? What if a mission critical element depends on keeping a certain individual alive? And how do an individual's decision-making attributes, values, and priorities influence their decision-making? These are just a few examples of the multitude of factors that make it challenging to concretely identify, measure, and algorithmically replicate a trusted human's decisions. However, for an ADM to be successful, identifying, measuring, and algorithmically replicating these factors is exactly what must be done.

6.2.2 *ITM Program Structure*

To develop an ADM that can be used for triage situations, and given the range of challenges highlighted above, ITM is structured with four Technical Areas (TA) of research: (TA1) Decision-maker characterization, (TA2) Human-aligned algorithmic decision-makers, (TA3) Evaluation and, (TA4) Policy and practice integration (See Fig. 6.1: ITM Technical Areas).

As the name suggests, TA1 researchers are focused on characterizing human decision-makers; specifically, the human attributes or values that may be relevant to triage decision-making. To that end, this requires TA1 researchers to create computational representations of decision-makers that summarize their attributes given a set of domain-specific circumstances. In other words, if a medical decision-maker encounters three patients with different injuries and physical characteristics, how can one quantitatively measure characteristics of the human decision-maker that define how they make their decisions about the three patients? To do this, decision-maker attributes will need to be identified and defined; the impact of situational information, domain knowledge, and other contextual elements on decision-maker attributes will need to be understood; and decision-maker responses to scenarios and decision-points will need to be represented in a computational framework.

TA2 researchers are focused on building human-aligned algorithms. To do this in a way that can be scientifically measured, TA2 researchers will need to build ADMs with quantifiable alignment to trusted human decision-maker attributes. Considering the example above, this means that an algorithm or set of algorithms will need to include variables that account for the characteristics of human decision-makers who

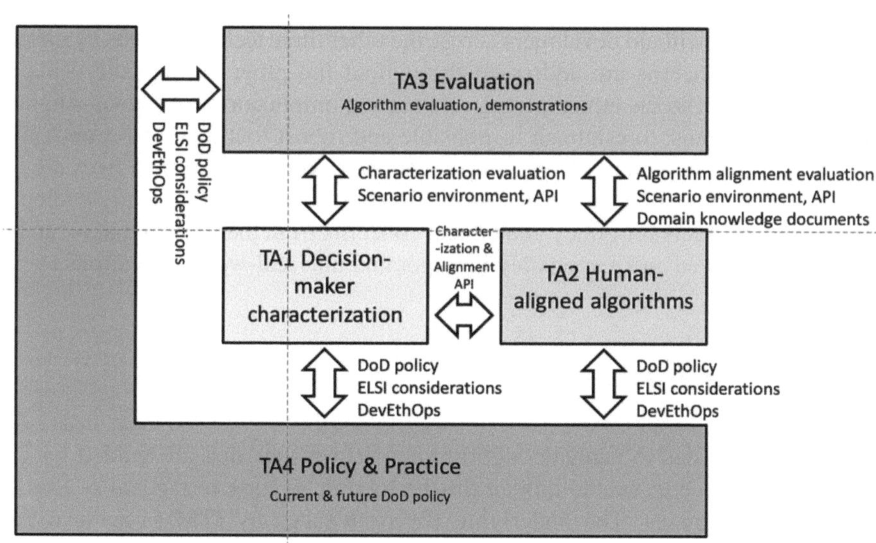

Fig. 6.1 ITM Technical Areas (DARPA 2024a)

are deciding how to triage the three patients in a way that is measurable. Such quantifiable alignment will allow for ADMs that can be adjusted to a group of trusted human decision-makers or even fine-tuned to a trusted individual decision-maker, such as the senior surgeon responsible for triage in a mass-casualty incident. Further, TA2 researchers must be able to integrate high-level goals and guidance such as DoD policy, Rules of Engagement, and commander's intent, into the ADMs.

TA3 researchers are responsible for evaluating the algorithms and demonstrating the technology. This means TA3 researchers must develop evaluation protocols, requirements, and metrics for triage decision-making in austere conditions and for a mass casualty event. Given the intent to discover if human decision-making attributes can be algorithmically encoded in an ADM, TA3 researchers must also design an environment that allows for data collection while accounting for psychological fidelity for human decision-makers. This will require a complicated array of objectives such as identifying a reference pool of trusted human decision-makers and ascertaining key knowledge in order to provide a control for ADM performance.

Ensuring that the systems being developed are in alignment with ethical and legal norms throughout the full system lifecycle is essential. Therefore, ITM includes an integrated policy and practice component via TA4. Specifically, TA4 is divided into two ELSI teams: one is responsible for internal ELSI components related to program design and ADM development and the other focuses on socializing the ITM program with a broad audience to build a community of practice and pathways to policy. This technical area is predicated on the understanding that long-term success of an ADM requires acceptance by the broader policy community as well as system end-users. Since there are limited policies governing ADMs to date, curating a multidisciplinary community of experts is a critical step in the conversation about potential policies that will be required for future technological capabilities. Additionally, incorporating policy and practice considerations from the start of the ITM program will aid developers across the other three technical areas by ensuring that ELSI concerns are addressed throughout the program lifecycle. This is especially relevant to the ethical, legal, and societal implications of human-aligned autonomous systems; to establish responsible and robust foundations for an ADM that will be used for human-off-the-loop decision-making when human lives are on the line and there is no clear right answer. In other words, ITM aims to develop a solution that accounts for policy and ethical concerns from the start so that it can be seamlessly deployed and responsibly incorporated into real-world operations.

6.2.3 ITM Metrics

ITM is using metrics to evaluate algorithmic performance that are guided by the program's objective to enable human-off-the-loop delegation to tactical ADMs in difficult DoD domains. The underlying approach taken by ITM to achieve this objective is to quantify the alignment of ADMs with trusted humans. This approach, and the related relationships between the TAs is visually shown in Fig. 6.2 below.

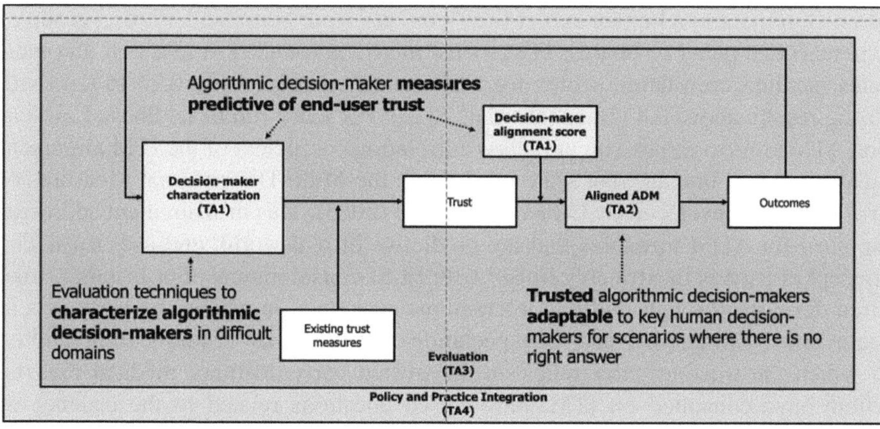

Fig. 6.2 ITM's approach to quantifying the alignment of ADMs with trusted humans where there is no right answer (DARPA 2024a)

A core hypothesis of ITM is that ADMs encoded with human decision-maker attributes and values will be trusted, and more likely adopted, by humans. To test this hypothesis ITM will measure: (1) delegation willingness, (2) trust, and (3) alignment.

The delegation willingness metric is a behavioral measure of the willingness of triage professionals to delegate to an aligned ADM. ITM aims to have an aligned ADM achieve a 60% delegation preference over a comparable baseline ADM for its Phase I evaluation. The target of 60% delegation preference is based on research that indicates triage accuracy for nurses in the U.S. is 58.7%—61.3% (Martin et al. 2014; Mistry et al. 2018). For reference, the best reported triage accuracy by nurses, found through a meta-analysis conducted by Tam et al., was 82.9% (2018). This measurement addresses the operational need for ADMs that are trusted by expert human decision-makers. Given this metric, one obvious ELSI consideration relates to the concept of automation bias, which is the tendency for humans interfacing with an algorithmic system to defer to the system if they know it is algorithmic. In other words, humans have a bias that favors ADMs, regardless of the system's performance that may contradict recommendations from a non-automated source (Skitka et al. 1999; Goddard et al. 2012). Therefore, for a measure of delegation willingness to be valid, a human expert evaluating an ADM's recommendation should not be able to tell if they are evaluating the recommendation of another human expert or an ADM.

The trust metric applied to ITM is intended to quantify a human expert's willingness to delegate to an algorithmic system's performance. Put simply, an ADM could be designed to optimize various results such as, for example, the likelihood of a prioritized patient surviving, the number of casualties that receive treatment based on available medical resources, or a number of other algorithmically programmable objectives. ITM aims to build ADMs that are quantitatively proven to have trust given alignment to a human expert (i.e. "you" or "your commander") or a group of experts (i.e. a panel or board). ITM's trust metric is founded in research that indicates medium correlation scores for trust measures range from 0.25 to 0.4, with strong results above 0.4 (Hancock et al. 2023). For a dry-run of its Phase I evaluation, ITM aims to achieve an intraclass correlation coefficient of the ITM alignment measure with a human trust scale of .3 using the Multi-Dimensional Measures of Trust v2 scale developed by Ullman and Malle (2023). This measurement addresses the need for ADM measures that are predictive of real-world, end-user trust. The concept of trust is inextricably linked with ELSI considerations. For instance, trust often develops through multiple interactions over time, in which one party acts in accordance with another party's expectations. Further, trust requires vulnerability, in which the trusting party relies on the trusted party. Military medical experts, whom have consulted on ITM, have raised questions related to the cadence of reevaluating the relationship between a system-user and the system itself as well as the process for reestablishing user expectations when they are not met by the system. The experts emphasized that this reevaluation cadence will be important for the operationalization of an ADM in often ambiguous, high-consequence DoD environments.

The alignment measurement refers to the ability to tune an ADM to a subset of the attribute space. This measurement will be evaluated according to the ADM's alignment to the largest cluster of human attributes. This measurement addresses the need for ADMs to be adaptable to key human decision-makers. Specifically, expert human decision-makers engaged in active combat on a high-priority operation will potentially make different triage decisions than an emergency medical professional in a civilian hospital. Decisions will be impacted by an individual's values and ethical judgments as well as organizational policies and legal mandates. For an ADM to be operationally relevant, the ability to align to a specific human end-user or group will likely be required, be they a special operations medic deployed behind enemy lines or a team of trauma-surgeons facing a mass-casualty event in Las Vegas. That said, alignment has its own set of ELSI concerns: it could lead to group think, or, on the positive side, increased critical thinking and greater awareness of weaknesses. In an effort to test ITM's hypothesis, it is equally important to consider broader questions, such as: Is alignment to a trusted human sufficient to establish trust in an ADM? How do we know if the alignment is "good enough"? Do we want to align an ADM to humans? And, if so, when is alignment appropriate?

Addressing these questions, as an integrated research area of ITM, encourages deeper consideration of the possible ethical, legal, and social implications that operationalizing an ADM for high-consequence decisions could pose.

6.3 A Deeper Look at ELSI

We have highlighted the integral nature of ELSI to the ITM program, but all of the issues raised require deeper discussion. At a fundamental level, ITM's approach to responsible AI is guided by, among others, the AI ethical principles of DoD's Chief Digital and AI Office (CDAO 2022) and those listed in the President's Executive Order on AI (The White House 2023). In fact, the CDAO's AI ethical principles and those elucidated in the 2023 Executive Order apply to all DoD AI capabilities, encompassing both combat and non-combat applications.

Clearly stating principles is a first step, but operationalizing ethical AI principles is challenging, requiring a practical approach based on understanding the real-world use case of any specific socio-technical system (Trusilo and Burri 2021). Therefore, ITM applies the CDAO AI ethical principles through an integrated technical area (TA4) that is focused on ethical, legal, and societal implications (ELSI) for the full program lifecycle including system development, testing, and evaluation. ITM, as a basic research program, does not include a deployment phase; however, TA4 research is informed by existing policies and practices, ensuring that ITM systems can be successfully operationalized, monitored, and revised as required. Additionally, TA4 researchers are socializing ELSI issues with a multidisciplinary audience of experts, hosting workshops designed to facilitate discussions among experts external to the ITM program on related policy, ethics, military medicine, triage, bioethics, AI alignment, and other relevant topics. These discussions play an essential role in establishing an interdisciplinary network that can be called upon to help identify and address gaps in existing policy.

To accomplish the required, full-lifecycle integration of ELSI, as described above, TA4 researchers are composed of two teams: (1) an internally facing advisory team led by the Institute for Defense Analysis (IDA), and (2) an outreach team led by the University of Maryland Applied Research Laboratory for Intelligence and Security (UMD ARLIS). The internally facing advisory team engages with ITM researchers from the other three technical areas in order to identify and advise on ELSI issues and provide expert guidance on relevant policies and practices.

The authors of this chapter are part of the outreach component of TA4, tasked with engaging with the DoD, academic communities, and other external stakeholders. In this role, we have organized two events designed to bring together those stakeholders and ITM researchers. We will now discuss some of the key points of discussion from the second ITM external outreach event.

6.3.1 *External Outreach Event Overview*

Long-term success of ITM depends in part on acceptance of the ADM by the policy community. Therefore, as part of the integrated ELSI effort, Phase I of the ITM program includes three external outreach events. These events are intended to engage policy and practice subject matter experts from outside of ITM, with the goals of socializing the program; building a community of interest; and fostering collaboration and debate on operational, as well as ELSI considerations. In March 2024, the second outreach event (workshop) was held, which this section will discuss.

Development of the workshop was guided by three key questions: (1) How does policy influence decision-making in practice? (2) How were decision-makers able to adapt to other innovative techniques that disrupted traditional approaches? and (3) What can be learned about the potential to strategically incorporate automated tools in life-and-death decision-making for optimal outcomes? The objectives of the workshop were to provide members of the policy community, stakeholders, and ITM researchers a better understanding of: (a) human decision-making in situations where there is a high level of uncertainty and no right answers, (b) factors that may shape the willingness of a human to delegate decision-making authority to AI systems for life-or-death decisions where there is no right answer, and (c) how innovation can influence decision-making and relevant policy. Additional objectives specifically supported ITM researchers by elucidating: (d) future design elements that should be considered in ITM developmental processes, and (e) the technical information that is important for shaping future policy.

Subject matter experts (SMEs) in areas such as medical policy and decision-making, combat casualty care, and integrated military medical capabilities were invited to participate as panelists and speakers. The SMEs were affiliated with Army Futures Command's Medical Capability Development Integration Directorate (CDID), Walter Reed National Military Medical Center, Special Operations Medical Association, Harvard Medical School, DEU Joint Command Special Operations (German Army), Barts Health National Health Service (NHS) Trust and UK Defence Medical Service, Defence Science Organisation (DSO) National Laboratories in Singapore, Duke University, and the Deputy Assistant Secretary of Defense for Health Policy Readiness and Oversight. There were three panel discussions and one keynote presentation that offered perspectives on the benefits, risks, and challenges of applying autonomous decision-making technology to life-or-death situations.

6.3.2 Workshop Insights

Insights from the workshop suggest the adoption of an ADM depends on regulatory and cultural factors, and that a human will be more likely to delegate to a system if the system can be trained as a colleague in a skillset, such as tactical combat casualty care (TCCC), alongside a human operator. That said, workshop experts also highlighted that they do not always have the opportunity to train with the same human colleagues with whom they are required to operate. More specifically, the workshop highlighted: (1) variable levels of desire for human oversight, (2) the importance of addressing impacts on end-users such as the possibility of moral injury, and (3) the challenge of rapidly establishing the trust of system operators and integrating new systems into existing military decision-making processes.

First, experts stressed the need for human oversight of an ADM but recognized the potential benefits of highly capable systems in high-stress, resource-constrained environments. During the workshop, international experts pointed out that military and medical training varies between countries and will impact the acceptance of ADM technologies. For example, cultural differences play a role in public perception and adoption of new technologies even though medical rules of engagement are standard across NATO and partner nations. Further complicating this challenge is the fact that cultural differences exist between services within any one country's military, which will impact any service branch's ability to successfully adopt disruptive technology. For example, U.S. Special Operations Forces (SOF) are more accepting of their highly trained medics making independent decisions that deviate from standard procedures.

Therefore, cultural differences must be accounted for when designing tactics, techniques, and procedures (TTPs) for an ADM use case. This is especially true because ITM is conceptualized as a human-off-the-loop system, designed to fill the space when human oversight is no longer possible because human decision-makers are overwhelmed or out of reach. In such an instance, will cultural differences matter or will the need to rapidly make high-consequence battlefield triage decisions in a highly variable environment force a non-conventional approach, such as delegation to an ADM? Ultimately, trust-building around ADM technology needs to be collaborative between government, public, and medical communities, taking into account the cultural contexts and maximizing touch points for system integration. Additionally, legal considerations for rapidly advancing technologies must be informed by existing law and detailed impact assessments of any ADM capabilities.

Second, the workshop highlighted the importance of addressing the possibility of moral injury of ADM end-users. In this context, the term moral injury was used broadly, referencing a range of definitions and implications in line with the wide-ranging research related to moral injury with regard to military populations reviewed by Richardson et al. (2020). Specifically, Richardson et al. state that the term *moral injury* broadly refers to the experience military service members often feel when "engaging in activities, witnessing acts, or immediate decision-making that may violate their moral codes and personal values. If unacknowledged, these factors can lead to injuries that can affect the physical, psychological, social, and spiritual health of military men and women" (2020).

An operational ADM presents the potential to lessen or exacerbate moral injury depending on the protocols applied to pre-, during-, and post-use. Additionally, consequences of such moral injury can vary from impacting a unit's overall mission readiness to creating new casualties. Therefore, choices that impact system use as well as the inherent Human-Computer-Interaction (HCI) of such use, must account for moral injury and the related design trade-offs.

At a basic level, it is widely accepted that an array of challenges exists when medical professionals choose to adopt AI technology that impacts treatment provision (Rajpurkar et al. 2022). For example, if during a high-stress event, a medical professional does not understand a new technology's limitations and failure points, they can make a bad situation worse and hold themselves responsible when there is an undesirable outcome. To begin to address this concern, end-users can build trust in a system by training alongside it in a safe environment while also independently mastering the basics of combat triage. Additionally, workshop participants highlighted that the potential for moral injury and combat operational stress disorders could be lessened if end-users have an option to override an ADM without retribution. Therefore, embedding a non-retribution component, which allows users to override an ADM's decision, may reduce the risk of user moral injury. However, more research, along with thorough testing and evaluation protocols, and system certification procedures will be required to fully address the complexities of moral injury.

A third major point of discussion during the workshop was the concept of calibrated trust. Establishing trust typically requires progressive, incremental steps over time and is not instantaneous. Further, there are arguments that AI systems do not have the capacity to be trusted, but rather human interactions with AI systems is about reliance (Ryan 2020). But the mission space ITM is intended to operate in may not allow much time for system integration. When discussing this challenge, experts stated that ADMs could potentially become "technological colleagues" if trained alongside humans. Such concurrent training would demonstrate system reliability, credibility, care, respect, equity, and transparency. If this concurrent training was completed in multiple iterations, metaphorical "sets and repetitions" alongside a human counterpart, end-user reliance in the ADM would be engendered. Workshop participants stated that, ideally, an ADM would be considered a colleague rather than a tool controlled by a human. Such a system would be especially helpful for a population of individuals without a skillset, such as a military unit in which the medic is incapacitated or unavailable.

Additionally, several experts stated that while fully automated "colleagues" might be ideal, especially given a high-casualty environment, creating human-controlled tools that transparently present information is a vital initial step. The key is to make the space to carry out collaborative work with human end-users before there is no choice, when we must rely on fully automated systems because there is no other option.

During the workshop, it was also suggested that ADMs developed with physiology-based algorithms may better predict patient outcomes compared to ADMs with provider-oriented algorithms. This suggestion is based on the notion that predictors of human decision-making will have greater variability due to provider responses to environmental factors and emotions, such as fear, anger, or frustration. This raises a range of questions about for what an ADM designed for human-off-the-loop operation in high-stakes environments should be optimized. Ultimately, ITM is conducting basic research on alignment of an ADM with human decision-makers, based on human attributes, but future research could seek to identify performance differences between a provider-aligned ADM and a physiology-based ADM.

6.4 ELSI Challenges and Future Work

The workshop described in Sect. 3, as well as ongoing ITM ELSI work, highlights two overarching challenges of operationalizing ELSI considerations for disruptive technology designed for high-stakes DoD domains. These two overarching challenges, described in more detail in Sect. 6.4.1, include: (1) the need to address an array of conflicting policies and practices, and (2) the fact that ELSI considerations are highly nuanced. With these challenges in mind and guided by the specific needs of the ITM program, we are able to elucidate future ITM ELSI related work in Sect. 6.4.2.

6.4.1 Overarching Challenges of Operationalizing ELSI Considerations

First, any new system must be built on essential foundations, such as regulations, policies, and TTPs. For example, a tactical ADM designed for triage in austere conditions must be informed by existing DoD policies. However, ITM work must also inform the development of future policies and concepts of operations (CONOPs) to address areas in which existing policies, practices, and regulations are inadequate, irrelevant, or out-of-date for real-world use of a human-off-the-loop ADM. The only way policy gaps can be identified is if: (a) the system's use cases, capabilities, and limitations, are well understood, and (b) the existing body of relevant policies, TTPs, and regulations are well understood.

Identifying and addressing the body of material that captures relevant policies and practices must be done in a transparent and inclusive way. Additionally, all key stakeholders must be involved, including intended system operators, system developers, commanders of units that will deploy the systems, and partner nation military personnel. Because military commanders are legally responsible for the actions of the units they are commanding, CONOPs that embody a commander's assumptions and intent must be developed. Related, system certification models must be established, so that a commander knows a system is safe and reliable. For a program such as ITM, in which basic research on a disruptive technology is the goal, expertise that goes beyond current practice is required.

Second, early integration of ELSI considerations benefits ITM researchers' and developers' design considerations and the systems' ELSI-related capabilities, but addressing specific concerns in a nuanced way takes time and concerted effort. For example, as shown above, an ADM can perform to design specifications and still lead to moral injury for end-users. Such a possibility is a result of the inherent disconnect between developers, who require a specific expertise based on years of experience developing highly technical algorithmic systems, versus system end-users, who have a very different kind of expertise, requiring a comparable amount of time and effort to develop. Simply put, it is not enough to recognize that there is potential for moral injury. Any program developing a system designed for high-stakes DoD missions, when there is no clear right answer, must be prepared to confront challenging questions and design tradeoffs. Not addressing the disconnect between system developers and end-users will have far-reaching impacts, such as negatively impacting an end-user's mission capability, even if a system operates exactly as designed. For this reason, ITM is committed to, for example, understanding the current degree of risk of moral injury for military medical personnel and how an ADM might lessen or intensify such a risk. Recognizing the challenge of addressing nuanced ELSI considerations is a fundamental reason why DARPA has chosen to integrate a policy and practice technical area for the ITM program.

6.4.2 *Future ELSI Work*

Additional ITM research effort must be put into defining gaps, uncertainties, and disconnects related to ELSI considerations with the objective of clarifying future AI policy development. For example, specific requirements for ADM user acceptance must be clarified and codified in related policy. Such work will make it clear what level of alignment is required, which will have tertiary impacts on training procedures, the specificity of user-data required to align a system, and the lifespan of a system-user relationship. Perhaps, research will indicate that alignment based on individual user feedback is highly correlated with user-trust, in which case it will be critical to know the minimum amount of time and energy required to provide a specific level of individual user feedback for any particular system. Alternatively, research may indicate that alignment to individual users is achievable and is correlated with higher levels of user trust, but that such alignment leads to poor medical outcomes, impacting overall system adoption and commanders' willingness to deploy such systems. Identifying gaps related to ELSI is crucial for clarifying the boundaries of ambiguous areas that will inform future policy development that applies to the full lifecycle of autonomous systems.

The example above raises another area that requires additional investigation. Namely, additional research is required to determine if human-AI alignment is a reliable and safe metric. In other words, how can ITM developers know that alignment to humans is sufficient? Should a system designed to make high-stakes decisions, that involve questions of life or death, be aligned to humans? And if so, which humans? Quantifying attributes related to human decision-making will require the consideration of human attributes that are likely to be unstable. Therefore, research must be done to determine if human decision-making attributes can be generalizable across high-stakes environments or if such attributes are domain-specific. Putting this into the context of ITM, we must ask, are the human decision-making attributes that are being used by ITM TA1 researchers sufficient? Or, does such alignment-related work require additional or other attributes? Military triage leaders with whom we have engaged have emphasized that in order to trust an ADM, evidentiary data indicating the system can make better decisions than a human is required. This is anecdotal evidence that the bar for an algorithmic system is higher than that for humans. Regardless of the validity of this statement, collecting useful data about system performance that is sufficient to support end-user buy-in when there is no "correct" answer, will be challenging.

Other use cases of an ITM ADM must be explored in greater detail as the ELSI challenges will likely vary depending on the context. For example, it will be important to consider the use of an ITM ADM in high-stakes environments that are more permissive than a near-peer conflict (e.g., natural disaster). Lessons learned from the war in Ukraine, as well as both domestic and international disaster response operations, will be leveraged to inform such research. Exploring other high-stakes domains outside of battlefield triage will contribute to the research of human decision-making and willingness to delegate and support the development of a tool that is useful in a range of dynamic, austere settings, in which resources are limited and time is of the essence.

Other future ITM-related work can explore ELSI considerations related to the personalization of an ADM to individual users by integrating user feedback. Will such personalization impact a user's willingness to delegate to an ADM system? And, would the integration of individual user feedback impact the medical outcomes? Such questions introduce the possibility of trade-offs between increased user trust in a system, which may increase its actual use, versus a reduction in ideal outcomes based on purely physiological measures that lead to ADM outputs that do not align to an individual end-user. These questions also raise an overarching consideration related to the way in which an ADM fits into existing workflows and TTPs, which will impact system adoption and, later, potential disuse. In other words, further exploration of ELSI challenges related to human-aligned autonomous systems and the impact of alignment on human trust to delegate decision-making authority to an ADM in high-stakes domains, is required.

6.5 Conclusion

This chapter provided an introduction to DARPA's "In The Moment" (ITM) basic research program, including the motivation behind the program, how the program's interdependent technical areas are structured, and the metrics that will be used to test the program's hypothesis that ADMs encoded with human decision-maker attributes and values will be more likely adopted by humans. With this background, we then presented details of ITM Technical Area (TA) 4: Policy and Practice, which includes the program's Ethical, Legal, and Societal Implications (ELSI) efforts. Though there are many outstanding questions, it is clear that integrating an ELSI component in basic research programs designed to develop revolutionary capabilities aligns with DARPA's comprehensive and innovative approach to pushing the limits of emerging technology in a responsible way. To that end, key points of discussion raised during ITM's March 2024 workshop included balancing human oversight with critical system needs, the importance of addressing impacts on end-users, and the challenge of establishing "trust" in an algorithmic system designed to independently operate in high-stakes environments when there is no clear right answer. By highlighting both the range of outstanding policy and practice questions and the work being done to address them, this chapter shows the importance of DARPA's emphasis on full integration of ELSI research. This research forces us to ask, how do we successfully and responsibly disrupt current military medical practices when time is of the essence? Ultimately, if human-off-the-loop systems become essential and the capability exists to build and deploy them, an approach that incorporates ELSI is not just best practice but essential to success.

Acknowledgments The work described in this chapter was only possible through the collaboration of dozens of individuals across multiple organizations. In particular, the authors wish to acknowledge the DARPA ITM program team, the members of other technical teams involved in the ITM program who actively participated in ELSI activities, and the many experts that provided candid and valuable insights at the ITM external events. The authors also deeply appreciate the contributions of their ITM ELSI teammates including David Danks, Brian Pierce, Harvey Rishikof, Rick Thomas, and Stephen Xenakis. Any errors or omissions are solely the responsibility of the authors.

References

Alexandrow, C. 2008. *The Story of GPS.* https://www.darpa.mil/attachments/(2O10)%20Global%20Nav%20-%20About%20Us%20-%20History%20-%20Resources%20-%2050th%20-%20GPS%20(Approved).pdf. Accessed 15 May 2024.

Axe, D. 2023. Did the Ukrainian Army Kill 1,100 Russians In A Single Day? It's Certainly Possible. *Forbes.* https://www.forbes.com/sites/davidaxe/2023/03/14/did-the-ukrainian-army-kill-1100-russians-in-a-single-day-its-certainly-possible/. Accessed 1 June 2024.

Center for Strategic & International Studies. 2024. *The DARPA Perspective on AI and Autonomy at the DOD.* Center for Strategic & International Studies Wadhwani Center for AI and Advanced Technologies. https://www.youtube.com/watch?v=1xSw835-rig. Accessed 20 October 2024.

Chief Digital and Artificial Intelligence Office (CDAO). 2022. *Responsible Artificial Intelligence (RAI): Transforming the Department of Defense Through AI.* https://www.ai.mil/docs/CDAO_SLICKSHEET_RAIv2_07_25_22.pdf. Accessed 15 May 2024.

DARPA. 2024a. *In the Moment (ITM).* https://www.darpa.mil/program/in-the-moment. Accessed 1 June 2024.

DARPA. 2024b. *DARPA's Stealth Revolution.* https://www.darpa.mil/about-us/timeline/darpas-stealth-revolution. Accessed 15 May 2024.

Goddard, K., A. Roudsari, and J. C. Wyatt. 2012. Automation Bias: A Systematic Review of Frequency, Effect Mediators, and Mitigators. *Journal of the American Medical Informatics Association.* 19 (1): 121–127. https://doi.org/10.1136/amiajnl-2011-000089.

Hancock, P. A., T. T. Kessler, A. D. Kaplan, K. Stowers, J. C. Brill, D. R. Billings, K. E. Schaefer, and J. L. Szalma. 2023. How and Why Humans Trust: A Meta-Analysis and Elaborated Model. *Frontiers in Psychology.* 14:1081086. https://doi.org/10.3389/fpsyg.2023.1081086.

Martin, A., C. L. Davidson, A. Panik, C. Buckenmyer, P. Delpais, and M. Ortiz. 2014. An Examination of ESI Triage Scoring Accuracy in Relationship to ED Nursing Attitudes and Experience. *Journal of Emergency Nursing.* 40 (5): 461–468. https://doi.org/10.1016/j.jen.2013.09.009.

Mayer, R. C., J. H. Davis, and F. D. Schoorman. 1995. An Integrative Model of Organizational Trust. *The Academy of Management Review.* 20 (3): 709–734. https://doi.org/10.2307/258792.
Mistry, B., S. Stewart De Ramirez, G. Kelen, P. S. K. Schmitz, K. S. Balhara, and S. Levin. 2018. Accuracy and Reliability of Emergency Department Triage Using the Emergency Severity Index: An International Multicenter Assessment. *Annals of Emergency Medicine.* 71 (5): 581–7.e3. https://doi.org/10.1016/j.annemergmed.2017.09.036.
Menes, K., Tintinalli, J., and L. Plaster. 2017. *How One Las Vegas ED Saved Hundreds of Lives After the Worst Mass Shooting in U.S. History*. https://epmonthly.com/article/not-heroes-wear-capes-one-las-vegas-ed-saved-hundreds-lives-worst-mass-shooting-u-s-history/ Accessed 2 June 2024.
Rajpurkar, P., E. Chen, and O. Banerjee. 2022. AI in Health and Medicine. *Nature Medicine.* 28:31–38. https://doi.org/10.1038/s41591-021-01614-0.
Richardson, N. M., A. L. Lamson, M. Smith, S. M. Eagan, A. M. Zvonkovic, and J. Jensen. 2020. Defining Moral Injury Among Military Populations: A Systematic Review. *Journal of Traumatic Stress.* 33:575–586. https://doi.org/10.1002/jts.22553.
Ryan, M. 2020. In AI We Trust: Ethics, Artificial Intelligence, and Reliability. *Science and Engineering Ethics.* 26:2749–2767. https://doi.org/10.1007/s11948-020-00228-y.
Skitka, L. J., K. L. Mosier, and M. Burdick. 1999. Does Automation Bias Decision-Making? *International Journal of Human-Computer Studies* 51:991–1006. https://doi.org/10.1006/ijhc.1999.0252.
Tam, H. L., S. F. Chung, and C. K. Lou. 2018. A Review of Triage Accuracy and Future Direction. *BMC Emergency Medicine* 1 (58): https://doi.org/10.1186/s12873-018-0215-0.
The Economist. 2024. *How Many Russian Soldiers Have Died in Ukraine*. https://www.economist.com/graphic-detail/2024/02/24/how-many-russian-soldiers-have-died-in-ukraine. Accessed 1 June 2024.
The White House. 2023. *Executive Order on the Safe, Secure, and Trustworthy Development and Use of Artificial Intelligence*. https://www.whitehouse.gov/briefing-room/presidential-actions/2023/10/30/executive-order-on-the-safe-secure-and-trustworthy-development-and-use-of-artificial-intelligence/. Accessed 2 June 2024.
Trusilo, D., and T. Burri. 2021. The Ethical Assessment of Autonomous Systems in Practice. *J* 4 (4): 749–763. https://doi.org/10.3390/j4040051.
Ullman, D., and B.F. Malle. 2023. *Measuring Human-Robot Trust with the MDMT (Multi-Dimensional Measure of Trust)*. https://doi.org/10.48550/arXiv.2311.14887.
Voices from DARPA. 2024. *83: When Should Machines Decide?* DARPA. https://www.youtube.com/watch?v=vMIXAcEyfeU. Accessed 30 October 2024.

Daniel Trusilo works at the intersection of AI, international security, and public policy. He is also a member of the Ethical, Legal, and Societal Implications team for the DARPA *In the Moment* (ITM) program. Dr. Trusilo earned a bachelor's degree from the US Military Academy at West Point, a Master of Arts in Law and Diplomacy from the Fletcher School at Tufts University, and Masters and Doctorate degrees in International Affairs from the University of St. Gallen, Switzerland.

Lauren Diaz is a research lead at the Applied Research Laboratory for Intelligence and Security (ARLIS), a University-Affiliated Research Center (UARC) at the University of Maryland (UMD), College Park. At ARLIS, Lauren supports intelligent human-machine systems research in the artificial intelligence, autonomy, and augmentation mission area. She is a policy and practice principal investigator for the DARPA ITM program. Lauren holds a Master of Public Health in Health Promotion, Education, and Behavior from the University of South Carolina, Columbia. Previously, Lauren worked as a senior research analyst at the University of Maryland, Baltimore's Institute for Innovation and Implementation. Additionally, Lauren coordinated large-scale projects funded by the National Institutes of Health (NIH) at the University of South Carolina, Columbia.

Ellie Tyler is a researcher at the Applied Research Laboratory for Intelligence and Security (ARLIS), at the University of Maryland. Joining ARLIS in 2023, she focused on the assessment of emerging technologies and their potential public health security implications. Ellie holds a bachelor's degree from Virginia Tech, where she studied Clinical Neuroscience alongside National Security and Foreign Affairs.

Chapter 7
A New Age of Dual-Use Technologies: Identifying and Evaluating AI-Induced Risks and Opportunities in Military Medical Ethics

Martin Hähnel

7.1 Introduction

The advent of artificial intelligence (AI) has brought about significant advancements and raised critical ethical concerns, particularly in the realm of dual-use technologies. Dual-use technologies are those that can be employed for both civilian and military applications. Dual use is also used to describe the potential of an item in question for good or bad use. We usually encounter the phenomenon of dual-use in the context of export control (Carrozza et al. 2022), but since new cross-border digital technologies such as AI have been increasingly developed and deployed, the dual-use problem has extended to a whole range of fields of application, from classic nuclear technology to unmanned aerial vehicles (UAVs or Drones).[1]

At this point we must note that dual use, especially of AI systems, is not genuinely a military problem, but is always confronted with the dual-use problem due to the general potential for harmless objects to be converted into weapons. AI systems could be weaponized for various malicious purposes, including cyberattacks, surveillance, and autonomous weapons development. Malicious actors could utilize AI algorithms to intensify propaganda, sway public opinion, or execute advanced phishing attacks. Additionally, the creation of autonomous weapons systems driven by AI presents ethical issues regarding the absence of human control and the risk of unintended escalation in conflicts. The potential for escalation can even multiply

[1] For an overview of various fields of technology and research where dual use issues play an important role, see Heinrichs et al. (2025).

M. Hähnel (✉)
University of Bremen, Bremen, Germany
e-mail: haehnel@uni-bremen.de

B. Koch, D. Winkler (eds.), *Artificial Intelligence Ethics in Military Medicine and Humanitarian Healthcare*, Military and Humanitarian Health Ethics,
https://doi.org/10.1007/978-3-032-11331-3_7

between areas where spin-offs traditionally occur or where the probability of repurposing is high, such as in the military and medical fields.[2]

As AI applications are increasing in both the medical and military sectors, it is not only important to analyze ethical challenges and dual-use risks for each individual area, but also to consider their positive and negative synergies. This essay explores the concept of dual-use, focusing on AI's implications in both military and medical fields, and examines the ethical challenges inherent in evaluating dual-use potentials in military medicine.

7.2 Outline of the Chapter

The following article begins by outlining the concept of dual-use technologies—tools or systems that can serve both civilian and military purposes or be used for both beneficial and harmful ends. As AI becomes more integrated into sensitive domains such as medicine and the military, its dual-use potential becomes more pressing and ethically complex. Understanding and addressing these challenges requires a nuanced, context-sensitive ethical framework.

In the second part, I delve deeper into the nature of dual-use technologies by highlighting how accelerating technological innovation and the fusion of disciplines have made traditional ethical frameworks inadequate. To bring order to the dual-use debate, I introduce a "trimodal property model" that assesses dual-use risks based on three dimensions: the intrinsic susceptibility to misuse, the intentions behind use, and the contextual environment. However, I emphasize that especially in the case of AI, this model struggles to fully capture the risks due to unknown variables and the complexity of AI systems.

The third section contrasts how AI manifests as a dual-use technology in the military versus the medical sector. In military contexts, AI is typically geared toward efficiency in operations such as surveillance, autonomous weapons, and decision-making support. Yet, because the misuse of military dual use technologies is inherently tied to their intended function, the ethical concerns around AI in the military often revolve more around boundary-blurring and unintended civilian applications than traditional notions of misuse. In contrast, medical AI—aimed at diagnosis, treatment, and healthcare optimization—carries dual-use risks related to data misuse, discriminatory algorithms, and technologies like brain-computer interfaces that could be used for therapeutic issues rather than for enhancement (Gielas 2025). Although the goals of medicine and the military differ, I try to point out that both sectors share implementation challenges such as ensuring human oversight, data protection, and responsible deployment of AI systems.

[2] Spin-offs, in this context, often involve the creation of new companies based on research or technology that could have applications in either the civilian (e.g., medical) or military sectors, or both.

The fourth section focuses on the ethical dilemmas of assessing dual-use potentials in military medicine by outlining three central issues: value conflicts, implementation problems, and the importance of human-centered design.[3] Value conflicts arise when core principles like transparency and security clash—particularly in research settings where openness can increase vulnerability to misuse. Implementation challenges stem from the inadequacy of top-down ethical guidelines to manage dynamic, unpredictable technologies like AI. In line with a human-centered perspective on AI, I advocate for a hybrid ethics-by-design approach that embeds ethical reasoning throughout the development process of dual use technologies in the field of military medicine. Finally, I argue that despite AI's increasing autonomy, human judgment and responsibility must remain central, warning against over-reliance on machines (*automation bias*). In response to these challenges, I propose two practical tools: *Accurate Risk Classification (ARC)* and *Problem Mirroring (PM)*. The ARC model categorizes dual-use risks based on whether they are direct or indirect, who the actor and the potential victim are, and considers even the possibility of AI systems themselves becoming agents or subjects of harm. PM emphasizes mutual learning between the medical and military fields, the need for shared expertise, and early collaboration to identify and mitigate dual-use risks. I also argue for the inclusion of AI ethics education in military medical training. The article concludes with some thoughts on the future of AI applications in military medicine.

7.3 Understanding Dual-Use Technologies

In an era of rapid technological advancement and multiple global crises that endanger prosperity, health, and peace, a new normative framework for application areas related to security—primarily bioethics, technology ethics, and research ethics—is emerging. We are observing profound shifts that challenge the theoretical and practical underpinnings of applied ethics, particularly research ethics, on several fronts:

(a) the quickening pace of innovation in life sciences and allied disciplines,
(b) the ongoing fusion of biology and biomedicine with fields such as mathematics, engineering, chemistry, computer science, and information theory
(c) the unchecked proliferation of biological and biomedical capabilities worldwide,
(d) the permanent transformation of science through novel digital tools that change the collection, management, dissemination, and access to information,
(e) and, amid current global military conflicts, a growing readiness to develop, manufacture, test, and utilize weaponry.

[3] I am not claiming that wherever medical AI encounters military AI, the classic questions of military medical ethics (e.g., dual loyalty, treatment of enemy combatants, scarce resource allocation) are automatically raised. Technological development and its ethical evaluation are still too much in progress and too complex to be able to make such a sweeping statement.

Accordingly, grasping research ethics and the ethics of science as interdisciplinary, multifaceted, and acutely risk-conscious domains of applied ethics becomes ever more crucial. Amidst epistemic uncertainty, changing social dynamics, unstable political decision-making, and unforeseeable economic constraints, ethical judgments must balance costs and benefits, possibilities and dangers, welfare and detriment, freedom of research or progress, and the importance of public safety. As a result, the future of applied ethics (and military medical ethics as a part of it), especially in the normative evaluation of security-sensitive research, might be characterized by an ethical ambivalence that mirrors competing aims and purposes. It seems we are still far from the end of technology diffusion, which is closely tied to the dissemination of technologies, including those with dual uses (Meier 2014, 9). But what makes a technology a dual-use technology?

Dual-use technologies encompass a broad spectrum of applications, balancing between beneficial and potentially harmful uses. Narrowly defined, dual use refers to the contrast between civilian and military use. Broadly speaking, it includes any technology that can serve acceptable purposes while also being susceptible to misuse for unacceptable purposes, often referred to as "security-relevant" technologies . While definitions of "dual use" may vary (Rath et al. 2014; Hähnel 2024), it commonly suggests that the same advancements can be used for positive or negative ends. It is important to note that research outcomes or technologies are not inherently abusive; misuse only occurs when humans enable or intentionally employ them for detrimental objectives. In a society deeply invested in technological and scientific advancement, the dual use conundrum, its widespread nature, and the imperative to confront it appear inescapable.

To bring some order to the dual-use discussion, I have developed a trimodal property model that offers a comprehensive framework for understanding dual-use technologies. This model describes the conditions and properties that are necessary for a good in question to be qualified as a dual-use good or dual-use technology: In doing so, we must examine

(a) the extent to which a good is susceptible to misuse due to its intrinsic properties, (b) the intentions associated with a particular use and (c) the context in which the use takes place or is intended to take place (Hähnel 2024).

However, this does not yet fully capture the problem of dual-use, as we are dealing with many unknown variables, especially in the case of higher-level dual-use risks, e.g. those caused by AI, which also increases the difficulty of identifying the number of stakeholders and the intentions they are pursuing.[4] Much therefore depends on the characteristics and customs of the context in which technologies with dual-use potential are used or are to be used in the future. In other words: "Dual use risks continue to exist as long as possible development paths, ambivalences, application possibilities, and intentions are not analyzed, made aware of and

[4] In Hähnel (2024), I also have developed a special knowledge matrix and a tailored stakeholder matrix to address dual-use issues, which are typically challenging to encapsulate.

assessed—with possible consequences for the design of further development." (Liebert 2021, 289).

7.4 How Can AI Appear as a Dual-Use Technology in Military Medicine?

7.4.1 AI as a Dual-Use Technology in the Military

The military sector is certainly one of the most advanced contexts for the application of new AI technologies that have found diverse applications in this area, including surveillance, target recognition, cyber defense, autonomous weaponry, and battlefield analytics. A range of military AI technologies have been created for generative tasks, such as intelligent decision support systems and aided target recognition (Larkin et al. 2021), which aid in decision-making, target identification, and field casualty care.

Now, as already mentioned above, there seems to be no genuine dual-use problem in the military sphere, since the misuse of weapons, e.g. by hammering a nail with a rifle or turning it into a work of art, is harmless and does not pose a major ethical problem (I do not want to discuss pacifist cases in which weapons are not used for self-defense here). Equally unproblematic is the fact that in the military sphere dual use is more a matter of incorrect use or behavior than of actual and deliberate misuse: if someone is unable to operate a weapon technology, he or she does not misuse it for a bad purpose. However, this does not mean that there should be no awareness of potential dual-use risks in a military context. Considering the trimodal property model discussed earlier, we might ask: How can the inherent characteristics of an AI-supported weapon (such as black-box mechanisms) lead to its misuse? What other 'good' purposes (that can turn out to be 'bad') might a soldier or military medic have for AI technology beyond the fulfilment of professional duties, protection and self-defense? Is there a dual-use dilemma if a soldier uses military technology for civilian purposes in exceptional circumstances (e.g. by using surveillance technology for spying on unsuspicious non-military targets)? And so on.

It is evident that military applications of AI introduce unique ethical and security challenges. These include the risk of hasty alarmism stemming from biased perspectives on specific technologies, overlooking the significance of civilian-military technology spin-offs, and the emergence of blurred boundaries between civilian and military interests (Liebert 2021). A key limitation is that the examination of military AI frequently focuses on its restricted dual-use concept, highlighting the necessity for broader viewpoints to comprehensively understand and address dual-use risks in this domain. For this reason, it is ethically more controversial when dual use AI technologies from the military sector encounter dual use AI technologies from the medical sector.

7.4.2 *AI as a Dual-Use Technology in Medicine*

In the medical field, AI's dual-use potential is equally significant but diametrically opposed in its outcomes compared to the military sector. While military AI aims to improve the efficiency, accuracy, and strategic potential of defensive and offensive maneuvers, medical AI seeks to enhance patient care, improve health outcomes, and optimize healthcare systems. Potential applications include personalized treatments, diagnostic accuracy, disease prediction, and streamlined administrative tasks (see Oniani et al. 2023). The various application fields of AI in medicine have been thoroughly characterized and assessed from an ethical standpoint (cf. Rubeis 2024). Despite frequent discussions about the inherently ambiguous nature of this technology, the specific dual-use potential of medical AI applications is seldom discussed. This ambiguity stems from the unique vulnerability of the ill and needy, including their data, and the rightfully stringent ethical standards in the healthcare sector. The question then arises: how does medical AI emerge as a dual-use technology?

The examples of AI technologies showing their Janus face in the healthcare sector are numerous and may become even more abundant in the future. The dual-use aspect of AI in medicine is paradigmatically exemplified by cases where AI-driven pharmaceutical software unintentionally proposed potential chemical warfare agents, highlighting the hazards and grave ethical challenges of such technologies (Urbina et al. 2022). Furthermore, so-called Brain-Computer Interfaces (BCI) combined with AI present a potent method for exploring brain functions, offering direct insight and control over neurons that govern behavior (Zhang et al. 2020). This could advance our understanding of the human brain and aid in the progress of rehabilitation medicine (Slutzky 2019). However, this technology possesses a tangible dual-use potential, as it can be utilized to either recover lost functions or enhance human capabilities, with the latter posing enormous ethical risks (Sattler and Pietralla 2022). Rather than fostering beneficial decisions for vulnerable individuals, AI systems can be detrimental as they may exhibit discriminatory behavior and exacerbate inequalities (Kaushal et al. 2020). Another commonly expressed concern regarding AI in medicine is the vast quantity of patient data required for collection and the associated risks of confidentiality breaches. The demand for medical data on the black market is substantial, and there is a significant inclination to target healthcare data and hospital systems, especially in the context of warfare—e.g., during the recent conflict in Ukraine, civilian hacker collectives from both Ukrainian and Russian sides have targeted hospitals and pharmacies (Tidy 2023).

The examples provided here are not exhaustive; the anticipated rise in AI application within medicine suggests an increased probability of discovering new dual-use potentials. To date, it is evident that both AI technology and the medical field are vulnerable to dual use. The convergence of these domains amplifies this susceptibility, underscoring the need for more robust regulations and safeguards (see Krauel and Frewer 2024).

7.4.3 *Common Focus, Common Challenges?*

It would now appear that the military and medical sectors have diverging interests regarding the use of AI. However, according to Oniani et al. (2023), this only seems to apply to the basic objectives, but not to the desire to use AI effectively and appropriately: "While we acknowledge the different ideological foundations in military and healthcare due to the contrasting objectives, we argue that both military and healthcare sectors illustrate a compelling convergence of priorities for the applications of AI." (ibid.). Rather, the military and medicine have the same interests when it comes to "application validity, attention to practical implementation, and the prioritization of a human-centered approach" (ibid.) Fundamentally, I concur with Oniani et al. at a basic descriptive level; however, at a more normative-ethical level, we must examine the 'different ideological foundations.' These underlying assumptions are crucial in highlighting the significant differences in addressing the dual-use dilemma. For instance, the normative rationale for employing medical knowledge for non-medical (military) purposes, such as neuroenhancement, must be unequivocally articulated (refer to the second section to understand the full extent of the dual-use issue). It must also be made clear that with the help of AI in the field of medicine, human lives are saved or not saved for *different* (!) moral reasons than in the military, although there are of course context-independent overlaps here.

AI solutions in the medical and military sectors not only share common strengths but also exhibit significant weaknesses. Thus, addressing the context-independent issues of AI systems in a context-sensitive manner becomes a task of both technical and ethical design. The challenges are similar across military and civilian healthcare sectors: overcoming the lack of accountability to retain direct control over AI systems, safeguarding highly sensitive military and health data,[5] and deciding whether to grant epistemic authority and decision-making power to AI, be it a medical recommender system or an autonomous weapon system.

7.5 Ethical Challenges in Evaluating Dual-Use Potentials in Military Medicine

As discussed in the previous section, assessing the dual-use potential of AI in military medicine poses distinct ethical dilemmas. The alignment of military and medical AI objectives leads to shared focuses and synergies, yet it also confronts us with

[5] The comparison between these two forms of data, which also overlap when it comes to the health data of an injured soldier, for example, is illuminating both in general and in relation to dual use. Generally speaking, military data focuses on readiness, operational effectiveness, and potential hazards, while civilian healthcare prioritizes individual well-being and broader population health metrics. In relation to dual use, it would be particularly important to identify the parameters that are typical of each data type, but also those that are common to both, which enable the harmful use of AI applications.

the challenges of resolving emerging value conflicts, surmounting unexpected barriers to implementation, and ensuring that humans remain integral to the process.

7.5.1 *Value Conflicts*

Values are central to ethical considerations, providing orientation for weighing benefits and risks, such as the dual use risks, in research and technology development. Applied ethics identify specific values relevant to contexts, such as transparency, fairness, reliability, and accountability, as noted in the HLEG handbook for Trustworthy AI (HLEG 2019). These values guide decision-making and legitimize choices in research and technology governance.

Identifying the shared values that should govern both the general ethical use of technology like AI and its application in specific domains such as medicine or the military is far from simple. Oniani et al. (2023) has attempted to filter out the values that are relevant for both military and medical AI.[6] However, these shared values say little about the way in which they should be implemented (cf. section 5.2) and do not solve the problem that arises when one value must be weighed against another one. For example, transparency can boost trust but may conflict with competitive advantages. In dual-use research, transparency is crucial for the democratization of research but presents a challenge due to the potential misuse of sensitive information. Nonetheless, value conflicts in the field of medicine and the military should not be seen solely as trade-off situations, because deontological constraints such as human dignity express an unconditionality at which benefit-risk calculations come to an end. High ethical standards must also be imparted to dual-use AI, posing a significant challenge in the ethical design of digital medical and military systems. AI systems in military medicine are required to navigate conflicts of values, as they must differentiate between beneficence towards civilians, their own wounded combatants, and those of the enemy, despite the principle of medical neutrality. However, the result of this differentiation should always be confirmed and, if necessary, falsified by humans.

7.5.2 *The Implementation Problem*

As just mentioned, the central question is how values and ethical principles can be implemented in medical and military systems without becoming ineffective or reinforcing existing conflicts of values. As we can see in the recent literature, classical (top-down) ethical guidelines are more and more challenged by the dynamic and

[6] These values or principles are traceability, reliability, lawfulness, accountability, governability ad equity.

unpredictable nature of AI technologies, prompting calls for a hybrid approach of ethics-by-design that combines both top-down principles and bottom-up processes (Hähnel and Müller 2025). This implementation process is accompanied by numerous ethical issues, with the question of responsibility playing a central role: an AI system can only be successfully implemented if responsibilities are clarified, i.e. who is praised when the system works well and who is to blame when it makes mistakes. This also raises important legal liability issues.

The classical structure of responsibility involves A being responsible for x toward B by reference to y, with A representing individuals, groups, or institutions, x referring to actions or decisions, and y encompassing reasons, social conventions, laws, or moral norms (Werner 2011). (Prospective) Responsibility hinges on the anticipation of harmful outcomes. When dual-use consequences are predictable, failure to mitigate them indicates negligence. Yet, predicting misuse in intricate and uncertain research domains is difficult. Developers and regulators are tasked with performing risk/benefit evaluations, weighing technical know-how against extensive impact studies. Effective responsibility requires pinpointing an appropriate level of diligence for managing Dual Use Research of Concern (DURC), comprehending decision-making amidst uncertainty, and ensuring that both developers and regulators execute their duties without redundancy. As dual-use risks persist alongside future advancements, heightened awareness within both medical and military realms becomes crucial. Despite a history of accepted risks, the dual-use dilemma, particularly with AI technologies, poses a unique challenge to all involved parties.

7.5.3 Human Centered Design

In both medicine and the military, the focus is (or should be) on human beings first and then on technologies. Nonetheless, advancements in technology, particularly those driven by AI, have resulted in a decreased need for human intervention in both the execution of processes and their outcomes. The aim of applied AI ethics is therefore to keep people in the loop and not to make them disappear in a socio-technical system. On the one hand, AI poses the dual-use risk of medical or military personnel over-relying on technology and thus ignoring the irreducible importance of humans in decision-making processes (*automation bias*). The human element also brings vulnerability and fallibility into play, which ensures that we remain skeptical of purely technological solutions that humans themselves have created. It has now become a commonplace that AI technologies should only serve humans by supporting them in the fulfilment of their tasks. This also means that humans as a dual-use factor, in that they can want good and bad things, must be distinguished from technology as a dual-use factor, which cannot want anything good or bad of its own accord.[7] The primordial focus of ethics on human beings (or persons) therefore also remains secure because the question of responsibility must not be abandoned. Whether it is military or medical AI, or a combination of both, the question of accountability and responsibility must be asked and answered satisfactorily in all areas; there must be no room for responsibility gaps.

7.6 Some Tools for Preparing Suitable Countermeasures: Accurate Risk Classification (ARC) and Problem Mirroring (PM)

To effectively assess and mitigate dual-use risks, I suggest developing a scheme for accurate risk classification (AC) and problem mirroring (PM). AC involves identifying *first-level* (direct misuse) and *higher-level risks*. AI as a technology entails dual-use problems in an intensified, higher-level form, which arise due to its character as an advanced epistemic technology. The reason for this is that (generative) AI can be used to distribute existing (technological) knowledge, including knowledge that is associated with dual-use risks. On the other hand, they could also be used to generate new technological knowledge or technologies, which are then potentially associated with dual-use risks. While, according to the classic definition, dual-use problems arise when a technology can be directly misused for harmful purposes, generative AI, e.g., in the form of Large Language Models (LLMs), thus pose an indirect risk of misuse—in addition to the direct risks of misuse that they also pose. A particular challenge in this case results from the fact that it is not known in detail which specific technologies could be constructed with the help of LLMs. Due to this higher level of uncertainty, the establishment of suitable strategies to contain the indirect dual-use risks is associated with special challenges that are not known in this form from the classic dual-use discussion. I would like to develop a three-dimensional classification scheme in which the misuse scenarios are classified according to (1) whether they involve a direct (first-level) or an indirect (higher-level) dual-use risk, (2) who the misusing actor is and (3) who the potentially harmed party is. In the case of dimensions 2 and 3, the following are possible in principle: a. the user of the LLM, b. the LLM itself, c. third parties.

With the help of realistic simulations (e.g., wargames), scenarios can be developed that enable dual-use risks to be identified at an early stage and classified accurately in order to counteract the radical ignorance that still prevails with regard to determining the future opportunities and risks of using AI in military medicine. For instance, imagine a military medic who has to take an injured soldier to a safe place suggested by AI. Is the place suggested by AI really safe? What happens if the enemy gets hold of this information? Or, an AI-supported armed drone delivers

[7] Floridi (2023) believes that a distinction must be made between ethical questions of dual-use and empirical questions of how a particular technology is or can be used.

medication to the specified location: how can it distinguish between the wounded soldier and the military medic, who are the intended recipients of the delivery, and the enemy, who want to shoot the drone down? If the drone detects the enemy instead of your own people, will it fire? What happens if the drone accidentally fires on your own people? Many questions, (still) unclear answers.

The ARC tool helps us understand which actors are confronted with which risks, which must be distinguished from one another in terms of their degree of complexity. It thus also contributes to identifying the relevant responsibilities in the event of unexpected damage or incorrect use.

The question of how this theoretical or hypothetical classification can become relevant in practice is certainly justified here. The scenarios we have played through, which could one day become reality, are particularly helpful in this regard, enabling us to take preventive measures to mitigate the risks. We can identify the right measures by using ethical abduction to derive adequate explanations and decisions from our observations in relation to the scenarios we have played through.

The second tool of PM, which applies the results of the ARC, emphasizes the need for a context-sensitive exchange of expertise and a cross-expertise ethical design of dual-use AI technologies.

(a) joint development of strategies for evaluating and mitigating first- and higher-level dual-use risks based on a context-sensitive exchange of expertise (*top-down*)
(b) cross-expertise ethical design of dual-use AI technologies in military medicine (*bottom-up*)[8]
(c) need for AI ethics curriculum in military medical education

The main goal of this mixed method is to enhance preventive measures by more effectively identifying responsibilities, thereby revealing previously hidden dual-use potential. The military and medical sectors must learn from each other—not only from mistakes due to underestimated dual-use risks but also by sharing insights from the beginning about where they perceive dual-use potential in themselves and others.

7.7 AI and Future Military Medical Ethics

What does all this mean for military medical ethics, especially about overcoming future challenges? The overarching objective in future military medical ethics is to develop context-sensitive normative frameworks that encourage the non-dual use of

[8] Here, it is also possible to draw on existing findings. For example, with regard to the use of AI systems, dual-use scenarios in the civilian medical sector could be compared with dual-use scenarios in the military sector, and conclusions could be drawn for dual-use scenarios in the military medical sector. However, this does not replace the need to run through realistic scenarios in the military medical field with its own characteristics and rules.

AI technologies. This involves robust testing, prioritizing data privacy, fostering transparency, and maintaining human oversight and accountability. Continuous monitoring and improvement, international collaboration, and shared best practices are essential for the responsible and ethical use of AI in military medical contexts. Military medical ethics, which will increasingly rely on AI in the future and thus also accept an increased risk of the emergence of first- and higher-level dual-use problems, must rely on proven mitigation strategies (such as those developed by Tucker 2012) and adapt them to their context-specific requirements. For this to succeed, it is not only important that, for example, military doctors and researchers in the grey area of civil-military spin-offs are aware of dual-use risks and are adequately trained in these issues. Training must also be provided from the outset by ethics committees, which at best have an insight into current technology research and are partially specialized in dual use concerns related to interfaces between the medical and the military. It must not happen here that the left hand does not know what the right hand is doing.

7.8 Conclusion

The dual-use nature of AI presents significant ethical and practical challenges in both military and medical fields. By adopting a multidimensional approach to evaluating dual-use potentials and fostering collaborative efforts to develop ethical frameworks, society can harness the benefits of AI while mitigating its risks. Future research and policy-making should continue to explore and address these challenges to ensure the responsible and ethical deployment of AI technologies. Military medical ethics can be a touchstone for this, as it should have knowledge of both the dual-use risks of medical AI and the increase in dual-use risks of military AI through so-called spin-offs. It can use this knowledge to mirror the risks and challenges that arise in one area for the other. Ultimately, our examination reveals that the ethics of medical AI can expose the blind spots of military AI, and conversely, medical AI can benefit from the insights of military ethics. It allows for a more profound comprehension of the potential and hazards associated with the use of AI in its contributing fields, as well as an awareness of the vulnerabilities within its own domain, notwithstanding the unique and overarching questions that emerge, which are not present in either civilian medicine or strictly military contexts.

References

Carrozza, I., N. Marsh, and G. Reichberg. 2022. *Dual-use AI Technology in China, the US and the EU Strategic Implications for the Balance of Power*. Oslo: Prio Paper.

Floridi, L. 2023. On Good and Evil, the mistaken Idea that Technology is Ever Neutral, and the Importance of the Double-Charge Thesis. *Philosophy and Technology* 36:60.

Gielas, A. 2025. Soldier Enhancement through Brain–Computer Interfaces: The Risks of Changing the Human Condition. *The RUSI Journal* 170 (1): 32–47. https://doi.org/10.1080/03071847.2025.2449894.

Heinrichs, J.-H., S. E. Aslan, K. Alex, N. H. Conradie, M. Hähnel, M. Kropf, J. Kuck, O. Lev, M. Philippi, and V. Risse. 2025. Guideline on Dual Use and Misuse of Research for Committees for Ethics in Security Relevant Research. *Berichte des Forschungszentrums Jülich* 4449:33. https://doi.org/10.34734/FZJ-2025-02029.

Hähnel, M. 2024. Conceptualizing Dual Use: A Multidimensional Approach. *Research Ethics* 21 (2): 205–227. https://doi.org/10.1177/17470161241261466.

Hähnel, M., and R. Müller. 2025. Ethical Theories for AI: Systematizing the Discourse. In *Blackwell Companion to Applied Philosophy of AI*, ed. M. Hähnel and R. Müller, 135–150. Hoboken: Wiley.

Kaushal, A., R. Altman, and C. Langlotz. 2020. Health Care AI Systems are Biased—we Need More Diverse Data to Avoid Perpetuating Inequality in Medicine. *Scientific American—Health & Medicine* 3 (1). Available at: https://www.scientificamerican.com/article/health-care-ai-systems-are-biased/. Accessed 30 May 2024.

Krauel, E., and A. Frewer. 2024. Dual Use Concerns in Artificial Intelligence and the Neurosciences: How Medical Research Can End Up in War. *Research Ethics* 0 (0): https://doi.org/10.1177/17470161241262149.

Larkin, G. B., et al. 2021. Human Performance with Complex Technology: How Visual Cognition +Is Critical to Enhanced Performance with Aided Target Recognition (AiTR). In *Advances in Neuroergonomics and Cognitive Engineering. AHFE 2020. Advances in Intelligent Systems and Computing, vol 1201*, ed. H. Ayaz and U. Asgher. Cham: Springer. https://doi.org/10.1007/978-3-030-51041-1_19.

Liebert, W. 2021. Dual-use-Forschung und -Technologie. In *Handbuch Technikethik*, ed. A. Grunwald and R. Hillerbrand, 289–294. Stuttgart: J.B. Metzler.

Meier, O. 2014. *Technology Transfers and Nonproliferation of Weapons of Mass Destruction: Between Control and Cooperation*. Oxon: Routledge.

Oniani, D., J. Hilsman, Y. Peng, R. K. Poropatich, J. C. Pamplin, G. L. Legault, and Y. Wang. 2023. Adopting and Expanding Ethical Principles for Generative Artificial Intelligence from Military to Healthcare. *Npj Digital Medicine* 6 (1): 225. https://doi.org/10.1038/s41746-023-00965-x.

Rath, J., M. Ischi, and D. Perkins. 2014. Evolution of Different Dual-Use Concepts in International and National Law and Its Implications on Research Ethics and Governance. *Science and Engineering Ethics* 20 (3): 769–790.

Rubeis, G. 2024. *Ethics of Medical AI*. Cham: Springer.

Sattler, S., and D. Pietralla. 2022. Public Attitudes Towards Neurotechnology: Findings from Two Experiments Concerning Brain Stimulation Devices (BSDs) and Brain-Computer Interfaces (BCIs). *PLoS One* 17 (11): e0275454.

Slutzky, M. W. 2019. Brain-Machine Interfaces: Powerful Tools for Clinical Treatment and Neuroscientific Investigations. *The Neuroscientist* 25:139–154. https://doi.org/10.1177/1073858418775355.

Tidy, J. 2023. Ukraine Cyber-Conflict: Hacking Gangs Vow To De-Escalate. *BBC.*. Available at: https://www.bbc.com/news/technology-67029296. Accessed 29 Nov 2023.

Tucker J.B. (2012): Innovation, Dual-use, and Security. Cambridge, MA: MIT.

Urbina, F., F. Lentzos, C. Invernizzi, et al. 2022. A Teachable Moment for Dual-Use. *Nature Machine Intelligence* 4:607.

Werner, Micha H. 2011. Verantwortung. In *Handbuch Ethik. Dritte, überarbeitete und ergänzte Auflage*, ed. Marcus Düwell, Christoph Hübenthal, and Micha H. Werner, 541–548. Stuttgart: J. B. Metzler.

Zhang, X., Z. Ma, H. Zheng, T. Li, K. Chen, X. Wang, C. Liu, L. Xu, X. Wu, D. Lin, and H. Lin. 2020. The Combination of Brain-Computer Interfaces and Artificial Intelligence: Applications and Challenges. *Annals Of Translational Medicine* 8 (11): 712. https://doi.org/10.21037/atm.2019.11.109.

Martin Hähnel has obtained a diploma in industrial engineering and studied philosophy at the Technical University of Dresden. In 2015 he finished his PhD studies in philosophy with a thesis on virtue ethics. He is pursueing various activities in externally funded projects on medical ethics. Since 2021 he is a coordinator of a joint project funded by the German Federal Ministry of Education and Research on the responsible use of AI in medicine. After several research stays abroad (University of Oxford, Boston College) and ethical counselling activities (University of Cambridge) he completed his habilitation process with a thesis on the Neoaristotelian justification of bioethics in 2024.

Chapter 8
Meaningful Human Control Over AI Military Decision Support Systems: Exploring Key Challenges

Atay Kozlovski

8.1 Introduction

The potential benefits of AI technology are by now widely recognized. In the military, AI systems are being integrated into a variety of domains. For instance, in logistics, AI can optimize resource allocation, manage inventory with precision, and streamline maintenance schedules. In weapon systems, AI innovations can enhance target recognition, improve missile guidance, and enable autonomous drones. In training, AI can monitor and assess physical fitness levels, provide real-time feedback during exercises, and optimize team coordination drills. In intelligence, AI can analyze vast amounts of data, identifying patterns beyond the capability of human operators, and deliver actionable insights in real time.

While AI systems can provide significant benefits, their use in the military, particularly in situations with potential life-or-death consequences, raises serious ethical and legal concerns. Much of the early ethical literature on this topic concentrated on the design and deployment of Lethal Autonomous Weapons Systems (LAWS), such as autonomous drones, loitering munitions, and autonomous defense turrets (del Valle and Moreno 2023). However, in light of the many challenges that these systems raise, the debate slowly shifted its focus to discussing hybrid systems in which we can use the benefits of novel AI technology while maintaining human involvement, flexibility, and control. This vision for the future of warfare is best encapsulated by Paul Scharre's concept of 'Centaur warfighting' (Scharre 2016)—a human-machine team merging the strengths of both.

In a more recent interpretation, Sparrow and Henschke (2023) introduced an additional layer to this metaphor, suggesting that the human-machine partnership might not always resemble a centaur—a human head atop a horse's body—but

A. Kozlovski (✉)
University of Zurich's Center for Ethics, Zürich, Switzerland

B. Koch, D. Winkler (eds.), *Artificial Intelligence Ethics in Military Medicine and Humanitarian Healthcare*, Military and Humanitarian Health Ethics,
https://doi.org/10.1007/978-3-032-11331-3_8

could instead take the form of a minotaur—a human body directed by the head of a bull. This shift highlights that advancements in AI have significantly outpaced those in robotics, urging us to focus our analysis on the implications of militaries delegating cognitive tasks, rather than merely operational ones, to AI systems. This will be the primary focus of this paper in which we will examine the challenge and possibility of ensuring that we maintain a meaningful form of human control over the use of AI based military decision support systems.

The chapter is organized as follows: Sect. 8.2 provides an overview of the ethical debate surrounding the use of LAWS and introduces the concept of meaningful human control. Section 8.3 offers background on the development of Decision Support Systems (DSS) (Sect. 8.3.1) and explores six ethical challenges that may arise from their use in the military (AI-MDSS) (Sect. 8.3.2). Section 8.4 presents the philosophical framework of meaningful human control (MHC) (Sect. 8.4.1), demonstrates how this framework can address the six ethical challenges outlined in Sect. 8.3.2 (Sect. 8.4.2), and concludes by discussing the key technical, normative, and design challenges that must be addressed to ensure AI-MDSS operates under meaningful human control (Sect. 8.4.3).

8.2 The Ethics of Lethal Autonomous Weapon Systems (LAWS)

In 2012, a coalition of political activists, academics, and other concerned individuals launched a campaign advocating for a legal ban on the development and deployment of 'Killer Robots', officially known as Lethal Autonomous Weapon Systems (LAWS). Since then, the core ethical debate in academia has centered on three primary critiques: the compliance problem, the potential for responsibility gaps, and possible dehumanization effects (Eggert 2024).

Starting with the issue of compliance, a major concern raised by critics of LAWS is whether such systems can meet the regulatory and moral demands of international humanitarian laws (IHL) and Jus in Bello (Leveringhaus 2022). Can these systems accurately distinguish between combatants and non-combatants? Is it possible to program a LAWS to 'calculate' the proportional benefit of an attack in relation to the overall outcome of a war? How much 'collateral damage' can be justified in a given attack? Critics argue that not only are current LAWS incapable of performing these tasks, but that ethics and morality, in principle, cannot be codified into algorithms (Purves et al. 2015).

From compliance issues, we turn to the concern that the use of LAWS will create a breakdown in responsibility attribution for unintended or negative outcomes caused by the system's actions. Much has already been written on the potential for responsibility gaps (Matthias 2004; Sparrow 2007); at its core, the concern is that due to the autonomous capabilities of LAWS and the involvement of 'many hands' (van de Poel et al. 2015) in their development and use, no single person will be able to meet the traditional criteria of knowledge and control (Fischer and Ravizza 1998) necessary to be deemed morally responsible for the system's actions. For instance, if an autonomous drone bombs a convoy of surrendering enemy combatants, it may be unclear who is to blame for this unlawful and morally repugnant action.

Finally, many critics contend that the use of LAWS is unacceptable because it dehumanizes both the enemy forces being targeted (Asaro 2012; Renic and Schwarz 2023a) and the decision-making process leading to the loss of life (Bender 2024). Regarding the latter, this critique may point to the concern that no human would be directly involved in the decision to take a life or that the threshold for engaging in war could be lowered, as there would be no need to risk our own forces (Sparrow 2016). As for the former, critics argue that LAWS fail to uphold the basic human dignity owed even to enemy combatants. For example, Sparrow argues that in deploying LAWS, "we treat our enemy like vermin, as though they may be exterminated without moral regard at all" (Sparrow 2007, 67).

Although these critiques are concerning, it is typically claimed that they must be balanced against the potential benefits these systems offer. Proponents argue that LAWS can enhance precision in the use of lethal force, thereby reducing the number of unnecessary casualties. Additionally, perhaps the strongest argument in favor of LAWS is that they can decrease casualties among the 'good guys' (Burri 2018). What General would willingly send soldiers into harm's way if a safer option were available? And what politician could hope to be reelected if they allowed citizens to die needlessly when a robot could have been used instead?

Given this interplay between the potential benefits and pitfalls, it has become a key issue to attempt to develop and deploy these systems in ways that would ensure they remain under human control so as to guarantee their safe and responsible use. Initially, it was argued that this could be achieved by keeping human actors either 'in-the-loop' or 'on the loop' (Cohen et al. 2023; Wagner 2019, 2011). However, it quickly became evident that mere human involvement would not ensure their effectiveness, especially if humans were expected to intervene with or supervise over systems operating at a speed and scale far beyond their own capabilities. Consequently, 'mere' human control was deemed inadequate unless it was also 'meaningful'. An example discussed by Horowitz and Scharre can help illustrate this point:

> Consider a person who sits in a room and is supposed to press a button every time a light bulb in the room goes on. If the person does this as instructed, and a weapon fires each time the person presses the button, a human has fired the weapon, but human control over the weapon is far from meaningful (Horowitz and Scharre 2015, 10).

So what makes human control meaningful? Amoroso and Tamburrini (2021) argue that for human control to be meaningful in the case of LAWS we must adhere to "distinctive human obligations regarding weapons systems control. These obligations constrain human-weapon shared control by retaining for human agents the roles of "fail-safe actor," "accountability attractor," and "moral agency enactor"" (Amoroso and Tamburrini 2021, 247). Each of these roles aims to address one of the three main critiques mentioned earlier. By functioning as 'fail-safe actors', humans could plausibly ensure compliance with the requirements of IHL. Moreover, if violations still occur, the role of 'accountability attractor' would establish a clear line of responsibility. Finally, by maintaining the role of 'moral agency enactor', human involvement would mitigate objections based on the dehumanizing effects of the use of LAWS. How precisely to design a system in this way, and whether these human roles effectively overcome the objections discussed above is debatable. However, this illustration serves to clarify one approach to achieving 'meaningful human control'.

8.3 AI Military Decision Support Systems (AI-MDSS)

8.3.1 Decision Support Systems (DSS)

Unlike LAWS, which are designed to replace human agents, Decision Support Systems (DSSs) are inherently intended to enhance and support human decision-makers rather than replace them. The origins of DSSs date back to the 1960s (Arnott and Pervan 2005), and in recent years these systems have greatly benefited from technological advancements, such as new machine learning methods, increased computing power, and access to vast amounts of data. A key motivation for developing and using DSSs is the fact that it is by now well established that humans are not fully rational decision makers—they suffer from mood swings, are susceptible to a vast number of behavioral and cognitive biases (Sunstein 2024), their decisions tend to be noisy (Kahneman et al. 2021), they are limited in the amount of information they can process or account for in their decisions, etc. For instance, studies have shown that, by a conservative estimate, in the USA alone, there are over 20,000 preventable hospital deaths due to human error every single year (Rodwin et al. 2020). Another example relates to judicial decision-making: "A study of thousands of juvenile court decisions found that when a local football team loses a game on the weekend, the judges make harsher decisions on the Monday (and, to a lesser extent, the rest of the week)" (Kahneman et al. 2021, 32).

Against this backdrop of flawed human decision-making, AI systems in the form of DSSs are viewed not only as tools that can help decision makers overcome their inherent biases and limitations, but also as instruments which can enhance the decision-making processes. By leveraging these systems' ability to rapidly analyze vast amounts of data, we can gain new insights and arrive at more optimal decisions. Typically, DSSs are distinguished according to the method by which these systems attempt to guide and influence the decision making process. In the DSS literature we find a distinction between systems which focus more on the decision making process ('process-oriented systems') and those which focus directly on the outcome of that process or the decision itself (outcome-oriented systems) (Poszler and Lange 2024).

For instance, a process-oriented system could provide the decision maker with curated important information (Klincewicz 2016), examples of past decisions in similar situations (Manríquez Roa and Biller-Andorno 2023), it may lead the decision maker through a series of steps by which she would need to justify her decision (Lara and Deckers 2020), or the DSS might play 'Devil's Advocate' in order to ensure that the decision-maker considers alternative options (Bang et al. 2023). In contrast, outcome-oriented DSSs are more directive and typically provide users with specific recommendations or evaluate decisions made by users. These DSSs support specific outcomes by being fine-tuned to the preferences and values of a specific user, or to an external set of preferences, values, and ethical theories introduced into the system during its training phase (Klincewicz 2016).

Although this distinction between outcome and process oriented DSSs is helpful, it is crucial to recognize that it is more a matter of degree than of strict categorization. While some DSSs may be purely process or outcome oriented, most systems will fall somewhere along a spectrum between these two extremes. This becomes even more evident when considering the socio-technical context in which the system is embedded. Social scoring DSSs and risk assessment systems are prime examples. Consider the 'Dutch childcare benefits scandal' (*toeslagenaffaire*):

In September 2019 it was reported that the Dutch Tax Authorities had developed and deployed a DSS aimed at identifying and preventing cases of child benefits fraud. According to a report by Amnesty International, the DSS functioned as a 'risk classification model' that assessed the likelihood of fraud in specific child benefits applications. Applications deemed low-risk by the model were almost always automatically approved, while those flagged as high-risk were forwarded to a civil servant for further investigation. However, the report highlights a critical flaw: the civil servant "was given no information as to why the system had given the application a high-risk score for inaccuracy" (Amnesty International 2021, 16). In other words, the system relied on an opaque, self-learning algorithm—commonly referred to as a "black box"—which did not allow users or even the system's designers to understand the rationale behind its classifications.

The scandal surrounding this story stems from two major issues. First, the DSS was discovered to produce biased recommendations, resulting in "a disproportionate focus on particular groups of people based on their ethnicity, and qualifies as racial profiling under the international human rights framework" (Amnesty International 2021, 22). Second, the tax agency imposed draconian penalties on applicants whose applications were flagged as likely fraudulent by the system. Politico reported that "Authorities penalized families over a mere suspicion of fraud based on the system's risk indicators. Tens of thousands of families—often with lower incomes or belonging to ethnic minorities—were pushed into poverty because of exorbitant debts to the tax agency. Some victims committed suicide. More than a thousand children were taken into foster care" (Heikkilä 2022).

The DSS used by the Dutch tax agency is an excellent example of how the distinction between outcome-oriented and process-oriented DSSs can be vague and often depends on how the system is integrated in the decision-making process. On the one hand, this DSS exhibits characteristics of an outcome-oriented system: it offered specific recommendations on which applications should be investigated and operated as a 'black-box', providing no detailed explanation for why a particular application was flagged. On the other hand, by merely identifying suspicious applications, the DSS can also be seen as process-oriented, as it only facilitated the initial step in the investigation process, helping civil servants prioritize their time and efforts. Furthermore, the DSS simply flagged applications without influencing how these applications were subsequently investigated or how the applicants were penalized. Therefore, it is evident that a DSS cannot be evaluated solely based on its design; rather, it must also be considered within the broader socio-technical system in which it operates. This is an important point to bear in mind as we turn now to examine the use of AI-DSS in the military.

8.3.2 The Ethics of AI-MDSS

While there are well-documented examples of DSSs being employed across various domains such as the COMPAS system used in the U.S. judicial system for assessing recidivism risk (Angwin et al. 2016), the Dutch system for detecting fraudulent child benefits applications (Amnesty International 2021), and the Viogen system utilized by Spanish police to assess the risk of repeated gender-based violence (Castro-Toledo et al. 2023), it has only come to wider public attention recently that militaries worldwide have also been developing and implementing DSSs. In the U.S., the Department of Defense (DoD) initially partnered with Google to develop an advanced targeting recommendation system called 'Maven'. After Google exited the project in 2019, 'Palantir' stepped in to continue the work, and a 2024 Bloomberg article revealed some details about the system's design and operation:

> In addition to video imagery, it can now incorporate data from radar systems that see through clouds, darkness and rain, as well as from heat-detecting infrared sensors—allowing it to look for objects of interest such as engines or weapons factories. It can also analyze nonvisual information, by cross-referencing geolocation tags from electronic surveillance and social media feeds, for example. [...] Temple estimates that, with Maven's assistance, he can now sign off on as many as 80 targets in an hour of work, versus 30 without it. He describes the process of concurring with the algorithm's conclusions in a rapid staccato: "Accept. Accept. Accept." (Manson 2024).

Another example is an experimental DSS called 'TAD' which is being developed by Parallax and funded by DARPA. According to the project description "TAD aims to improve the critical decision-making process for triage and point-of-injury care through clear explanations and readily accessible information [...] In the future, our work could help in mass casualty care situations with a hundred people in beds and five doctors [...] TAD will also be important in small-unit triage situations, where inexperienced personnel must choose how to care for soldiers immediately after they are wounded" (Hall 2023).

A final example worth discussing in more detail is the system known as 'Lavender.' According to reports, 'Lavender' is an outcome-oriented DSS developed by the Israeli Defence Forces (IDF) and has been utilized in the ongoing war in Gaza (Abraham 2024). The system is reportedly trained on vast amounts of data to generate profiles of 'enemy operatives' and assign a 'risk assessment score' (Chanenson and Hyatt 2016) to individuals within the general population in order to flag potential enemy operatives. Those whom 'Lavender' identifies as 'high risk' were placed on an attack list, with the system allegedly identifying 37,000 targets at its peak (McKernan and Davies 2024).

At the beginning of this chapter we outlined three categories of objections commonly raised against the use of LAWS: non-compliance with IHL, the creation of responsibility gaps, and the dehumanizing effects of such technologies. The report by Abraham on the use of 'Lavender' demonstrates how an AI-MDSS can also be vulnerable to each of these criticisms (Kozlovski 2024).

Starting with the question of compliance, it is important to remember that the central concern of Jus in Bello is ensuring that the attacking party accurately distinguishes between combatants and noncombatants, and that every attack adheres to the principle of proportionality—meaning that the harm inflicted must be proportional to the anticipated military advantage (Leveringhaus 2022). However, according to Abraham's report 'Lavender' "makes what are regarded as 'errors' in approximately 10 percent of cases, and is known to occasionally mark individuals who have merely a loose connection to militant groups, or no connection at all." Moreover, "One source stated that human personnel often served only as a 'rubber stamp' for the machine's decisions, adding that, normally, they would personally devote only about "20 seconds" to each target before authorizing a bombing" (Abraham 2024). Similar to the motivations behind developing 'Maven', the development of a system like 'Lavender' is driven by the desire to accelerate the target recommendation and decision-making process in both speed and scale (Renic and Schwarz 2023b). However, this approach appears to be at odds with the requirements of IHL. If approximately 10% of the system's recommendations are false positives, and an analyst spends only 20 seconds examining each recommendation before approving it, it seems highly improbable that these errors will be caught and that only legitimate targets, as defined by IHL, will be approved for attack.

Turning to the question of responsibility, while one might argue that in LAWS, where the system is fully autonomous, there are significant challenges in attributing responsibility, a DSS is different. A DSS merely provides recommendations, making the human agent who approves these recommendations the clear candidate for responsibility. However, as seen in the Dutch system case discussed earlier, the way in which 'Lavender' was used also raises potential issues of responsibility attribution. Abraham writes that "sources said that if 'Lavender' decided an individual was a militant in Hamas, they were essentially asked to treat that as an order, with no requirement to independently check why the machine made that choice or to examine the raw intelligence data on which it is based" (Abraham 2024). This practice suggests a troubling erosion of human oversight and accountability, potentially leading to responsibility gaps similar to those observed in more autonomous systems.

The dehumanization effects of such an AI-MDSS are glaringly obvious in the description of how 'Lavender' and its supporting systems were designed and used:

> According to the sources, "There was no 'zero-error' policy. Mistakes were treated statistically," said a source who used Lavender. "Because of the scope and magnitude, the protocol was that even if you don't know for sure that the machine is right, you know that statistically it's fine. So you go for it." [...] The sources [...] also described a similar system for calculating collateral damage [...] "the collateral damage calculation was completely automatic and statistical"—even producing figures that were not whole numbers (Abraham 2024).

Here, we see how the AI-MDSS both dehumanized the decision-making process itself by effectively removing the human from the decision-making loop and dehumanized the individuals who were the targets of analysis, reducing them to mere numbers within the system's calculations. While expected collateral damage might be expressed as partial numbers like 5.5 or 3.5, in reality, there is no such thing as half a human being, and treating the system's targets in this way represents the ultimate dehumanization of those individuals.

To this point we have shown that an AI-MDSS can raise the same ethical concerns as LAWS do. However, in addition to these three critiques, we must also recognise the traditional ethical challenges associated with the integration of AI systems into the decision-making process such as algorithmic bias, automation bias, and cognitive deskilling (French and Lindsay 2022). Concerns over algorithmic bias refer to "the worry that an algorithm is, in some sense, not merely a neutral transformer of data or extractor of information" (Danks and London 2017, 4691). That is, while the goal of using a DSS is to assist decision makers to arrive at objective and good decisions, algorithmic bias threatens that recommendations provided by the DSS will be skewed or unfair. Often this is referred to as the 'garbage in garbage out' phenomenon—if the system is trained on bad data it will provide bad answers. However, this slightly simplifies the breadth and scope of algorithmic bias. In actuality bias can arise in any stage of the machine learning process—data collection, data preparation, model development, model evaluation, model post-processing, and model deployment (Baker and Hawn 2022)—and can be categorized into different forms—Historical bias, Representation bias, Measurement bias, Aggregation bias, Evaluation bias, and Deployment bias (Suresh and Guttag 2021).

For our purposes there is no need to expand on each of these categories and one example will suffice to illustrate why this is an important issue of concern. In a much discussed case of algorithmic bias Amazon decided to scrap its hiring algorithm after it was discovered that the system was not evaluating candidates in a gender neutral way. In fact, it was discovered that the system "penalized resumes that included the word 'women's', as in 'women's chess club captain'. And it downgraded graduates of two all-women's colleges" (Dastin 2018). In effect, the system had 'learned' that female candidates were not as good as their male counterparts and as a result produced algorithmically biased hiring recommendations. Imagine the implications of such a bias in a system like 'Lavender'.

Turning now to the problem of 'Automation Bias' (Cummings 2006, 2012), this issue refers to the human tendency to uncritically accept recommendations or data provided by computational systems. In some amusing instances, this bias has led to tourists following faulty GPS directions, resulting in them driving into bodies of water (Bharade 2023). However, in more dangerous and tragic cases, automation bias can have devastating consequences. A well-known example is the 1988 downing of Iran Air Flight 655. A radar system mistakenly identified the civilian aircraft as an Iranian fighter jet, and despite signs that the system had made an error, the crew of the USS Vincennes relied on the computer's recommendation and authorized the attack, leading to the deaths of all 290 passengers on board (Singer 2009, 186).

Lastly, the possibility of 'cognitive deskilling' (Schwarz 2021), or simply skill degradation, is also concerning in that an overreliance on DSSs may lead decision makers to lose their ability to act effectively without the aid of the DSS. Scholars have raised concerns that a proliferation of AI systems may lead to a process of deskilling in both the 'know-how' of practical actions and the 'know-what' of ethical deliberation and moral reasoning. For instance, Shannon Vallor argues that as we delegate different activities and decision-making tasks away from human actors, we also remove the very activity by which they would typically exercise and cultivate their moral virtues. In the military context Vallor writes that the danger of such deskilling may have a significantly negative impact in that "the conduct of killing in war demands considerable moral skill if it is not to descend into utter moral chaos, in which the lines between civilian and combatant, friend and foe, military necessity and mindless vengeance do not just get blurred (as they do in all wars), but are wholly abandoned" (Vallor 2015, 114). As such, moral deskilling will not only pose a problem for acting without the aid of the DSS, it may also create difficulties in supervising or criticizing the recommendations of the system.

8.4 AI-MDSS and Meaningful Human Control (MHC)

The previous section discussed six ethical concerns regarding the design and use of AI-MDSSs: non-compliance with IHL, potential responsibility gaps, dehumanization effects, algorithmically biased outputs, potential for automation bias, and possible ethical and professional deskilling.[1] In Sect. 8.2 of this chapter we explained that a central response in the literature to the critique against LAWS is to seek ways to ensure a meaningful form of human control over these systems. Although 'Lavender', and DSSs in general, are not autonomous in the same way as LAWS, I will nevertheless argue in this section that the philosophical framework of MHC can be fruitfully applied to the evaluation of DSSs and offer us a standard against which we can assess whether such a system can be safely and responsibly used. I will first discuss the MHC framework in general, then show how the framework addresses

[1] I do not claim that this is an exhaustive list of the ethical concerns but rather ones that have received much attention in the literature.

each of the six ethical challenges discussed above, and then explore key challenges for achieving MHC over an AI-MDSS.

8.4.1 *Meaningful Human Control (MHC)*

Although the call for ensuring meaningful human control over AI systems has become increasingly widespread, there remains significant ambiguity about what this actually entails and how to achieve it. From a legal perspective, the requirements for achieving meaningful human control are particularly vague and contested (Davidovic 2023; Ekelhof 2019; Robbins 2023; Vignard 2014). However, at the philosophical level, various theories have been proposed to clarify the type of control we should aim to achieve over AI systems and the conditions that must be met to realize this form of control. These include Effective Human Oversight (Sterz et al. 2024), Comprehensive Human Oversight (Verdiesen 2024), Variable Autonomy (Methnani et al. 2021, 2024), Human-Machine Teaming (Andreas et al. 2023), and Meaningful Human Control (MHC) (Santoni de Sio and van den Hoven 2018), among others. Here, I will focus on the MHC framework developed by Santoni de Sio and Van den Hoven (2018), as it has been especially influential and has already been successfully applied to various design contexts (Mecacci et al. 2024), including Surgical Robotics (Ficuciello et al. 2019), medical diagnosis algorithms (Hille et al. 2023), Smart-Home Systems (Umbrello 2020), Autonomous Vehicles (Calvert et al. 2021; Heikoop et al. 2019; Santoni de Sio et al. 2023; Struik 2021), and Military Drone Systems (Steen et al. 2023).

Santoni de Sio and van den Hoven explain that the philosophical framework of MHC attempt to define "the sort of control humans need to have over (semi)autonomous systems such that unreasonable risks are avoided, that human responsibility will not evaporate, and that is [sic] there is a place to turn to in case of untoward outcomes" (Santoni de Sio and van den Hoven 2018, 2). Typically, when we think about autonomy and control, we tend to see them as being in opposition—like two sides of a rope in a game of tug-of-war. In this view, increasing a system's autonomy necessarily reduces the human user's control over it. However, the MHC framework challenges this perspective by shifting the concept of control from a direct operational form control to a notion of indirect guidance control (Santoni de Sio et al. 2023).

The notion of guidance control is rooted in the works of Fischer and Ravizza (1998) on moral responsibility. In their book, Fischer and Ravizza outline two key conditions for attributing moral responsibility to an agent for a particular outcome: (1) Moderate-Reasons-Responsiveness and (2) Ownership. The first condition, reasons-responsiveness, evaluates whether the agent was, in principle, capable of being both receptive and reactive to relevant reasons in a given situation. This involves assessing different factors, such as whether the agent was aware, or should have been aware, of certain pertinent reasons for acting, and whether the agent had the capacity to respond to these reasons in making a decision. If both the receptivity and reactivity aspects are fulfilled, the agent meets the requirement of moderate reasons-responsiveness, thereby qualifying for being held morally responsible for the outcome. The second condition, ownership, examines whether the decision-making mechanism that led to the agent's action can genuinely be attributed to the agent herself. This condition allows for the possibility of mitigating the attribution of moral responsibility in certain situations, such as when the agent's actions are influenced by external factors like being under the influence of drugs, manipulated by an external party, or brainwashed into acting in a specific way.

Adapting Fischer and Ravizza's conditions of 'reasons-responsiveness' and 'ownership' to the context of AI, the MHC framework posits that an AI system is under meaningful human control if it fulfills two key conditions: Tracking and Tracing. Briefly, the Tracking condition assesses whether the system is properly attuned and functions as intended, while the Tracing condition addresses the question of responsibility for the system's actions. Together, these conditions provide a more nuanced understanding of control than the traditional concept of having a 'human in-the-loop'. Instead of focusing solely on the necessity of human involvement at specific decision points, the MHC framework evaluates whether a system meets specific standards, regardless of whether control is exerted by a human, an AI-human team, or a fully autonomous AI system. This approach suggests that, in principle, even a fully autonomous system could be under meaningful human control. However, as we will discuss below, achieving the Tracking and Tracing conditions is highly demanding, making it unlikely that current AI systems can meet these standards without human involvement.

Having laid out the overview, we can now turn to a more detailed discussion of the MHC framework. But before delving into the conditions of Tracking and Tracing, it is crucial to clarify that the MHC framework uses the term 'system' to encompass not just the AI algorithm or the hardware comprising the technological apparatus, but also the broader socio-technical environment in which the technology is embedded (van Diggelen et al. 2024). For instance, when considering an 'autonomous vehicle', the MHC framework takes into account that "a driving system includes human agents and vehicles as well as the whole traffic environment and the social, legal, and political infrastructures" (Mecacci and Santoni de Sio 2020, 106). Therefore, when assessing how meaningful human control can be achieved within a 'system', the framework extends its analysis and recommendations beyond the technology itself to include a variety of stakeholders and their direct or indirect roles in the system's operation.

Building on this understanding, I will now discuss the two conditions underlying the MHC framework. Starting with the Tracking condition, Santoni de Sio and van den Hoven offer the following definition:

> In order to be under meaningful human control, a decision-making system should demonstrably and verifiably be responsive to the human moral reasons relevant in the circumstances—no matter how many system levels, models, software, or devices of whatever nature separate a human being from the ultimate effects in the world, some of which may be lethal. That is, decision-making systems should track (relevant) human moral reasons. (Santoni de Sio and Van den Hoven 2018, 7)

To clarify, the concept of (moral) reasons in MHC is used both in its traditional practical role, as indicating a consideration which favors a specific course of action (Dancy 2000), and as a placeholder for a variety of other concepts such as goals, plans, norms, intentions, and values (Mecacci and Santoni de Sio 2020). That is, the Tracking condition focuses on whether the system accounts for all relevant considerations that a human agent would have considered in that case. Accordingly, the Tracking condition requires that a system, in the broader socio-technical sense, achieve an acceptable level of reason-responsiveness. That is, just like in Fischer and Ravizza's discussion, Tracking requires that a system be receptive, selective, and reactive towards the relevant reasons for the decision-making process. Receptive, in that the system must be able to identify reasons; selective, in that it distinguishes between relevant and irrelevant reasons, and reactive, in that its outputs or actions are based on, or guided by, those identified and selected reasons.

Naturally, every design context will differ in terms of whose reasons should be considered, which of those reasons are relevant, and to what degree each reason should influence the system's behavior. The MHC framework does not propose a 'one-size-fits-all' model; it acknowledges that these questions will require different answers depending on the specific context. For example, consider the design context of an autonomous vehicle (AV). When addressing the question of whose reasons the system should track, the most obvious agent is the 'driver' or passenger of the vehicle. However, the driver cannot be the only agent whose reasons are considered. The AV must also account for other factors, such as road conditions and infrastructure, weather conditions or time of day, traffic laws and norms, and the actions of other vehicles on the road. While the operator of the AV clearly has some priority in influencing the vehicle's actions, a range of other stakeholders and environmental factors must also be tracked to ensure safe and responsible operation. Simply knowing all these reasons, however, is not enough. The system must also be capable of determining the relevance of each reason in a given situation and have a method for resolving conflicting or contradictory reasons (Mecacci and Santoni de Sio 2020). Thus, an AV can only be deemed under meaningful human control if it successfully identifies, prioritizes, and responds appropriately to all relevant reasons in any given action it takes.

Shifting now to the Tracing condition, this condition emphasizes the need to ensure that some human agent meets the required conditions to be held morally responsible for any potential harm caused by the AI system:

> In order for a system to be under meaningful human control, its actions/states should be traceable to a proper moral understanding on the part of one or more relevant human persons who design or interact with the system, meaning that there is at least one human agent in the design history or use context involved in designing, programming, operating and deploying the autonomous system who (a) understands or is in the position to understand the capabilities of the system and the possible effects in the world of the its use; (b) understands or is in the position to understand that others may have legitimate moral reactions toward them because of how the system affects the world and the role they occupy. (Santoni de Sio and van den Hoven 2018, 9)

The primary concern of the Tracing condition is to ensure that there is no room for potential responsibility gaps. In Sect. 8.2 we already explained that the concern here relates to the potential that no single individual will meet the traditional criteria of knowledge and control for being held morally responsible for the actions or output of the AI system. However, it is important to note that the very existence of responsibility gaps is contested in the literature (Tigard 2020). For example, Hindriks and Veluwenkamp argue that alleged 'responsibility gaps' are either situations where an agent can be held indirectly responsible for the harm caused or instances where the harm constitutes a case of blameless harm (Hindriks and Veluwenkamp 2023, 21). The MHC framework remains neutral as to the possible existence of responsibility gaps and merely strives to ensure that the conditions for holding some actor responsible will be built into the design of the system. As such, if responsibility gaps do exist, then MHC can be seen as offering a way to 'fill-in' these gaps. Alternatively, if responsibility gaps do not exist, then MHC offers a method for producing design recommendations which ensure that human controllers can meet the necessary conditions to effectively act on their responsibility.

For instance, in 2018, a tragic accident occurred between an Uber-operated autonomous vehicle and a pedestrian named Elaine Herzberg, resulting in her death (Nyholm 2023). This incident raised significant questions regarding the responsibility of both Uber and Rafaela Vasquez, the human test driver seated in the vehicle at the time of the crash. De Sio and Van den Hoven discuss such cases and emphasize that "designing for satisfying the tracing condition means ensuring that different human agents along the chain are technically and psychologically capable of complying with their tasks and are well aware of their responsibility for the behavior of the autonomous system" (Santoni de Sio and van den Hoven 2018, 12). The tracing condition, therefore, aims not merely to identify who is responsible for preventing negative outcomes but also to provide socio-technical recommendations to ensure that such prevention is achievable. In other words, MHC cannot be achieved simply by assigning responsibility to a particular individual—X—for the actions of the AV. Rather, it requires that X meets the necessary conditions, such as having relevant knowledge of the system's capabilities, receiving adequate physical and/or psychological training for fulfilling this role, and being properly equipped to handle the responsibilities associated with overseeing the AV's operation.

Note that although achieving the Tracing condition requires that a human agent (the controller) (1) understands the system's capabilities and (2) appreciates their own moral responsibility for its behavior, the specifics of what this entails are left to the design context. For example, in the AV scenario above, understanding the system's capabilities might involve knowing the conditions under which the AV is prone to misidentify objects or being trained to take control over driving functions promptly. However, it likely does not require Rafaela Vasquez to grasp the exact electrical signals transmitted from the AV's computer or the data volume used to train its algorithms. The level of understanding needed for Tracing is highly contextual and must be tailored to each specific design situation.

Table 8.1 The ethical challenges addressed by the conditions of tracking and tracing

Tracking	Tracing
Compliance with IHL	Responsibility gaps
Dehumanization	Dehumanization
Algorithmic Bias	Automation Bias
	Moral deskilling

8.4.2 MHC and the Ethics of AI-MDSS

In this section I will look at how the conditions of Tracking and Tracing can potentially address each of the six ethical challenges discussed in Sect. 8.3.2 (Table 8.1).

Starting with Tracking, if an AI-MDSS were to successfully meet the Tracking condition of MHC it could plausibly alleviate much of the concern regarding potential problems of compliance with IHL, dehumanization effects, and algorithmic bias in its recommendations. Let's look briefly at each in turn.

Algorithmic bias involves the risk that an AI-MDSS might base its recommendations on incorrect assumptions about which criteria are relevant or how significant those criteria should be for its output. For instance, consider the case of Amazon's hiring algorithm, which exhibited bias against female candidates. This bias could stem from the system either incorrectly treating 'gender' as a relevant criterion in its recommendations or from giving undue weight to 'gender' in its calculations, either positively or negatively. Regardless of the source of the bias, the criteria themselves and their relative weight should be understood as reasons which the system needs to consider in its calculations. As such, the Tracking condition of MHC directly addresses this issue in that a case of algorithmic bias would entail a failure in Tracking.

Similarly to concerns about algorithmic bias, if AI-MDSS's recommendations must adhere to IHL rules, then a system that fails to consider these rules is not appropriately responding to relevant reasons, and thus fails to meet the Tracking condition for meaningful human control. However, a complication arises with principles like proportionality in Jus in Bello, which require balancing harm against anticipated military advantage and are inherently vague, leaving much to human judgment. If this judgment must indeed be made by a human, then achieving MHC might seem unattainable for such systems. Although the burden of proof for this claim lies with those making it, this objection may not be as significant as it first appears. The socio-technical perspective of MHC suggests a possible resolution: if proportionality judgments must be human-driven, then for an AI-MDSS to meet the Tracking condition and be under meaningful human control, it should integrate human agents to assess the proportionality of every recommendation provided by the system. Thus we see that an advantage of the MHC framework is that it can provide such design recommendations to be implemented into the system.

Finally, regarding the issue of dehumanization, this issue is only partly addressed by the Tracking condition of MHC and will also be discussed below with regard to the Tracing condition. First, like with algorithmic bias, if dehumanization is caused by a lack of accounting for specific reasons in the system's 'reasoning' then this can ostensibly be fixed by ensuring that the system takes those reasons into consideration. Second, if instead, the problem of dehumanization stems from the fundamental motivation behind deploying an a AI-MDSS in the first place, its capability to generate recommendations at high speed and scale, then a way to address this may be by limiting the system's outputs or raising the threshold for positive classification such that the system would be more selective in its recommendations.

Third and final for the discussion on Tracking, if the objection from dehumanization stems from an objection to the system's logic, that is, to representing humans as mere numbers in a calculation which may result in a life or death decision, then it may be that MHC cannot be achieved over an AI-MDSS in that the system would be unable to Track this reason. To illustrate this point, consider the following:

> The very logic of AI rests on this classification and codification of life into computable data to identify objects, and patterns between objects. As John Cheney-Lippold notes, "To be intelligible to a statistical model is . . . to be transcoded into a framework of objectification" and become defined, cross-calculated, as a computationally ascertained, actionable object. This epistemic grounding produces not only a pure objectification but also, if the target is human, a desubjectification and deindividualization. (Renic and Schwarz 2023a, 335)

Of course, one might object to the inherent dehumanization argument by pointing out that we do not necessarily find it objectionable to use AI-DSSs in other contexts, such as cancer diagnosis or content recommendation and moderation.

Moving on to the Tracing condition, recall that this condition requires that some human agent must (1) understand the capabilities of the system and (2) appreciate their own moral responsibility for its behavior. In the context of an AI-MDSS tracing will strongly relate to how the system is designed to produce its recommendations, the ability of human users to interpret those recommendations, and the type of explanation that the system can provide for its recommendations. With this in mind, achieving the Tracing condition in the design and use of an AI-MDSS may allow us to address concerns related to potential responsibility gaps, dehumanization, automation bias, and moral deskilling.

Starting with the issue of responsibility gaps, as explained in the previous section, the Tracing condition is specifically designed to prevent such gaps from arising. By ensuring that a system is designed in a way that allows a human agent to meet both requirements of the Tracing condition, clear lines of responsibility can be maintained. However, it's crucial to recognize that this relies not only on the technical design of the system but also on the social context in which the system is embedded. We will explore this aspect in greater detail in the next section.

Regarding dehumanization, beyond the three Tracking-related points discussed earlier, one could argue that a clear understanding of why the system made certain recommendations could help mitigate concerns about the objectification of human targets. If the system's reasoning were transparent and a human agent could review and endorse the decision-making process that led to its conclusions, this might be considered a sufficiently dignified and respectful procedure such that concerns over dehumanization would be mitigated. However, if this is indeed the solution to the problem of dehumanization then it would imply that the AI-MDSS must be part of a broader system that includes human oversight, rather than functioning fully autonomously throughout the entire 'kill-chain'.

Finally, if Tracing indeed requires that a human user will be able to understand the recommendations of the AI-MDSS, either by assessing the explanation provided by the system or by evaluating the data on which this recommendation is based, then it seems that we have the necessary means for avoiding the problems of automation bias and moral deskilling. Moreover, taking into consideration the second condition of Tracing, that a human agent understand their own personal responsibility for the system's actions/outputs, it seems reasonable to assume that analysts using an AI-MDSS will be incentivised to assess the system's recommendations, rather than merely pass them along automatically, and in so doing also gain the needed experience to avoid 'deskilling'.

8.4.3 Challenges for Achieving MHC

While not an ethical framework in itself, the previous two sections have demonstrated that the MHC framework addresses many, though not all, ethical concerns related to the design and use of AI systems. In fact, proponents of the MHC framework acknowledge that achieving meaningful human control is only a necessary and not a "sufficient condition for a system to be morally or societally good" (Santoni de Sio 2024, 158). For example, a repugnant system, such as the recent attempt to use AI to detect people's 'sexuality' (Cockerell 2023), could still be considered under meaningful human control if it meets the necessary conditions of Tracking and Tracing. Therefore, although designing a system to meet the conditions of MHC does not constitute an endorsement on the use of that system, the framework does offer a method for identifying design requirements that must be met to claim that the system can be safely and responsibly used. With that in mind, in this final section I will highlight some of the key technical, normative, and design challenges for designing an AI-MDSS to meet the Tracking, Tracing, and Socio-technical embedding conditions for achieving MHC (Table 8.2).

Table 8.2 Key challenges for achieving MHC over AI-MDSS

Tracking	Tracing	Sociotechnical Embedding
Defining DSS Objective	The Black-Box problem	Pace and Scale
Identifying Relevant Stakeholders	Type of system Output	Training
Resolving Conflicts	Type of Explanation	Contestation

Tracking

In the previous sections we described the Tracking condition as concerned with the 'reasons-responsiveness' of the system being designed or assessed. Furthermore, we explained that the MHC framework uses the concept of 'reasons' as a place-holder for a variety of other concepts such as goals, intentions, plans, norms, values, etc. While the concept of 'reasons-responsiveness' remains faithful to the work of Fischer and Ravizza, another way to conceptualize the Tracking condition is as an 'alignment problem' (Santoni De Sio and Mecacci 2021; Nyholm 2023). The 'Alignment Problem' (Christian 2020; Gabriel 2020) refers to a set of questions revolving around which or whose values ought to guide the design and decision-making of an AI system (Bostrom 2016; Russell 2019). This involves not only the technical aspect of how to ensure that the AI system bases its decisions on the 'correct' reasons/values, but also the normative question regarding which reasons and values are relevant in a given situation.

Considered as an alignment problem, we can see three key challenges for achieving the Tracking condition—(1) Properly defining the objective of the DSS, (2) Identifying relevant stakeholders and their corresponding reasons, (3) Establishing a method for resolving conflicts within the system.

1. While it might seem obvious that an AI system should be designed to achieve a 'well-defined' objective, past design failures reveal just how challenging this can be, especially when it comes to producing normative recommendations. Take, for example, Amazon's AI hiring system. What was the goal of this system? To identify the best possible candidate? But what does it actually mean to be the best candidate? The answer can vary depending on the specific position, the company's culture and norms, the current employee makeup, and so on. Moreover, while there are clearly 'wrong' or 'unacceptable' answers to this question, this doesn't necessarily mean that there is only one 'correct' profile that is the best.

   Applying these questions to the design of an AI-MDSS like 'Lavender', it's essential to clearly define the system's goal/s. Is the objective to assess how likely it is that a person is affiliated with a terrorist organization? To determine if they are sympathetic to the cause? To identify if they have participated as a combatant, or if they are currently an active combatant? Each of these objectives would require a different system design. The defined objective will also influence the type of data needed to be used to train the system, the system's adaptability to changing circumstances, and more. To reiterate, my point here is that without a well-defined, tractable objective for the system, achieving the Tracking condition of MHC is impossible.
2. A key challenge for achieving Tracking is identifying all stakeholders whose reasons need to be considered by the system. In the case of an AI-MDSS, this obviously includes the military designers and operators of the system, but it would likely also need to incorporate considerations based on IHL, and possibly even the reasons of individuals being targeted by the system. For example, while

the military might prefer to classify all suspected enemy targets under a single category, complying with IHL's distinction requirement might necessitate that the system differentiate between 'enemy combatants' and 'enemy non-combatants', such as financial or administrative personnel. Similarly, while it might be more effective for the system to incorporate as much data as possible, there could be legal or moral reasons to exclude certain information, such as medical records.

3. Lastly, depending on the exact goal/s of the system and the variety of (stakeholder's) reasons that the system needs to account for, it is likely that there will be conflicts between competing reasons which would need to be resolved (Kozlovski 2022, van den Hoven et al. 2012; van de Poel 2015). These conflicts can present challenges at both the design stage and the level of algorithmic recommendations. During the design phase, difficult questions must be addressed, such as what constitutes an acceptable level of system reliability and how to balance the need for accuracy with the military's demands for scale and pace.

At the algorithmic level, conflicts of reasons become most apparent when the system's recommendations are evaluative and actionable. A DSS can be designed to produce purely descriptive outputs—such as categorizing an image—or evaluative outputs—such as determining that a person poses a danger. In the case of descriptive outputs like image recognition, the system must be trained on a sufficient number of 'good examples' to accurately identify what it is supposed to recognize. However, even this relatively straightforward task can be technically challenging and prone to errors. For instance, in 2015 Google's photo app mistakenly labeled two Black individuals as gorillas (Kasperkevic 2015). More concerning is when a system is designed to produce evaluative outputs. In these cases, the system must learn to weigh different values and reasons against one another. While this can be approached by assigning specific weights to each parameter, theorists argue that such evaluative judgments often involve incommensurable aspects, making the resolution of these comparisons highly contestable and subjective (Dobbe et al. 2021; Goodman 2021; Chang 2024).

Tracing

Recall that the Tracing condition requires that a human agent (1) understand the capabilities of the system and (2) appreciate their own moral responsibility for its behavior. While the second aspect will be addressed in the Socio-technical Embedding section below, here I want to focus on the challenges related to ensuring that an agent understands the system's capabilities. In this context, if Tracking was interpreted as an 'alignment problem', then Tracing, as the condition for ensuring responsibility attribution, can be best described as a problem of Explainability. Floridi et al. (2018) and Baum et al. (2022) have both made this connection arguing that explainability is a key condition for responsibility attribution. As such, this raises three challenges for achieving Tracing: (1) the Black-Box problem, (2) the type of system output, (3) the type of explanation provided by the system.

1. Much has already been written about the so-called 'Black Box' (Schlicker et al. 2021) problem which refers to the difficulty, or even impossibility, of precisely mapping and predicting the system's 'reasoning'—the process by which an AI system transforms inputs into outputs. The sheer number of variables and data involved, the complexity of the algorithms, and the computational power required for these massive calculations make the decision-making process of such systems incomprehensible not only to the average user but even to the system's designers. As a result, while a user can see the input provided to the system (such as a query or data) and the output it generates (like a recommendation), they won't be able to understand how or why the system arrived at that recommendation.

   The primary concern for Tracing over the use of Black-Box models is that users will have no explanation for the system's output and it will be difficult to predict future system recommendations (Manríquez Roa and Biller-Andorno 2023). There are two ways to address the 'Black-Box' problem—using methods from the field of Explainable AI (XAI) to interpret the 'Black-Box' model (Adadi and Berrada 2018), or replace the model with an interpretable 'Glass Box' model. Regarding the latter, "Interpretable models can entail significant effort to construct, in terms of both computation and domain expertise" (Rudin 2019, 9) making it a challenging approach to implement. Additionally, there is an ongoing debate about whether there is a trade-off between accuracy and interpretability (Bell et al. 2022). As to the former, XAI methods involve designing a secondary model to interpret the output and process of the original Black-Box model. This approach raises concerns about whether the interpretation is truly accurate or merely offers a plausible explanation for the original model. Furthermore, using multiple models can create additional distance between the user and the actual data or world being analyzed, potentially increasing the likelihood of errors.
2. A second challenge for ensuring Tracing relates to how the system presents its recommendations. In theory, there are countless ways a DSS could be designed to communicate its output. However, in practice we usually see a handful of common methods: a numerical score in risk assessment tools like COMPAS (Angwin et al. 2016), categorization in image recognition software (Cummings 2019), or natural language output in systems using large language models (LLMs). In the case of 'Lavender' it has been described in the following way: "According to sources, the machine gives almost every single person in Gaza a rating from 1 to 100, expressing how likely it is that they are a militant" (Abraham 2024). The challenge here is designing the system's output in a way that enables the user to fully understand its meaning and how to act based on it. In other words, while it might be straightforward to respond to an assessment of 1 or 100, a middling score could create confusion. In high-stakes decision-making situa-

tions, it's crucial to ensure that the analyst using the system understands the appropriate response to a score of 63 versus a 71.

3. A third challenge concerns the type of explanation that the AI-MDSS should provide for its recommendations. This issue is closely tied to the previous challenges; even if we avoid using a 'Black-Box' model and carefully consider how the output is presented, there remains the question of what type of explanation is needed to best achieve Tracing. For example, Baum et al. (2022) argue that for responsibility attribution, we need a 'reasons-explanation' for the actions and decisions of an AI system: "Just like human experts would provide reasons for their recommendations, so should decision support systems" (Baum et al. 2022, 17–18). They suggest that this explanation should indicate the 'motivating' reasons that led the system to make its recommendation. Of course, for an explanation to be effective, it must be limited in scope, meaning the system should prioritize which reasons played a central role in its analysis and highlight them.

Socio-Technical Embedding

Finally, the successful achievement of the Tracking and Tracing conditions will heavily depend on the broader socio-technical structure in which the AI-MDSS is embedded. If the system is not used as intended or for its designed purpose, there will inevitably be challenges in achieving MHC. Therefore, it's not enough to simply design the algorithm or the DSS interface; the entire socio-technical system must be designed with the goal of achieving MHC in mind. I will highlight three such challenges related to AI-MDSS: (1) pace and scale of recommendations, (2) Training, and (3) contestation methods.

1. One of the primary reasons for implementing an AI-MDSS is its ability to generate recommendations quickly and in large quantities. While this motivation doesn't inherently conflict with the conditions of Tracking and Tracing, it's easy to see how, as demonstrated in the case of 'Lavender', prioritizing the scale and pace of recommendations over quality and accuracy could lead to the removal of many safeguards designed to ensure meaningful human control. Therefore, to achieve MHC, the conduct norms and procedures must be designed to help the unit operating the AI-MDSS withstand external pressures to act in such a way that compromises MHC.
2. As was discussed in the analysis of the Tracing condition, the operators of the AI-MDSS must receive specialized training for their role. While it might seem obvious that a military organization would only allow properly trained individuals to operate advanced technologies, I'm emphasizing that this training should specifically focus on ensuring meaningful human control. Operators shouldn't just learn how to use the AI-MDSS; they should also be trained to challenge certain recommendations, recognize the system's limitations, and refuse to cooperate if they are required to use the system in ways that would compromise MHC.

3. Lastly, it is crucial to design a mechanism within the unit's operation that clearly outlines the procedure for rejecting or contesting any recommendation made by the AI-MDSS. Without such a mechanism, no explanation of how and why the system generated a specific result would be sufficient to hold human operators accountable for the system's output and the use of its recommendations. While MHC doesn't mandate that every system include such a mechanism, if Tracking and Tracing require human involvement, then operators must have a way to intervene in the system's operation when necessary.

8.5 Conclusion

This chapter has provided an initial exploration of the theory of Meaningful Human Control as applied to AI-based Military Decision Support Systems. Although MHC has traditionally been discussed within the context of LAWS, this chapter underscores the importance of broadening this focus to encompass the wider array of AI applications in the military. I have tried to show how the MHC framework can function both as a critical tool for assessing the safe and responsible use of AI systems and as a foundation for developing design recommendations. These recommendations are essential to ensuring that AI systems operate in a manner that preserves human control and responsibility, even when dealing with highly autonomous AI technologies.

We began the chapter by referencing the contrasting Centaur and Minotaur visions for the future of AI in warfare. As the trend toward delegating cognitive tasks from humans to AI systems continues, it is imperative that we approach the deployment of such technologies with a healthy skepticism and caution. The MHC framework provides a straightforward yet powerful method for evaluating these innovations, ensuring that the solutions proposed by technological advancements do not become more problematic than the issues they seek to resolve.

References

Abraham, Y. 2024. 'Lavender': The AI Machine Directing Israel's Bombing Spree in Gaza. *+972 Magazine*. https://www.972mag.com/lavender-ai-israeli-army-gaza/. Accessed 29 Aug 2024.

Adadi, A., and M. Berrada. 2018. Peeking Inside the Black-Box: A Survey on Explainable Artificial Intelligence (XAI). *IEEE Access* 6:52138–52160. https://doi.org/10.1109/ACCESS.2018.2870052.

Amnesty International. 2021. Xenophobic Machines: Discrimination Through Unregulated Use of Algorithms in the Dutch Childcare Benefits Scandal. https://www.amnesty.org/en/documents/eur35/4686/2021/en/. Accessed 29 Aug 2024.

Amoroso, D., and G. Tamburrini. 2021. Toward a Normative Model of Meaningful Human Control over Weapons Systems. *Ethics & International Affairs* 35 (2): 245–272. https://doi.org/10.1017/S0892679421000241.

Andreas, T., Luciano, F., & Mariarosaria, T. (2023). Human Control of AI systems: from Supervision to Teaming. Available at SSRN: https://ssrn.com/abstract=4504855 or http://dx.doi.org/10.2139/ssrn.4504855

Angwin, J., J. Larson, S. Mattu, and L. Kirchner. 2016. Machine Bias. *ProPublica* https://www.propublica.org/article/machine-bias-risk-assessments-in-criminal-sentencing. Accessed 29 Aug 2024.

Arnott, D., and G. Pervan. 2005. A Critical Analysis of Decision Support Systems Research. *Journal of Information Technology* 20 (2): 67–87.

Asaro, P. 2012. On Banning Autonomous Weapon Systems: Human Rights, Automation, and the Dehumanization of Lethal Decision-Making. *International Review of the Red Cross* 94 (886): 687–709.

Baker, R. S., and A. Hawn. 2022. Algorithmic Bias in Education. *International Journal of Artificial Intelligence in Education* 32:1052–1092. https://doi.org/10.1007/s40593-021-00285-9.

Bang, Y., N. Lee, T. Yu, L. Khalatbari, Y. Xu, S. Cahyawijaya, and P. Fung. 2023. Towards Answering Open-Ended Ethical Quandary Questions. https://doi.org/10.48550/arXiv.2205.05989.

Baum, K., S. Mantel, E. Schmidt, et al. 2022. From Responsibility to Reason-Giving Explainable Artificial Intelligence. *Philosophy & Technology* 35 (12): https://doi.org/10.1007/s13347-022-00510-w.

Bell, A., I. Solano-Kamaiko, O. Nov, and J. Stoyanovich. 2022. It's Just Not That Simple: An Empirical Study of the Accuracy-Explainability Trade-Off in Machine Learning for Public Policy. In *Proceedings of the 2022 ACM Conference on Fairness, Accountability, and Transparency (FAccT '22)*, 248–266. New York: Association for Computing Machinery. https://doi.org/10.1145/3531146.3533090.

Bender, E. M. 2024. Resisting Dehumanization in the Age of "AI". *Current Directions in Psychological Science* 33 (2): 114–120. https://doi.org/10.1177/09637214231217286.

Bharade, A. 2023. Tourists in Hawaii Followed Their GPS and Drove Their Car Straight into a Harbor: "Pretty Sure That Was Not Supposed to Happen". *Business Insider*. https://www.businessinsider.com/tourists-hawaii-gps-drove-car-into-water-2023-5#:~:text=A%20pair%20of%20tourists%20drove,Hawaii%2C%20per%20The%20Washington%20Post. Accessed 29 Aug 2024.

Bostrom, N. 2016. *Superintelligence: Paths, Dangers, Strategies*, Reprint edition. Oxford: Oxford University Press.

Burri, S. 2018. What Is the Moral Problem with Killer Robots? In *Who Should Die? The Ethics of Killing in War*, ed. J. B. Strawser, R. Jenkins, and M. Robillard, 163–185. New York: OUP, Online edn. https://doi.org/10.1093/oso/9780190495657.003.0009.

Castro-Toledo, F. J., F. Miró-Llinares, and J. C. Aguerri. 2023. Data-Driven Criminal Justice in the Age of Algorithms: Epistemic Challenges and Practical Implications. *Criminal Law Forum* 34:295–316. https://doi.org/10.1007/s10609-023-09454-y.

Calvert, S. C., van Arem, B., Heikoop, D. D., Hagenzieker, M., Mecacci, G., & de Sio, F. S. (2021). Gaps in the control of automated vehicles on roads. In *IEEE Intelligent Transportation Systems Magazine 13*(4), 146–153. https://doi.org/10.1109/MITS.2019.2926278

Chanenson, S., and J. Hyatt. 2016. The Use of Risk Assessment at Sentencing: Implications for Research and Policy. Villanova Law/Public Policy Research Paper No. 2017-1040. Available at SSRN: https://ssrn.com/abstract=2961288. Accessed 29 Aug 2024.

Chang, R. 2024. Human in the Loop! In *AI Morality*, ed. David Edmonds. Oxford: Oxford University Press.

Christian, B. 2020. *The Alignment Problem: How Can Artificial Intelligence Learn Human Values?* London: Atlantic Books.

Cockerell, I. 2023. Researchers Say Their AI Can Detect Sexuality. Critics Say It's Dangerous. *Coda Story*. https://www.codastory.com/authoritarian-tech/ai-sexuality-recognition-lgbtq/. Accessed 27 Aug 2024.

Cohen, I. G., B. Babic, S. Gerke, Q. Xia, T. Evgeniou, and K. Wertenbroch. 2023. How AI Can Learn from the Law: Putting Humans in the Loop only on Appeal. *npj Digital Medicine* 6 (160): https://doi.org/10.1038/s41746-023-00906-8.

Cummings, M. L. 2006. Integrating Ethics in Design Through the Value-Sensitive Design Approach. *Science and Engineering Ethics* 12:701–715. https://doi.org/10.1007/s11948-006-0065-0.

Cummings, M. L. 2012. Automation Bias in Intelligent Time Critical Decision Support Systems. In *AIAA 1st Intelligent Systems Technical Conference*. Chicago, IL: American Institute of Aeronautics and Astronautics. https://doi.org/10.2514/6.2004-6313.

Cummings, M. L. 2019. Lethal Autonomous Weapons: Meaningful Human Control or Meaningful Human Certification? [Opinion]. *IEEE Technology and Society Magazine* 38 (4): 20–26. https://doi.org/10.1109/MTS.2019.2948438.

Dancy, J. 2000. *Practical Reality*. Oxford: Oxford University Press. https://doi.org/10.1093/0199253056.001.0001.

Danks, D., and A. J. London. 2017. Algorithmic Bias in Autonomous Systems. In *Proceedings of the Twenty-Sixth International Joint Conference on Artificial Intelligence*, 4691–4697. Melbourne, Australia: International Joint Conferences on Artificial Intelligence Organization. https://doi.org/10.24963/ijcai.2017/654.

Dastin, J. 2018. Amazon Scraps Secret AI Recruiting Tool That Showed Bias Against Women. *Reuters*. https://www.reuters.com/article/world/insight-amazon-scraps-secret-ai-recruiting-tool-that-showed-bias-against-women-idUSKCN1MK0AG/. Accessed 29 Aug 2024.

Davidovic, J. 2023. On the Purpose of Meaningful Human Control of AI. *Frontiers in Big Data* 5:1017677. https://doi.org/10.3389/fdata.2022.1017677.

del Valle, J. I., and M. Moreno. 2023. Ethics of Autonomous Weapon Systems. In *Ethics of Artificial Intelligence. The International Library of Ethics, Law and Technology*, ed. F. Lara and J. Deckers, 169–188. Cham: Springer. https://doi.org/10.1007/978-3-031-48135-2_9.

Dobbe, R., T. Gilbert, and Y. Mintz. 2021. Hard Choices in Artificial Intelligence. *Artificial Intelligence* 300:103555. https://doi.org/10.1016/j.artint.2021.103555.

Eggert, L. 2024. Rethinking 'Meaningful Human Control'. In *Responsible Use of AI in Military Systems*, ed. J. M. Schraagen, 213–231. Chapman and Hall/CRC.

Ekelhof, M. 2019. Moving Beyond Semantics on Autonomous Weapons: Meaningful Human Control in Operation. *Global Policy* 10 (3): 343–348.

Ficuciello, F., G. Tamburrini, A. Arezzo, L. Villani, and B. Siciliano. 2019. Autonomy in Surgical Robots and Its Meaningful Human Control. *Paladyn, Journal of Behavioral Robotics* 10:30–43. https://doi.org/10.1515/pjbr-2019-0002.

Fischer, J., and M. Ravizza. 1998. *Responsibility and Control: A Theory of Moral Responsibility*. Cambridge, UK: Cambridge University Press.

Floridi, L., J. Cowls, M. Beltrametti, R. Chatila, P. Chazerand, V. Dignum, C. Luetge, R. Madelin, U. Pagallo, F. Rossi, B. Schafer, P. Valcke, and E. Vayena. 2018. AI4People—An Ethical Framework for a Good AI Society: Opportunities, Risks, Principles, and Recommendations. *Minds and Machines* 28 (4): 689–707. https://doi.org/10.1007/s11023-018-9482-5.

French, S. E., and L. N. Lindsay. 2022. Artificial Intelligence in Military Decision-Making: Avoiding Ethical and Strategic Perils with an Option-Generator Model. In *Emerging Military Technologies*, ed. B. Koch and R. Schoonhoven, 53–74. Leiden: Brill Nijhoff. https://doi.org/10.1163/9789004507951_007.

Gabriel, I. 2020. Artificial Intelligence, Values, and Alignment. *Minds and Machines* 30 (3): 411–437. https://doi.org/10.1007/s11023-020-09539-2.

Goodman, B. 2021. Hard Choices and Hard Limits for Artificial Intelligence. In *Proceedings of 2021 AAAI/ACM Conference on AI, Ethics, and Society (AIES'21), May 19–21, 2021*, 112–121. New York: ACM. https://doi.org/10.1145/3461702.346253.

Hall, H. 2023. Parallax Advanced Research Wins DARPA in the Moment Award Totaling $4.067m. *Research & Development World*. https://www.rdworldonline.com/parallax-advanced-research-wins-darpa-in-the-moment-award-totaling-4-067m/. Accessed 19 Aug 2024.

Heikkilä, M. 2022. Dutch Scandal Serves as a Warning for Europe over Risks of Using Algorithms. *Politico*. https://www.politico.eu/article/dutch-scandal-serves-as-a-warning-for-europe-over-risks-of-using-algorithms/. Accessed 29 Aug 2024.
Heikoop, D. D., M. P. Hagenzieker, G. Mecacci, S. C. Calvert, F. Santoni de Sio, and B. van Arem. 2019. Human Behaviour with Automated Driving Systems: A Quantitative Framework for Meaningful Human Control. *Theoretical Issues in Ergonomics Science* 20:711–730. https://doi.org/10.1080/1463922X.2019.1574931.
Hille, E. M., P. Hummel, and M. Braun. 2023. Meaningful Human Control over AI for Health? A Review. *Journal of Medical Ethics*. https://doi.org/10.1136/jme-2023-109095.
Hindriks, F., and H. Veluwenkamp. 2023. The Risks of Autonomous Machines: From Responsibility Gaps to Control Gaps. *Synthese* 201:21. https://doi.org/10.1007/s11229-022-04001-5.
Horowitz, M., and P. Scharre. 2015. *Meaningful Human Control in Weapon Systems: A Primer*. CNAS Working Paper, March 2015. Center for a New American Security.
Kahneman, D., O. Sibony, and C. R. Sunstein. 2021. *Noise: A Flaw in Human Judgment*. New York: Little, Brown Spark.
Kasperkevic, J. 2015. Google Says Sorry for Racist Auto-Tag in Photo App. *The Guardian*. https://www.theguardian.com/technology/2015/jul/01/google-sorry-racist-auto-tag-photo-app. Accessed 29 Aug 2024.
Klincewicz, M. 2016. Artificial Intelligence as a Means to Moral Enhancement. *Studies in Logic, Grammar and Rhetoric* 48 (1): 61. https://doi.org/10.1515/slgr-2016-0061.
Kozlovski, A. 2022. Parity and the Resolution of Value Conflicts in Design. *Science and Engineering Ethics* 28 (22): 1–18.
Kozlovski, A. 2024. When Algorithms Decide Who Is a Target: IDF's Use of AI in Gaza. *Tech Policy Press*. https://www.techpolicy.press/when-algorithms-decide-who-is-a-target-idfs-use-of-ai-in-gaza/. Accessed 29 Aug 2024.
Lara, F., and J. Deckers. 2020. Artificial Intelligence as a Socratic Assistant for Moral Enhancement. *Neuroethics* 13 (3): 275–287. https://doi.org/10.1007/s12152-019-09401-y.
Leveringhaus, A. 2022. Morally Repugnant Weaponry?: Ethical Responses to the Prospect of Autonomous Weapons. In *The Cambridge Handbook of Responsible Artificial Intelligence: Interdisciplinary Perspectives*, ed. S. Voeneky et al., 475–487. Cambridge: Cambridge University Press.
Manríquez Roa, T., and N. Biller-Andorno. 2023. Black Box Algorithms in Mental Health Apps: An Ethical Reflection. *Bioethics*. https://doi.org/10.1111/bioe.13215.
Manson, K. 2024. AI Warfare Is Already Here. *Bloomberg*. https://www.bloomberg.com/features/2024-ai-warfare-project-maven/. Accessed 19 Aug 2024.
Matthias, A. 2004. The Responsibility Gap: Ascribing Responsibility for the Actions of Learning Automata. *Ethics and Information Technology* 6 (3): 175–183.
McKernan, B., and H. Davies. 2024. 'The Machine Did It Coldly': Israel Used AI to Identify 37,000 Hamas Targets. *The Guardian*, April 3.
Mecacci, G., and F. Santoni de Sio. 2020. Meaningful Human Control as Reason-Responsiveness: The Case of Dual-Mode Vehicles. *Ethics and Information Technology* 22:103–115.
Mecacci, G., D. Amoroso, L. Cavalcante Siebert, D. A. Abbink, M. J. van den Hoven, and F. Santoni de Sio, eds. 2024. *Research Handbook on Meaningful Human Control of Artificial Intelligence Systems*. Cheltenham: Edward Elgar. https://doi.org/10.4337/9781802204131.
Methnani, L., A. Tubella, V. Dignum, and A. Theodorou. 2021. Let Me Take Over: Variable Autonomy for Meaningful Human Control. *Frontiers in Artificial Intelligence* 4:737072. https://doi.org/10.3389/frai.2021.737072.
Methnani, L., M. Chiou, V. Dignum, and A. Theodorou. 2024. Who's in Charge Here? A Survey on Trustworthy AI in Variable Autonomy Robotic Systems. *ACM Computing Surveys* 56 (7): Article 184. https://doi.org/10.1145/3645090.
Nyholm, Sven. 2023. Responsibility Gaps, Value Alignment, and Meaningful Human Control over Artificial Intelligence. In *Risk and Responsibility in Context*, ed. A. Placani and S. Broadhead, 191–213. New York: Routledge.

Poszler, F., and B. Lange. 2024. The Impact of Intelligent Decision-Support Systems on Humans' Ethical Decision-Making: A Systematic Literature Review and an Integrated Framework. *Technological Forecasting & Social Change* 204:123403. https://doi.org/10.1016/j.techfore.2024.123403.

Purves, D., R. Jenkins, and B. J. Strawser. 2015. Autonomous Machines, Moral Judgment, and Acting for the Right Reasons. *Ethical Theory and Moral Practice* 18:851–872. https://doi.org/10.1007/s10677-015-9563-y.

Renic, N. C., and E. Schwarz. 2023a. Crimes of Dispassion: Autonomous Weapons and the Moral Challenge of Systematic Killing. *Ethics and International Affairs* 37 (3): 321–343. https://doi.org/10.1017/S0892679423000291.

Renic, N. C., and E. Schwarz. 2023b. Inhuman-in-the-Loop: AI-Targeting and the Erosion of Moral Restraint. *OpinioJuris*. https://opiniojuris.org/2023/12/19/inhuman-in-the-loop-ai-targeting-and-the-erosion-of-moral-restraint/. Accessed 19 Aug 2024.

Robbins, S. 2023. The Many Meanings of Meaningful Human Control. *AI and Ethics*. https://doi.org/10.1007/s43681-023-00320-6.

Rodwin, B. A., V. P. Bilan, N. B. Merchant, C. G. Steffens, A. A. Grimshaw, L. A. Bastian, and C. G. Gunderson. 2020. Rate of Preventable Mortality in Hospitalized Patients: a Systematic Review and Meta-analysis. *Journal of General Internal Medicine* 35 (7): 2099–2106. https://doi.org/10.1007/s11606-019-05592-5.

Rudin, C. 2019. Stop Explaining Black Box Machine Learning Models for High Stakes Decisions and Use Interpretable Models Instead. *Nature Machine Intelligence* 1:206–215. https://doi.org/10.1038/s42256-019-0048-x.

Russell, Stuart. 2019. *Human Compatible: AI and the Problem of Control*. New York: Viking.

Santoni de Sio, F., and G. Mecacci. 2021. Four Responsibility Gaps with Artificial Intelligence: Why They Matter and How to Address Them. *Philosophy & Technology* 34:1057–1084. https://doi.org/10.1007/s13347-021-00450-x.

Santoni de Sio, F., and J. van den Hoven. 2018. Meaningful human control over autonomous systems: a philosophical account. *Frontiers in Robotics and AI. Sec. Ethics in Robotics and Artificial Intelligence* 5:1–14.

Santoni de Sio, F., G. Mecacci, S. Calvert, D. Heikoop, M. Hagenzieker, and B. van Arem. 2023. Realising Meaningful Human Control Over Automated Driving Systems: A Multidisciplinary Approach. *Minds & Machines* 33:587–611. https://doi.org/10.1007/s11023-022-09608-8.

Santoni de Sio, F. 2024. Human freedom in the age of AI. New York: Routledge, Taylor & Francis Group.

Scharre, P. 2016. Centaur Warfighting: The False Choice of Humans vs. Automation. *Temple International & Comparative Law Journal* 30:151–165.

Schlicker, N., M. Langer, S. K. Otting, K. Baum, C. J. König, and D. Wallach. 2021. What to Expect from Opening Up 'Black Boxes'? Comparing Perceptions of Justice Between Human and Automated Agents. *Computers in Human Behavior* 122:1–16.

Schwarz, E. 2021. Silicon Valley Goes to War: Artificial Intelligence, Weapons Systems, and the De-Skilled Moral Agent. *Philosophy Today* 65 (3): 549–569. https://doi.org/10.5840/philtoday2021519407.

Singer, P. 2009. *Wired for War*. New York: Penguin.

Sparrow, R. 2007. Killer Robots. *Journal of Applied Philosophy* 24 (1): 62–77.

Sparrow, R. 2016. Robots and Respect: Assessing the Case Against Autonomous Weapon Systems. *Ethics and International Affairs* 30 (1): 93–116. https://doi.org/10.1017/S0892679415000647.

Sparrow, R., and A. Henschke. 2023. Minotaurs, Not Centaurs: The Future of Manned-Unmanned Teaming. *Parameters* 53 (1): https://doi.org/10.55540/0031-1723.3207.

Steen, M., J. van Diggelen, T. Timan, and N. van der Stap. 2023. Meaningful Human Control of Drones: Exploring Human–Machine Teaming, Informed by Four Different Ethical Perspectives. *AI and Ethics* 3:281–293. https://doi.org/10.1007/s43681-022-00168-2.

Sterz, S., K. Baum, S. Biewer, H. Hermanns, A. Lauber-Rönsberg, P. Meinel, and M. Langer. 2024. On the Quest for Effectiveness in Human Oversight: Interdisciplinary Perspectives.

In *Proceedings of the 2024 ACM Conference on Fairness, Accountability, and Transparency (FAccT '24)*, 2495–2507. New York: Association for Computing Machinery. https://doi.org/10.1145/3630106.3659051.

Struik, A. 2021. *Meaningful Human Control over Automated Driving Systems: Driver intentions and ADS Behaviour*. Utrecht University.

Sunstein, C. R. 2024. Choice Engines and Paternalistic AI. *Humanities and Social Sciences Communications* 11 (888): https://doi.org/10.1057/s41599-024-03428-0.

Suresh, H., and J. Guttag. 2021. A Framework for Understanding Sources of Harm Throughout the Machine Learning Life Cycle. In *Proceedings of the 1st ACM Conference on Equity and Access in Algorithms, Mechanisms, and Optimization (EAAMO '21)*, 1–9. New York: Association for Computing Machinery, Article 17. https://doi.org/10.1145/3465416.3483305.

Tigard, D. W. 2020. There Is No Techno-Responsibility Gap. *Philosophy & Technology* 34 (3): 589–607.

Umbrello, S. 2020. Meaningful Human Control Over Smart Home Systems: A Value Sensitive Design Approach. *Humana Mente Journal of Philosophical Studies* 13 (37): 40–65.

Vallor, S. 2015. Moral Deskilling and Upskilling in a New Machine Age: Reflections on the Ambiguous Future of Character. *Philosophy & Technology* 28:107–124. https://doi.org/10.1007/s13347-014-0156-9.

van den Hoven, J., G.-J. Lokhorst, and I. van de Poel. 2012. Engineering and the Problem of Moral Overload. *Science and Engineering Ethics* 18 (1): 143–155. https://doi.org/10.1007/s11948-011-9277-z.

van de Poel, I. 2015. Conflicting Values in Design for Values. In *Handbook of Ethics, Values, and Technological Design*, ed. J. van den Hoven, P. Vermaas, and I. van de Poel. Dordrecht: Springer.

van de Poel, I., L. Royakkers, and S. D. Zwart. 2015. *Moral Responsibility and the Problem of Many Hands*. New York: Routledge. https://doi.org/10.4324/9781315734217.

van Diggelen, J., K. van den Bosch, M. Neerincx, and M. Steen. 2024. Designing for Meaningful Human Control in Military Human-Machine Teams. In *Research Handbook on Meaningful Human Control of Artificial Intelligence Systems*, ed. G. Mecacci, D. Amoroso, L. Cavalcante Siebert, D. A. Abbink, M. J. van den Hoven, and F. Santoni de Sio, 232–252. Cheltenham: Edward Elgar.

Verdiesen, E. P. 2024. *Comprehensive Human Oversight over Autonomous Weapon Systems*. Dissertation (TU Delft), Delft University of Technology. https://doi.org/10.4233/uuid:5d444c43-0e3a-4912-838c-5a9c20ffee97.

Vignard, K. 2014. The Weaponization of Increasingly Autonomous Technologies: Considering How Meaningful Human Control Might Move Discussion Forward. *UNIDIR Resources*, Vol. 2. http://www.unidir.org/files/publications/pdfs/considering-how-meaningful-human-control-might-move-the-discus-sion-forward-en-615.pdf. Accessed 29 Aug 2024

Wagner, M. 2011. Taking Humans Out of the Loop: Implications for International Humanitarian Law. *Journal of Law Information and Science* 21: https://ssrn.com/abstract=1874039.

Wagner, B. 2019. Liable, but Not in Control? Ensuring Meaningful Human Agency in Automated Decision-Making Systems. *Policy Internet* 11 (1): 104–122.

Atay Kozlovski is a Swiss National Science Foundation postdoctoral mobility grant researcher and a visiting research fellow at the 'Sociotechnical AI Systems Lab' at the Delft University of Technology in the Netherlands. He holds a PhD in philosophy from the University of Zurich and is a member of the International Committee for Robot Arms Control (ICRAC). His research focuses on the theory of meaningful human and control and the ethical and societal impact of emerging technologies.

Chapter 9
Respecting Autonomy in AI-Supported Military Medicine Decision-Making: A Conceptual Overview

Florian Demont-Biaggi

9.1 Introduction

Relational approaches are common in contemporary ethics, but there are not many applications to the military domain.[1] Initially designed to disclose structural dimensions of exploitation, relational approaches were soon applied in bioethics, AI-ethics, and elsewhere (Gary 2023; Mackenzie 2022; Dignum 2022). They promise not only to disclose structural problems, but also to deepen our understanding of concepts such as autonomy or equality (Stoljar and Voigt 2022). The central question raised here is this: Do relational approaches help us understand the ethics of AI-supported military medicine decision-making? The answer to this question to be developed below is: Yes, they do, especially regarding accountability. The answer does, however, involve a little twist on the concept of autonomy, which in turn will yield a somewhat particular view on relationality. Overall, it seems to relational approaches to military medical ethics have good prospects.

The topic will be approached through two fictive vignettes involving medicine decision-making during a crisis. The vignettes contain elements which are plausible, but are not meant to describe factual cases. They present opportunities for counterfactual reasoning and thus constitute a testing bed for ethical concepts and

[1] Of the many different ways that obligations can be understood in ethics, relational approaches are those which construe ethical obligations as grounded in (or emerging from) relations between persons. They explicitly distinguish themselves from more traditional views which seek to reduce ethical obligations to properties of individuals (like moral sentiments, emotions, or forms of judgment) or to insist on irreducible moral facts.

F. Demont-Biaggi (✉)
Military Academy (MILAC) at ETH Zurich, Zurich, Switzerland

B. Koch, D. Winkler (eds.), *Artificial Intelligence Ethics in Military Medicine and Humanitarian Healthcare*, Military and Humanitarian Health Ethics,
https://doi.org/10.1007/978-3-032-11331-3_9

intuitions. One vignette presents a civilian and the other a military situation, both involving AI-supported decision-making. The relational properties of both vignettes will then be spread out and compared. After an overview of the conceptual space encompassed by the vignettes has been set out, accountability issues will be focused on in detail. Based on Saba Bazargan-Forward's (2022) analysis of distributed agency, attention will be drawn to the role accountability can and should come to the fore in the vignettes. It will then be argued that human autonomy plays a central ethical role for accountability in these cases.

9.2 Relationality and AI: Two Fictive Scenarios

Relational approaches in bioethics and elsewhere are highly variegated. At least in bioethics, differing relational approaches should be held distinct, for combining them sometimes yields contradictory results (Gary 2023, 738–739). Mercer Gary (2023, 734–738) provides a conceptual overview by distinguishing four axes of difference for relational theories: (1) scope of relations considered, (2) nature of relations considered, (3) their determining power of selfhood, and (4) the resulting integrity of that selfhood. There are, however, no relational accounts of the ethical dimension of AI-supported military medicine decision-making yet. And simply projecting an existing theory from the civilian domain onto the military domain risks missing some important details, since the context of war and the role military medicine plays in it potentially differ substantially from the sort of contexts and cases relational approaches to bioethics usually deal with. There is also the important basic question of whether any relational approach can have the explanatory and normative power military medicine requires.

There is hence room for conceptual exploration. One standard way of beginning such an exploration in philosophy is through thought experiments. More precisely, I shall consider vignettes which are fictional, but plausible enough. One presents a civilian case of AI-supported medical decision-making and the other a military case of AI-supported medical decision-making. To keep the general focus on crisis leadership, the civilian case is also a case involving situational pressure, especially scarcity of resources. After the cases have been described, I shall go through Gary's four axes of difference to extract possible and plausible pathways into further theorizing for a relational approach to these cases.

9.2.1 The Civilian Case

This is the civilian case:

In the middle of a pandemic, medical resources are scarce and emergency rooms must make difficult triage decisions. Most of them involve deciding on whether to prioritize vaccinated persons over persons who refused to get vaccinated on non-medical grounds. Luckily, they employ an AI-support system, which has access to medical files of patients coming in, compares it to medical data of all other patients in the nation's healthcare system, and tracks nationwide distribution of medical resources in real time. The system also tracks triage decisions in other healthcare facilities. For every triage decision to be made, the system swiftly produces a recommendation, but it is often unclear how it came up with the recommendation.

Based on this case, the question is what the scope and nature of relations come to. And there are questions about how these relations affect selfhood and its integrity. Let us start with the patients. They are obviously related to healthcare providers, particularly those making the decision about their treatment. Through the AI-support system, there are relations to all other patients in the nation's healthcare system and particularly to those in a similar situation as they are. When triage is necessary, patients are also in a relation to other patients with whom they compete for healthcare. Note that some of these relations depend on past decisions: the patient's personal decision whether to get vaccinated and triage decisions (perhaps among other decisions) taken in other facilities do affect the boundaries within which patients compete for healthcare.[2]

Apart from that we have the relations healthcare providers are in. There is a distinction between those making decisions and those carrying them out. Those carrying decisions out are related to the patients and to their decision-makers. For both roles, persons' ethical intuitions may influence their behaviour. The decision-makers are related to the patients about whose treatment they decide, their followers (who may approve of their decision or not), and other (future) decision-makers and (future) patients who will be affected by the decision through the AI-support system.

Do note that the AI-support system is not taken to stand in any relation to persons.[3] It merely mediates relations, connecting a large set of past, current, and future patients as well as decision-makers with each other. It can be thought of as a sort of relation-accelerator. But not only that. It also influences some of the relations that decision-makers and ordinary healthcare providers enter into, because it issues recommendations. The system not only transmits information, it alters information too, and it is often unclear what was altered and to what extent. So, even though the AI-support system is not, in a narrow sense, taken to stand in any relation to persons, which also holds between persons, there is a broader sense of relationality in which the AI-support system has much weight: the AI-support system has the

[2] For present purposes it is important that decisions not to get vaccinated were motivated by non-medical reasons.

[3] Initially, I leave this assumption unargued for, well aware that some new materialists (Coole and Frost 2010) would want to find AI-support systems as well as other artifacts and things recognized as standing in relevant relations to persons. The points to be illustrated here can be made independent of the claims of new materialisms. This is not meant to imply that a more complete analysis might consider such intuitions. Later on, below, when we turn to accountability, some reasons will be provided for why AI-support systems should not be recognized as standing in relevant relations to persons.

potential to change, reshape, and even constitute particular decision-making practices, whereby it is an influential factor in the overall social system—a system of relations as described in the vignette.[4]

For this civilian case, the scope of the relations is mostly dyadic: these are relations between decision-makers, medical doctors, or caregivers on one side and patients on the other. Relations between patients that prevail due to competition, may involve several individuals, but can be reduced to discrete dyads. Through the AI-support system, however, there also exists an extensive network of relations between a large set of persons with considerable interdependencies irreducible to discrete dyads. There are, hence, two distinct scopes of relations in the case.

The nature of the relations in the vignette is structural, "determining the conditions of interpersonal relationships" (Gary 2023, 735). This is a common type of relation often employed in bioethics, as analysing such relations may help to identify some potential unequal standing among persons. Structural relations hence give rise to questions about fairness and justice, thus making ethical issues tangible. More precisely, patients depend on others—decision-makers, medical doctors, caregivers, other patients—to get their medical needs met, even though their past decisions concerning vaccination may influence whether they do have a claim-right. This in turn grounds responsibilities for others to respond.[5] Those providing healthcare must recognize and assess medical needs, decide on whether they can or should help and then act in accord with decisions made. Note that keeping the AI-support system up and running, which includes monitoring it for biased patterns, hallucinations, and other technical shortcomings affecting automated altering of information, is an integral part of providing healthcare in this case.

The notion of autonomy naturally comes in together with the question how these relations affect individuals' selfhood. However, looking at the vignette, it is hard to say whether any of these relations influence anybody's selfhood in a decisive way. It is also hard to say what role a notion of autonomy can play, since the sort of medical crises under consideration are interesting precisely because they, among other things, curb autonomy as they do (i.e. through situational pressure). What makes autonomy-issues hard to assess is that limits to autonomous decision-making and action go hand in hand with the sort of dependencies that patients experience, which in turn provide a footing for rights and duties at play. In other words, what is ethically relevant in the vignette seems not to centrally depend on a value of autonomy

[4] This broader sense of relationality can be spelled out in terms of an actor-network-theory (Latour 2005). Below I shall argue that ethical accountability does require relationality in the narrow sense and provide some reasons why an AI-support system as described here does not qualify for this more demanding sort of relationality.

[5] A tenet often associated with relational approaches is that dependency relations generate responsibilities (Collins 2015, 97–123). In fact, it is hard to come up with any right or duty which is not grounded in a dependency relation in an almost trivial sense, because any bearer of a right or a duty who cannot refer to such a footing cannot answer the question why he or she *should* act in accord with that particular right or duty. Without dependency relations, they need not care (at least not for tangible reasons). And for present purposes, why they should care is to a large degree due to structural relations partly constitutive of the social institutions within which present issues appear.

from which oughts can be derived. Rather, all is about restoring patients' health and, thereby, a good part of autonomous action currently (hopefully temporarily) suspended, in a context in which resources to do so are scarce. What is important here is that the relations under consideration do not constitute, influence, hinder, or even exploit individuals' selfhood and are still ethically relevant.

The relations are, however, connected to whether individuals will be able to fully live and enjoy their selfhood in the future after their stay at the medical facility or if they will have to adjust how they live their lives, because their health could not be fully restored. If they retain a trauma, must cope with a new organ or prosthetics, or if they have to undergo therapies and other interventions to relearn capabilities they had before or acquire new capabilities, their subjective experience of their body and maybe their environment will change so much that their self-image changes together with it and, thereby, the integrity of selfhood must be seen as affected. Note, however, that only in a few instances the relations in the case will impinge on the integrity of individual selfhood in such a way. More often, it is the medical condition (which made them seek out medical help in the first place) that eventually affects integrity.

Another factor potentially affecting the integrity of selfhood is the AI-support system and how it tracks, infers, and possibly alters information. Due to biases in the dataset, on which it was trained, due to patterns it finds in real time medical data (medical files, overall allocation of medical goods, decisions made elsewhere etc.), or because of a random quirk resulting in hallucinations, information alteration can be ethically relevant, but it may not be clear exactly what information was altered, how and to what extent. Obvious examples would be cases in which socio-economically marginalised persons receive no treatment (or lower-priority treatment) more often than persons with affluent backgrounds for no evident reason other than their socio-economical standing. There could also be sexists, racist, or other unjust treatments due to automated information altering that reproduces, even augments, or invents unethical patterns. It is, however, also possible that AI-altered information failed to track such unethical patterns, decreased their import, or simply invented alternatives yielding ethically better outcomes. The potential randomness in information alteration can thus be disruptive in two ways: aggravating injustice or instigating ethical innovation. To be sure, people working in healthcare also do that, but they can be asked for their reasons for doing so and even if their reasons are bad, their contribution to the overall ethical situation can be assessed due to the structural relations they stand in. For an AI-support system as we find it in the vignette, this is not possible, because it is often not clear what was contributed and why. In other words, it is possible that the AI-support system altered information in a way that affects the integrity of a patient's selfhood (positively or negatively), but nobody will ever be in a position to tell whether it actually did. The AI-support system hence adds an element of moral luck for patients.[6]

[6] It does not add an element of moral luck for healthcare providers, either decision-makers or others, because the structural relations they stand in accord them enough control to make them responsible for what they do independent of AI-support.

There are obviously several points at which further enquiries are possible and sensible. At any rate, the vignette plus the short remarks just provided should suffice to make plausible that crisis leadership in civilian medical contexts can come with special ethical challenges on its own.

9.2.2 The Military Case

Now, the civilian case is to be contrasted with a military case in order to clarify what is special about the context of military medicine and what role relational perspectives plus AI-supported decision-making may play there, that cannot already be found in the civilian case. Consider, therefore, the military medical ethics case:

In the middle of an armed conflict, medical resources are scarce and military emergency facilities must make difficult triage decisions. Most of them involve deciding on whether to prioritize soldiers eager to go back to battle over soldiers who would prefer not to go back for personal reasons. Luckily, they employ an AI-support system, which has access to military medical files of soldiers coming in, compares it to medical data of all other soldiers in the armed forces' healthcare system, and tracks overall distribution of medical resources in real time. The system also tracks triage decisions in other military emergency facilities. For every triage decision to be made, the system swiftly produces a recommendation, but it is often unclear how it came up with it.

Regarding the scope and nature of the relations at play, the military case does not run counter to much also found in the civilian case. One difference is that the soldiers are unlike in their eagerness to return to battle, while in the civilian case patients are unlike due to a past decision on whether to get vaccinated. Another difference lies in the nature of the crisis. In the civilian case, crisis leadership became necessary due to a pandemic. The military case is situated in armed conflict. While, in principle, the civilian case is best understood as still governed by standard considerations for civilian medical ethics, this is not so for the military case. Military medical ethics has its distinct issues and proposes different solutions. This is best seen when contrasting pandemic medical necessity with military medical necessity.

The primary objective of crisis leadership is to get back to a normal state. In order to do that, some things are more helpful than others. Some things are necessary others impossible. What is necessary in a pandemic to get back to a normal state does influence how scarce resources are managed. This directly affects how scarce medical resources are allocated and how decisions in emergency facilities are taken. But what is necessary in a pandemic is often up to discussion, since it involves decision-making on the political level and for democracies this does involve public discourse. Why should a patient accept some understanding of pandemic medical necessity, especially if he or she consciously made a vaccination decision for non-medical reasons that does not accord with it, thus exercising a right for self-determination usually accorded in normal civilian circumstances? Here it is hard to invoke broad beneficence—an appeal to the collective good "of an entire political commonwealth" (Gross 2021, 38–31)—to override a patients' self-determination in both medical and political matters in a general way. In cases like this, where public health is at stake, there is a proportionality question according to which it must be determined under which circumstances aggregated health interests outweigh an individual's. This is mainly a question about the threshold at which individual autonomy is curbed too much. Upshur (2002, 103) points out an important observation about the evidential basis for answering such questions:

In public health practice, the evidence may not be clear or the evidence may be characterized by underdetermination. [footnotes omitted] This commonly occurs in public health. We shall never have randomized control trial evidence of many environmental exposures such as chemicals, and many proposed interventions are subject to long lag times before effects are noted. Underdetermination occurs when the data can be interpreted in many ways that are plausible but conflicting. This can occur for statistical reasons such as model selection, or because of unexpressed or unacknowledged value or epistemic commitments. The problem of underdetermination is not limited to observational studies. [footnote omitted] It may be a generalized feature of knowledge acquisition.

If this is true for ordinary circumstances, it will be even more acute in a crisis such as a pandemic. The way the vignette is designed, much pressure is exerted on decision-making: resources are scarce, there is (especially early in a pandemic involving a barely known virus) more lack of evidence, time is essential, and there might be no stringent guidelines from organisational or political leadership applicable to issues at hand. From an epistemic point of view, this is a shaky foundation for deciding on what precise threshold is acceptable to curb individual autonomy for reasons of beneficence for overall public health. Appealing to broad beneficence may have some rhetorical power in crisis leadership and hence contribute to crisis management efforts by increasing influence, but from an epistemic point of view it is merely a stab in the dark.

In addition to that, public health should be sensitive to community sentiments, since it receives its money from the public, gains legal powers from it, and must be judged by the effectiveness of its service to the public (Callahan and Jenning 2011). Patients as described in the vignette have a right to political participation and are thus part of the public to which public health institutions and arrangements are answerable. This makes it very problematic to justify curbing individual patient autonomy by simply referring to overall beneficence. And crisis leadership is not the context for protracted and thorny elaborations of reasons for a much-needed decision: speed is of the essence.

The AI-support system does not matter much if we regard the person making the decision as fully accountable.[7] And then there is the question whether its potential unreliability outweighs the speed in decision-making it affords. Humans can also be biased and it should be recalled that the potential randomness in information alteration may lead to ethical innovation too. So, not all random information-alteration is

[7] Accountability will be discussed in more detail below.

necessarily bad in an ethical sense. Still, reliance on an AI-support system does suggest an epistemicism about ethically relevant information-alteration at play in the decision-making process: there is ethically relevant (possibly even decisive) information-alteration involved in the decision-making process, but we might never know what it is. This need not amount to reducing decision-making to a form of gambling. It is an empirical question whether randomness is an issue that emerges at frequencies and with a scope which render AI-generated recommendations proportionate due to decision-making speed and potential ethical innovation due to pattern-disruption.[8] What is interesting from a philosophical point of view is the possibility of ethically relevant information-alteration independent of human cognition, thought, and discourse. After all, in this lies a potential of ethically relevant agency for which accountability cannot be ascribed to any human agent. The consequences of this pose theoretical and practical problems that merit further reflection.

Overall, however, the inclusion of an AI-support system in the civilian vignette does not change ethical matters much from a relational point of view. Exploring the intricacies of appeals to pandemic medical necessities appears to be a much more fruitful pathway to pursue for future studies. But even there, if we focus on crisis leadership and the options the decision-maker does have, we may adopt a pragmatic attitude, according to which no matter what the AI-support system recommends and no matter how or what is decided in the end, a patient will be treated and that will constitute some contribution to overall efforts to deal with the pandemic. This is a plausible option precisely because questions about pandemic medical necessity and the import of public health issues through broad beneficence considerations are so complex. No matter how these considerations all will be spelled out, it cannot be done in situ and treating somebody is always better than treating nobody. The gain in decision-making speed probably outweighs the drawbacks of fully relying on the AI-support system. It is plausible that the disruptive potential of AI-support systems is innocuous in such contexts.

This is not the end of the line, however. Appealing to military medical necessity is very different from appealing to pandemic medical necessity.[9] There are several reasons for this. First of all, the soldiers to be treated in military emergency facilities do not decide on what counts as military necessity. Even if they happen to be operational-level officers whose post was bombed, they do not have a decisive say in what counts as overall military necessity (even if they are in a better position to track it than their subordinates). Military necessity, at least its general shape, is

---

[8] Many common AI-models (especially large-language models with standard machine-learning capabilities) have possibly reached an upper performance limit or soon will do so, because increase in performance requires exponential training data input (Udandarao et al. 2024). And for models at the upper performance limit we can test scope and frequency of what appear to be random quirks much more easily, because it can be ruled out that further increases in performance will substantially change scope and frequency.

[9] To keep things as neat as possible, I shall basically assume that Michael Gross (2021) is right about military medical necessity. The relational perspective will bring forth a few points that Gross does not discuss, but this does not amount to anything contrary to the conceptual framework he proposed.

determined on higher levels, since it is a strategic issue. Second, soldiers are accustomed to curbed individual autonomy because of military necessity; this is a defining mark of military organizations, since they bundle, coordinate, and focus individual capabilities and efforts to attain collective goals. Ethically, this is bound to just war theorizing. Michael Gross (2021, 31–32) writes:

> Military necessity refers to the military means to effectively pursue just war, whether national self-defense or humanitarian intervention. In contrast to [civilian] medical necessity, military necessity sanctions the least costly means to protect individual, aggregate, and collective interests. Fusing the ends and means of military and medical necessity, *military-medical necessity* designates the least costly medical means a military force requires to effectively pursue just war.

So, in the military case we have a much clearer standard for assessing decision-making, autonomy curbing, and AI-support to decision-making than in the civilian case. This is true even though both cases are cases of crisis leadership in a medical context and it testifies to the proposition that the military domain is distinct.

Turning to autonomy-curbing, the armed forces of some democratic countries only know voluntary military service. For their soldiers, consent to autonomy curbing can be assumed and implies acceptance of military necessity as a standard for what counts as broad beneficence to which they contribute. In democratic countries with compulsory military service, there is awareness that there are advantages to only employ soldiers in combat who are ready, willing, and able. The military vignette is not restricted to soldiers directly involved in combat, but includes those close enough to get wounded and close enough to count as being directly contributing to battle-efforts. At any rate, in the vignette soldier-patients differ in their eagerness to return to battle and that is meant to indicate whether they are motivated to still accept military necessity as the right standard to judge their personal case. Even when military service is compulsory, that acceptance does not make much of a difference in ethics or law, but it does make a difference in morale and, consequently, overall battle performance of a formation. Hence, there may be prudential reasons to take soldiers' motivation into account in order to better respond to what is militarily necessary. In that sense, military necessity provides solid ethical and prudential guardrails for human decision-making. Because of this, it cannot be held pragmatically—unlike in the civilian case—that all is fine as long as somebody is treated, since there is a clearer standard for what counts as an acceptable contribution to overall beneficence. In other words, decision-making speed never outweighs other considerations if that involves straying from what military necessity establishes.

Military necessity as a yardstick also changes perspectives on the AI-support system. Merely speeding up decision-making is not good enough, since fast decisions going against military necessity are to be ruled out categorically. The question then is whether an AI-support system can be expected to track military necessity reliably enough and implement this into its recommendations.

Turning to AI-support for military leadership in general, the prospects are not all bright. James Johnson (2024), for example, argues at great length that current AI-support does not provide what is needed to have humans and machines cooperate on a par in military decision-making. He writes (Johnson 2022, 253):

> Commanding war in complex and uncertain strategic environments entails more than voluminous, cheap (and often biased) data sets, and inductive machine logic. Until AI systems can produce testable hypotheses or reason by analogy and deductively reason (using "top-down" logic) like humans, they will not understand the real world and not be fully able to make decisions in non-linear, complex, and uncertain environments (Norvig 2014). [footnote omitted] Commanders' intentions, the rules of law and engagement (e.g. the principle of proportionality), and the exhibiting of ethical and moral leadership in the execution of strategic objectives are critical features of ethical, moral, and tactically effective military decision-making (e.g. highly context-dependent targeting decisions) (Roff 2014, 211–227). If we hold AI-ML [artificial intelligence—machine learning] systems to be incapable of properly performing these intrinsically human traits, the role of human agents in "mission command"—the implicit communication and bond of trust between tactical leaders and the political-strategic leadership—will be even more critical in future AI-enabled warfare (Goldfarb and Lindsay 2022; Kramer 2015; Beyerchen 1992–1993).

Crisis leadership, be it in a medical setting or not, requires understanding the overall situation and to navigate it successfully. Multi-modal large-language models, which are the sort of model most plausibly employed for AI-support in decision-making, exhibit systematic shortcomings already when they are to solve problems like visual pattern recognition (Tong et al. 2024).[10] This makes navigating the physical world very challenging and it also limits support in cases for which such things as visual assessment of a wound are centrally important for decision-making.

In military contexts, social navigation and collateral learning has been identified as playing an important role when dealing with extreme situations (Shachar et al. 2017; Kayes et al. 2017). Exhibiting good judgment in the sort of extreme situations common in military engagement at the echelon under consideration in the vignette involves a great amount of adaptability in order to deal with situations for which training did not fully prepare. It also involves inventiveness. At the same time, commanders' intent and military necessity have to be heeded, even if they or their interpretation change from time to time, or if their applicability to the situation at hand changes over time or even becomes questionable. In the passage quoted above, Johnson underlines the role of implicit communication and trust, which are relational qualities. In fact, social navigation and collateral learning can be interpreted as attempts to define, negotiate, revise, or abandon the relations governing dependencies, duties, and possibilities at play during crisis leadership, especially the extreme situations common at military frontlines.

It hence seems that relationality is something we should not entrust AI-systems with, at least in military contexts. Of course, there are other shortcomings in what AI-systems can do. But if relationality is at the very centre of what ethical decision-making in military leadership (be it medical or not) comes to, there is no plausible AI-support for such decision-making. On the other hand, arguments and reasons adduced so far merely suggest that AI-systems are not good enough now. AI-enthusiasts may still want to argue that new models will eventually deal with all

[10] Integrating visual self-supervised learning features attenuates the issues somewhat, but the open challenge remains.

these issues and that for some issues solutions are already at the horizon.[11] The prospects of this enthusiasm can be better assessed when considering accountability—a topic to which we turn now.

9.3 Accountability

One way of bringing the topic of accountability into focus is through considering the ethical relevance of the sort of randomness associated with AI-support. But this does require a bit of stage-setting. Intuitively, a person is accountable for things she does or did. In cooperative action, where she participated in a group doing things together, she can be thought to be accountable for her contribution. One might be tempted to think that this can be further specified by saying that a person is accountable for her causal contribution to a cooperative action. After all, things to which she did not contribute causally are beyond what she could control or wanted to influence. In war ethics and related topics in the philosophy of law, this intuition has, however, been questioned: Victor Tadros (2016) and Saba Bazargan-Forward (2022) have, for example, argued that there are cases where agents are accountable for wrongful actions in ways that go beyond their causal contributions.[12]

Consider structural relations involving authority. In the vignette we had decision-makers and healthcare providers acting in accord with these decisions. In this context Bazargan-Forward (2022, ch. 1) speaks of division of agential labour, so that we have deliberators deciding what to do and executors acting in accord with it. The central mark of authority here is that it involves a practical claim against somebody that they act in a specific way (Hart 1990, 101). For hierarchical organizations this can be seen as embedded in those structural relations constituting authority and, if aggregated, in an organizational hierarchy. If the healthcare providers do not act in accord with what the decision-makers set down and if there is no good reason to question whether the decision-makers have made a grave mistake (such as committing an obvious war crime), they are liable to suffer consequences.

Deference to authority can be captured in terms of protected reasons. A protected reason for an executor combines one or a set of first-order reasons to act in accord with what a deliberator (who has a suitable authoritative claim against an executor) has decided on one side with one or many second-order reasons, which exclude one or many first-order reasons from deliberation (even though they may compete with what the deliberator had furnished) on the other side (Raz 1977, 1990, 35–84). In the vignette the decision-maker may have decided to treat a specific soldier in accord with what the AI-support system had recommended. As far as the healthcare providers supposed to act on this decision are concerned, there is nothing obviously

[11] A promising approach seems to be neurosymbolic AI (Sheth et al. 2023). But even though its central concepts (viz. neural networks) have been around for quite some time, current research efforts in AI (und research funding) do not primarily go into this subdiscipline.

[12] For ease and shortness of exposition I shall focus on Bazargan-Forward's (2022) discussion.

wrong with this decision and there is no time to dig deeper anyway. The decision-maker therefore has an intact practical claim against the healthcare providers that they treat the soldier in accord with what has been decided. Now that arrangement excludes (for the healthcare providers' own deliberations about what particular steps are to be taken) reasons that compete with the first-order reasons the decision-maker had to adopt what the AI-support system recommended. The healthcare providers thus have a protected reason to do what was decided upon and that is a central feature of the structural relation constitutive of a deference of authority.

Now, in deference to authority, healthcare providers do many things potentially going beyond what the decision-makers do or even are capable of doing themselves. Still, if dutiful actions of the healthcare providers along these lines turn out to be ethically or legally wrong, the decision-makers will be accountable for it. It is in this sense that accountability in cooperative actions can exceed causal contributions. And it is a central feature of the sort of relationality we find in the divisions of agential labour common for hierarchical organizations.

AI-support systems for decision-making tend to be challenging for views of accountability that focus on causal contributions. After all, their potential randomness makes it unclear what causal contribution the AI-support system made, even if we knew what data went into the system, the general formal features of computational processes involved, and what it produced as a recommendation. There might have been a causally relevant information-alteration in the computational process, but we do not know whether there was one and what it was. Does Bazargan-Forward's notion of a division of agential labour and especially his notion of authority-based accountability help us evaluate the ethical dimension of employing an AI-support system for decision-making?

Answering this question first requires asking whether the AI-support system may count as a full-fledged deliberator. This, of course, amounts to asking whether AI-support systems can play a role in the sort of relationality between deliberators and executors for which deference of authority is reasonable. Here we should recall, first, that humans can also be biased and that, second, some potential randomness in information-alteration may lead to ethical innovation: it is an empirical question whether randomness is an issue that emerges at frequencies and with a scope which render AI-generated recommendations proportionate due to gains in decision-making speed and due to potential ethical innovation because of random pattern-disruptions. It is plausible to argue that while an AI-support system's causal contribution is negligible in the civilian case, but it seems not to be so in the military case. These points do clarify some ethical aspects of employing, but they do not substantially contribute to solving the question whether the AI-system may count as a full-fledged deliberator.[13]

In the initial analysis of the relations in the vignettes provided, the AI-support system was not seen as standing in the sort of structural relations with human agents

[13] At the most, these points may be adduced for arguing that—from an ethical point of view—the AI-support system can be useful in the civilian crisis setting.

that we find between human agents. A good intuitive reason for this is that commitment matters for accountability.[14] AI-support only matters if what it delivers is what decision-makers commit themselves to in their decisions. But is that plausible?

Consider where human autonomy plays a role for relationality in the vignettes. In the civilian case, patients have some say regarding broad beneficence and may adduce this to defend themselves against certain forms of autonomy-curbing. In the military case, soldiers may not want to return to battle and even if that does not formally allow them to fend off autonomy-curbing, it is something decision-makers have to consider if they are prudent about fulfilling their mission. If the soldiers' unwillingness becomes too strong, he or she might be ready to disobey and risk a court martial.

Particularly interesting is the relation between decision-makers and healthcare providers when there is deference to authority involving protected reasons. If the healthcare providers, being executors, have good reasons to believe that the decision-makers deliberations were unlawful or unethical, they have a reason to refuse to defer to them. Unlawful or unethical deliberations undo the decision-maker's practical claim against an executor that they act in a specific way.[15] This is so, because the division of agential labour in hierarchical settings is based on a presumption of lawfulness and ethical correctness (which is not to claim that there are no such things as coercion and duress in reality).[16]

It is questionable whether an AI-support system can ever meet minimal epistemic standards, since random quirks are commonly described as hallucinations. Apart from that, it is questionable whether AI-support systems can be considered autonomous in the sense just illustrated. Human agents do consider themselves as standing in some relation to others or not—and their judgments about it usually count for determining whether they are. The structural relations in the vignettes concern the human agents who are standing in these relations to each other and that is why they recognize themselves as having certain rights and duties. Human agents also recognize others as being concerned by a relation or not. Two human agents related to each other also do recognize themselves as being concerned by a relation and thereby agree on what their mutual rights and duties are. Recognizing myself, you, or us as standing in a certain relation is a necessary precondition for me, you, or us being subject to duties, rights, obligations, or rules.[17] This is what it means to be bound by an ought.

---

[14] Bazargan-Forward does not discuss commitment explicitly. But he discusses motivating reasons and admits that he believes they are deontically relevant (2022, 65). My discussion of commitment here does not flow naturally from his account, but I surmise it is compatible with it.

[15] Typically, military regulations contain that sort of provision in their basic documents.

[16] Bazargan-Forward (2022, 29–34) holds the weaker view that executioner's autonomy can overrule deference to authority, especially when a deliberator does not meet minimal epistemic standards, because she or he hallucinates, is manic, suffers from panic attacks and so on.

[17] The wording I employ here should make clear that I construe autonomy as self-determination in a broadly Kantian fashion. The understanding of the role of recognition put to use is the one Axel Honneth identifies as stemming from Kant and Hegel (Honneth 2020, ch. 4).

Under which circumstances can we withhold recognition of others as being subject to some rule (be it legal, ethical, conventional, or else)? Maybe there is evidence that they are not truthful, that there is something wrong with their cognition, or that they cannot be coherent. At any rate, we need specific and solid evidence to question a person's first-person authority when she claims to consider her own thought, speech, or action as being subject to some rule. For an AI-support system, we have the sort of evidence we need to withhold recognition of them as being subject to some rule. We may not always know the precise sequence of computational processes undertaken and, thus, are not always able to identify random information-alteration. But we know the general form of the computational processes employed: for a given input string of characters the most probable output string of characters is calculated based on probability-tables. This is not the right basis for ascribing the sort of first-person authority necessary for ethically relevant relations, let alone mutual recognition. If it was, autonomy qua self-determination would not involve truthfulness vis-à-vis the physical and social (i.e. relational) environment, to logical rules, or psychological reactions and especially not vis-à-vis self-ascriptions where first-person authority is not suitably challenged. Autonomy would be reducible to a string of characters produced by a calculation serving as a new input for the same or another calculation process.[18] The biggest problem with this is that we would lose the phenomenon of ethics and such things as accountability as we are familiar with them in everyday life.

9.4 Conclusion

The relational perspective on military medical ethics has proven useful. First of all, it made possible a new distinction between a civilian medical crisis case and a military medical case. It did so by drawing attention to some details about the role of autonomy in both cases. It did, however, also raise questions about the usefulness of an AI-support system in both cases. While the usefulness of an AI-support system in a civilian medical crisis situation (at least as captured through the civilian vignette) seems to be an empirical matter, its usefulness in the military case is categorically doubtful, because it fails to track such normative guardrails as military necessity or commander's intent.

[18] There is a large literature on rule-following starting with Kripke (1982) and continued by Boghossian (1989), which argues that rule-following cannot be construed in dispositional terms. Under the assumption that an algorithmic characterization of rule-following is a dispositional characterization (which Kripke endorses in his discussion), there are hence some considerable difficulties for those wanting to argue that an AI system follows rules just like humans do. It would be too much of a digression to go into this here, but it is worthwhile to point out that there is a well-established literature that considerably raises the threshold for convincing arguments by AI-enthusiasts.

Turning to accountability, the division of agential labour and especially the phenomenon of deference to authority as instantiated in the cases have turned out to be of central importance. It has been argued that an AI-support system cannot be considered as fully participating in such relational arrangements. In order to strengthen the argument against according AI a full standing in human ethical relationality, I have drawn on the idea that human agents consider themselves as being subject to rules. Furthermore, human agents consider other human agents as subjects to rules. Together with others they can even consider themselves as dyad or as a group as being subject to shared rules. These suggestions were not fully worked out, because they are—for present purposes—just meant to suggest a pathway that is plausible enough for further explorations of the topic. It by no means should be thought to settle the matter, even though it is meant to raise the bar substantially for AI-enthusiasm in military medical ethics.

What has been established, though, is the claim that a relational perspective can be applied to military medical ethics and that by doing so, new insights and new pathways for further enquiries become possible. The discussion on accountability suggests, however, that not any relational approach will do. It has been argued that a conception of relationality bound up with autonomy as self-determination and an emphasis on the role of recognition is one particularly promising option. How good it actually is, however, will have to be shown when considering other areas of military medical ethics and related fields. As far as the arguments presented here go, we may nevertheless presume good prospects.

References

Bazargan-Forward, Saba. 2022. *Authority, Cooperation & Accountability*. Oxford: OUP.

Beyerchen, Alan. 1992–1993. Clausewitz, Nonlinearity, and the Unpredictability of War. *International Security* 17 (3): 59–90.

Boghossian, Paul A. 1989. The Rule-Following Considerations. Reprinted in *Rule-Following and Meaning*, ed. A. Miller and C. Wright. 2004, 141–187. Chesham: Acumen.

Callahan, Daniel, and Bruce Jenning. 2011. Ethics and Public Health: Forging a Strong Relationship. *American Journal of Public Health 92* (2): 169–176.

Collins, Stephanie. 2015. *The Core of Care Ethics*. Basingstoke: Palgrave.

Coole, Diana, and Samantha Frost, eds. 2010. *New Materialisms: Ontology, Agency, and Politics*. Durham: Duke University Press.

Dignum, Virginia. 2022. Relational Artificial Intelligence. https://doi.org/10.48550/arXiv.2202.07446.

Gary, Mercer. 2023. Relational Approaches in Bioethics: A Guide to Their Differences. *Bioethics* 37:733–740.

Goldfarb, Avi, and Jon Lindsay. 2022. Prediction and Judgment: Why Artificial Intelligence Increases the Importance of Humans in War. *International Security* 46 (3): 7–50.

Gross, Michael. 2021. *Military Medical Ethics in Contemporary Armed Conflict. Mobilizing Medicine in the Pursuit of Just War*. New York: OUP.

Hart, Herbert L. A. 1990. Command and Authoritative Legal Reasons. In *Authority*, ed. J. Raz, 92–114. New York: New York University Press.

Honneth, Axel. 2020. *Recognition. A Chapter in the History of European Ideas*. Cambridge: Cambridge University Press.

Johnson, James. 2022. The AI Commander Problem: Ethical, Political, and Psychological Dilemmas of Human-Machine Interactions in AI-Enabled Warfare. *Journal of Military Ethics* 21 (3–4): 246–271. https://doi.org/10.1080/15027570.2023.2175887.

Johnson, James. 2024. *The AI Commander. Centaur Teaming, Command, and Ethical Dilemmas*. Oxford: OUP.

Kayes, Christopher, Nate Allen, and Nate Self. 2017. How Leaders Learn from Experience in Extreme Situations: The Case of the U.S. Military in Takur Ghar, Afghanistan. In *Leadership in Extreme Situations*, ed. M. Holenweger, M. K. Jager, and F. Kernic, 277–294. Cham: Springer.

Kramer, Eric-Hans. 2015. Mission Command in the Information Age: A Normal Accidents Perspective on Networked Military Operations. *Journal of Strategic Studies* 38 (4): 445–466.

Kripke, Saul A. 1982. *Wittgenstein on Rules and Private Language*. Oxford: Blackwell.

Latour, Bruno. 2005. *Reassembling the Social. An Introduction to Actor-Network-Theory*. Oxford: OUP.

Mackenzie, Catriona. 2022. Vulnerability, Exploitation and Autonomy. In *Thick (Concepts of) Autonomy*, ed. J. F. Childress and M. Quante, 175–187. Cham: Springer.

Norvig, Peter. 2014. *Artificial Intelligence: A Modern Approach*. 3rd ed. Harlow: Pearson Education.

Raz, Joseph. 1977. Promises and Obligations. In *Law, Morality and Society: Essays in Honour of H.L.A. Hart*, ed. P. Hacker and J. Raz, 210–228. Oxford: OUP.

Raz, Joseph. 1990. *Practical Reasons and Norms*. Princeton: Princeton University Press.

Roff, Heather M. 2014. The Strategic Robot Problem: Lethal Autonomous Weapons in War. *Journal of Military Ethics* 13 (3): 211–227.

Shachar, Ophir Weinstall, Henrietta Cons Ponte, and Ayal Ben-Ari. 2017. Social Navigation and the Emergence of Leadership: Tactical Command in the IDF Ground Forces in the Second Lebanon War. In *Leadership in Extreme Situations*, ed. M. Holenweger, M. K. Jager, and F. Kernic, 181–194. Cham: Springer.

Sheth, Amit, Kaushik Roy, and Manas Gaur. 2023. Neurosymbolic Artificial Intelligence (Why, What, and How). *IEEE Intelligent Systems* 38 (3): 56–62. https://doi.org/10.1109/MIS.2023.3268724.

Stoljar, Natalie, and Kristin Voigt. 2022. *Autonomy and Equality. Relational Approaches*. London: Routledge.

Tadros, Victor. 2016. Causation, Culpability, and Liability. In *The Ethics of Self-Defense*, ed. C. Coons and M. Weber, 110–130. Oxford: OUP.

Tong, Shengbang, Zhuang Liu, Yuexiang Zhai, Yi Ma, Yann LeCun, and Saining Xie. 2024. Eyes Wide Shut? Exploring the Visual Shortcomings of Multimodal LLMs. https://doi.org/10.48550/arXiv.2401.06209.

Udandarao, Vishaal, Ameya Prabhu, Adhiraj Ghosh, Yash Sharma, Philip H. S. Torr, Adel Bibi, Samuel Albanie, and Matthias Bethge. 2024. No 'Zero-Shot' Without Exponential Data: Pretraining Concept Frequency Determines Multimodal Model Performance. https://doi.org/10.48550/arXiv.2404.04125.

Upshur, Ross E. G. 2002. Principles for the Justification of Public Health Intervention. *Canadian Journal of Public Health* 93 (2): 101–103.

Florian Demont-Biaggi After studies in English literature, linguistics, and philosophy at Basle University, the University of Birmingham, King's College London, and a PhD in philosophy of language from Zurich University, Dr. phil. Florian Demont-Biaggi has been a lecturer at the Military Academy (MILAC) at ETH since 2013. There he has specialised in applied ethics with an emphasis on leadership and military ethics. Due to his penchant for interdisciplinary approaches, he also remains interested in epistemology and the philosophy of science. After writing the monograph *Rules and Dispositions in Language Use* (Palgrave 2014), he edited *The Nature of Peace and* *the Morality of Armed Conflict* (Palgrave 2017). Peer-reviewed contributions to journals and edited books on applied ethics, philosophy of language, leadership theories, and other topics form his research profile. His recent monography *Elements of Leadership Ethics* was published by Springer in 2025. In his current research he focuses on the moral dimension of military leadership, paying special attention to civil-military relations.

Chapter 10
Integration, Epistemic Responsibility, and Seamlessness

Hadeel Naeem

10.1 Introduction

In this chapter, I examine how we can responsibly form beliefs with AI technologies while relying on them seamlessly. Generally, we use technology seamlessly when we employ it without paying direct attention to the technology or our use of it. Technologies we use regularly for a significant period can become seamless in this way. Consider, for example, how we seamlessly reach for our phones when we look up directions in a new city. Other examples are smartwatches and virtual reality goggles that may be used seamlessly, even more quickly.

In this chapter, I undertake an epistemological inquiry. I aim to understand how we seamlessly rely on AI systems to *form beliefs* and when such beliefs are *epistemically responsibly* formed. Put another way, I intend to explore the conditions required for (what I call) *epistemic responsibility in seamless cases*. In general, we form beliefs responsibly when we base them on good reasons, properly consider the evidence, or reflect on the reliability of the belief-forming mechanisms. In seamless reliance on technology, it is unclear how we epistemically responsibly employ technology. This is because we effortlessly integrate technology without the conscious effort that is considered essential for rationality.

My investigation is distinct from the broad literature that explores moral responsibility questions about AI systems. This literature discusses, for instance, the moral responsibility gap (Matthias 2004; Champagne and Tonkens 2015; Königs 2022) and the permissibility of designing killer robots Himmelreich (2019). While distinct, the ethics and epistemology of AI aren't without important links, and researchers working on the ethics of AI will find plenty of food for thought in the pages that

H. Naeem (✉)
University of Erlangen-Nuremberg, Erlangen, Germany
e-mail: hadeel@hadeelnaeem.com

B. Koch, D. Winkler (eds.), *Artificial Intelligence Ethics in Military Medicine and Humanitarian Healthcare*, Military and Humanitarian Health Ethics,
https://doi.org/10.1007/978-3-032-11331-3_10

follow. Consider, for instance, a medical practitioner who endangers a patient's life because they follow an AI-suggested course of treatment. If we can show that the medical practitioner's belief about the course of treatment was responsibly produced, we have evidence that the medical practitioner did not recklessly endanger the patient.

This chapter argues that epistemic responsibility, at least as necessary for knowledge, requires that the agent become sensitive to the reliability of her belief-forming process. I argue that such a sensitivity can operate even during seamless uses of technology. Some virtue reliabilists defend such an account of epistemic responsibility by linking it with an account of cognitive integration. Cognitive integration explains how an agent's new belief-forming process (of employing an AI, say) becomes a cognitive ability (or skill) and a part of the agent's cognitive system. With the virtue reliabilist's integration-centred account of epistemic responsibility, I show how an agent can responsibly use technology even when relying on it seamlessly.

In keeping with the scope of this collection, I illustrate my discussion by referring to an example of a medical military context technology. In particular, I spotlight how medical practitioners employ AI systems to help with medical triages. A triage is a decision medical practitioners take to prioritise patient care based on injury, illness, severity, resource availability, and so on. *Triage decision support systems* implement algorithms that can help practitioners process a lot more information faster and, by doing so, help with making better triage decisions.[1]

Overall, the first goal of this chapter is to understand how we epistemically responsibly form beliefs with AI systems when we rely on them seamlessly. The second goal consists of applying these findings to cases involving military medical practitioners who seamlessly employ triage decision support systems.

The structure of this chapter is as follows: Sect. 10.2 discusses why the seamless use of AI technology raises important questions, Sect. 10.3 introduces seamlessness and how I intend to use the term, and Sect. 10.4 outlines epistemic responsibility and why epistemologists care for it. Section 10.5 elaborates on how an agent integrates a new belief-forming process and, hence, learns to use it responsibly even when employing it seamlessly. Section 10.6 concludes this chapter.

10.2 Significance

Sometimes we carefully and reflectively employ technology. In these cases, it's often clear that we are using technology responsibly because of the various methods we deploy. For example, carefully employing an instrument in a laboratory may involve reflecting on how to use it properly, what makes it reliable, and so on. Often, we employ *new* technologies carefully as we learn about how the technology

[1] See Molineaux et al. (2024) for more on triage decision support systems.

functions and how to use it properly. All these ways of responsibly employing technology require attention and careful deliberation. Here, attention, reflection, deliberation, and so on allow us to responsibly employ technologies.

In contrast, when we depend on an artefact seamlessly, we do not pay attention to it or how we use it. Often, we learn to rely on technologies seamlessly when we use them frequently over a period. Some technologies may be wearable or implantable, and so we may learn to rely on them seamlessly quite quickly. To use technology seamlessly doesn't require that the resource must never come to our attention. It simply means that we usually use it or we are disposed to employ the technology without paying attention to it or how we are using it.

For instance, while typing these words, I don't have to look at the keys on my keyboard. I don't reflect on where a certain letter key is situated and if I am pressing the right one. Similarly, when I have to look up a reference, my fingers automatically swipe the keyboard to submit a search in my browser. Looking up references is a crucial part of my writing and thinking process, and I have to perform this task several times a day. While I am consciously and deliberately reflecting on this task in the moment, I usually perform these actions seamlessly and without thinking about them. Similarly, I seamlessly scroll, click, and open a map app to get to 53rd Street. I form the belief that the building I need to reach is on 53rd Street. In all of these seamless, automatic tasks that I perform throughout the day, it isn't clear which practices of epistemic responsibility I deploy. How do I form these beliefs epistemically responsibly?

Another reason for this study is the peculiar nature of AI systems. For one, these systems are autonomous and self-learning, and some can set their own goals. They can also process a lot more information than their users and designers. In addition, most of these systems are epistemically opaque. That opacity doesn't seem to detract from their usefulness, and users still flock to them in droves. In many ways, AI technologies are like calculators—simply helping us in our cognitive tasks—but in other ways, they are akin to having a friend or collaborator who helps us accomplish our tasks. Hence, forming beliefs with these systems can be construed as forming beliefs with a mundane sort of tool (such as a calculator) or receiving testimony from an expert. These characteristics make AI systems epistemically salient as well as disconcerting.

Our cognitive systems are designed to automate oft-repeated cognitive tasks so we can focus our conscious attention on the tasks that demand it. A chess champion, for instance, has to think less deeply about the different moves she can make with a Queen compared to someone who is just learning to play the game. Because of this phenomenon, when we use certain tools frequently to perform a cognitive task, our use of them becomes more fluent and seamless as our cognitive systems automate the task. For instance, contrast how an accountant employs a calculator compared to a child. Or consider how some of us use computers to write, think, look up facts, and much more, and compare such people to those who have only used a computer once or twice in their lives. The tools we use fairly regularly become fluent, effortless, automatic, and seamless for us.

With AI systems permeating more and more areas of our lives, we'll likely depend on these systems to perform more and more cognitive tasks. Cognitive activities such as writing, thinking, planning, deciding, and so forth are all likely to involve AI systems in the future. The seamless use of AI technologies is therefore likely to become a common feature of our everyday lives, making the question of how to use them in an *epistemically responsible* fashion ever more important.

The clear usefulness of AI systems may be even more important in a military medical setting. Medical professionals in an emergency health centre have to make triage decisions in an extremely stressful and high-stakes environment to best allocate medical resources to the patients. Many of these professionals use charts and logs and distribute tasks amongst the team to better manage and responsibly make triage decisions. These professionals decide who should receive health care first, who is most likely to survive, etc. In the context of a war zone, such a decision may even have to be taken when enemy fire endangers the professional's very life. It makes sense for these medical practitioners to employ triage decision support systems. Such decision support systems can help medical practitioners make better decisions faster (at least based on much more information processing). Moreover, as time is of the essence in this context, there is an even stronger pressure to design these systems to be used with as little conscious processing as possible, making the question of their epistemically responsible seamless use even more pressing.

10.3 Seamlessness

Let me begin by giving an overview of what I mean by employing technology seamlessly. First of all, I want my characterisation of the seamless use of technology to be relatively general to not exclude relevant phenomena by fiat. Hence, and roughly speaking, we employ technology seamlessly when we recruit it without paying direct attention to it or our use of it. This is often due to us having employed the technology frequently over some time, so that the artefact has become invisible to us and its use has become incorporated as a new skill. Especially in cases where employing an artefact helps us regularly fulfil an important cognitive task, our reliance on it becomes seamless, and employing the artefact becomes our cognitive skill. A fitting example of the seamless reliance on technology is how we automatically and effortlessly reach for our phones when we need to get somewhere in a new city. Our hands tap the phone screen and bring up the maps app without us paying attention to what we are doing.

Recent philosophical literature describes the seamless use of technological artefacts in terms of embedded and extended cognition (Clark and Chalmers 1998; Clark 2008b; Pritchard 2018). The embedded cognition theory postulates that our cognitive processes rely in an especially significant way on the resources in our environment. Rob Rupert writes that according to the thesis of embedded cognition, "cognitive processes depend very heavily, in hitherto unexpected ways, on organismically external props and devices and on the structure of the external environment in which cognition takes place." (Rupert 2004, 393). The extended cognition thesis postulates an even stronger and more active dependence of our cognition on technology. According to the extended cognition theory, we sometimes depend on technological artefacts in a way that extends our cognitive processes outwith our skin and skull boundary, so that part of our cognitive process occurs in the artefact. One of the major differences between these two accounts is that extension requires a coupling between the artefact and the agent, whereas embedded cases only require a heavy reliance on the artefact for cognitive tasks.

Clark employs the concept of *seamless technology* to motivate the theory of extended cognition (2008a). He understands seamless technology as technology that easily inserts itself into our everyday lives in a way that makes our use of it fluent and effortless. His main argument for the link between seamless technology and extended cognition is that while the information contained in clunky technologies isn't easily accessible, seamless technologies can readily meet this constraint. Seamless technologies are therefore more likely to meet the conditions required for cognitive extension.

Duncan Pritchard (2018) uses the term "seamless" for technology that is used in the sort of fluent way we command our biological cognitive mechanisms. He writes, "...information-processing technology that is so seamlessly integrated with our on-board cognitive processes that the subject is often unable to distinguish between her use of those on-board processes and the technology itself" (2018, 329). His aim, like Clark's, is to motivate the extended cognition theory (and also to push for an extended knowledge theory). The main idea here is that when we employ external resources as seamlessly as we rely on our biological cognitive faculties, our cognition extends with these resources.[2]

However, there is very little agreement regarding when a given case of technology use qualifies as one of extension or embeddedness. Some philosophers maintain that it is not easy—or even possible—to tell the extended cognition and embedded cases apart (Heersmink 2018; Cassinadri 2024). We can empirically establish that cognition heavily depends on external resources (such as technologies), but there is no consensus on the kind of coupling that is sufficient for cognitive extension. Since demarcating cases of embedded and extended cognition is problematic, and since we can observe the seamless use of technology in both kinds of cases, I will focus on seamlessness instead of embedded or extended cognition.

Another way to understand seamlessness is with the concept of *phenomenal transparency*, but I find this concept also unjustifiably restrictive. It risks excluding certain cases that deserve to be looked at under the heading of the seamless use of technology. Heidegger (1976) illustrates phenomenal transparency, or what he calls 'ready at hand', by drawing attention to how an expert carpenter uses her hammer. While a novice carpenter carefully attends to the hammer and how it hits the nail, for the expert carpenter, the hammer disappears as a thing to attend to. She can focus

[2] The idea that when we employ the external resource the same way we employ our biological faculties then we observe cognitive extension is often called the *parity principle*. See, Sutton (2010) for a discussion on the parity principle.

on the nail and how she wants it to join the two pieces without consciously considering the hammer and how to move it. This disappearance of the object as an object—and our experience of the object as a part of our body—is called phenomenal transparency.[3]

However, there is disagreement about the relevance of phenomenal transparency in determining whether we incorporate a new skill when employing some technology. Some argue that phenomenal transparency is required, while others caution against it (Clark 2008b; Wheeler 2022; Sutton et al. 2011; Andrada 2020; Farina and Lavazza 2022; Hauser and Naeem forthcoming). This is another reason why I focus on the more general notion of the seamless use of technology.

Consider the seamless reliance on technology in the military medical context. Medical professionals who use triage support systems regularly and over extended periods are likely to learn to use them seamlessly. Now, we could ask whether these are cases of extended or embedded cases: are these medical professionals cognising in ways that merely depend on technology, or do they extend to the triage systems? But doing so gets us mired in theoretical matters that distract us from our goal, which is, after all, the investigation of epistemic responsibility practices in cases where we use technology in a fluid way and without paying direct attention to them. Similarly, we could ask whether these are cases of transparency—that is, whether the medical professions stop consciously apprehending the triage support systems as objects. But even if we found a way to settle this, it's not clear why, just because they do consciously apprehend them in some manner, their seamless use isn't problematic in the manner discussed in the previous section. It is, hence, more fruitful to focus on the notion of seamlessness directly.

To sum up, the discussion so far, understanding epistemic responsibility in cases where we seamlessly use artefacts is crucial because it's not clear what measures an agent takes to make sure that she is employing her process responsibly when she is not thinking about the resource or how she is using it. AI technologies bring their own problems, and it seems even more disconcerting to employ them seamlessly. To deal with the various ways we depend on technologies seamlessly, I outline seamlessness broadly. Let's turn to how the epistemic responsibility accounts present to us, and which of these helps us make sense of responsibility in seamless cases.

10.4 Epistemic Responsibility

Before exploring epistemic responsibility in cases where we depend on technology seamlessly, I first describe epistemic responsibility *simpliciter* and its significance in epistemology. This section then details why epistemic responsibility is necessary for knowledge and what kind of responsibility would work in seamless cases.

[3] Merleau-Ponty's and Landes' blind man and his cane exemplify a similar phenomenon (Merleau-Ponty and Landes 2012).

The discourse in epistemology once revolved around a kind of epistemic deontology. The main idea was that epistemic agents ought to fulfil important epistemic duties, and these duties were intertwined with the concept of justification (Greco 1990). Epistemologists were concerned with how agents ought to have good reasons for their beliefs. For instance, if I check my watch and it shows 5 pm, then I have a good reason to form the belief that it is 5 pm, and since I have this good reason, I am responsibly forming the belief that it is 5 pm. If I were to form the belief that it is 5 pm simply because of wishful thinking, then I would be forming a belief without a good reason, and the belief would be irresponsibly formed.

Note that not all true beliefs are responsibly formed. I might wishfully form the belief that it is 5 pm when it happens to be 5 pm. In this case, I form a true belief but not one that is responsibly produced. The truth of my belief is a mere accident; it is a matter of luck. A responsibly formed belief is not just accidentally true.

Why should we care about responsibly formed beliefs? Shouldn't true beliefs be sufficient? The consensus in epistemology is that knowledge is more valuable than true belief. True belief can be a lucky accident, but knowledge isn't. An agent who knows, rather than merely holds true beliefs, can depend on her beliefs providing her with a grasp on the world. In other words, were the state of the world different, her beliefs would change so that they track what's actually the case.

Are good reasons sufficient for responsibly forming true beliefs and therefore acquiring knowledge? Yes. Sometimes, good reasons are all we need to responsibly form true beliefs. However, our beliefs are not always in our control in this way, and we do not form all beliefs based on reason. Also, note that the subject of this chapter is the beliefs we form by seamlessly relying on technology. We form such beliefs without conscious and reflective effort. Moreover, belief formation of this sort is not unique to the seamless use of technology—we form many, if not most, of our beliefs in this non-reflective way. For instance, consider how our perceptual beliefs happen to us (so to speak). When we look at a tree, we automatically believe that there is a tree. Reasons seem to have no import here. Similarly, we form testimonial beliefs based on what others tell us or what we read in a book and often don't ask for reasons or look for reasons.[4]

Reliabilism attempts to offer a solution. According to reliabilists, knowledge requires reliably produced true beliefs, and whether the agent is aware that her belief is reliably produced or not is not relevant. A reliably produced belief is produced by a source that can produce a higher ratio of true beliefs than false Goldberg (2010). At first, the reliabilist solution seems to meet the minimal responsibility requirement for knowledge. The main idea is that reliable belief-forming mechanisms do not accidentally or luckily produce true beliefs; they consistently, and therefore responsibly (so to speak), produce true beliefs. Therefore, reliabilists maintain that our biological cognitive faculties, such as perception and memory, help us acquire knowledge because these are reliable belief-forming processes.

[4] I have simplified the debate about internalism and externalism about justification and presented it in my own words and without referring to these notions explicitly. For a more detailed description of these ideas, refer to Greco (1990); Alston (1986); BonJour (1988).

However, at a closer look, mere reliabilism (also called 'process reliabilism') fails to properly capture epistemic responsibility. Let me illustrate this failure with an example. Temp forms beliefs about the ambient temperature by looking at a thermometer on his living room wall.[5] His process of using the thermometer to form beliefs is reliable. However, one unfortunate day, Temp's thermometer breaks, and he fails to notice it. Luckily, and unbeknownst to Temp, an invisible genie takes it upon himself to help Temp out. Whenever Temp checks his thermometer to form a belief about ambient temperatures, the genie fixes the thermostat to match the thermometer reading. Hence, while Temp's thermometer is broken, his overall belief-forming process is still reliable. Reading the thermometer gives him far more true beliefs than false ones. However, is Temp forming beliefs in an epistemically responsible manner?

The consensus is that Temp doesn't know as his beliefs aren't responsibly formed. While his beliefs are true in a non-accidental and non-lucky way, they are still not in the running for knowledge. The reason for this is that Temp seems to be missing a connection to the reliability of the source of his beliefs. This is the reason Temp's beliefs aren't responsibly formed. If the genie were to take a vacation, Temp would go on to form beliefs in the same way, and his beliefs would turn out false.

With the Temp case, we have a clearer picture of the kind of epistemic responsibility we are looking for. It seems that the agent must have some connection to the reliability of her process, and as the Temp case shows, when this is missing, knowledge is missing. However, we cannot demand that the agent always have reflective access to the reliability of her process because, as I noted earlier, we form many of our beliefs in an unreflective and automatic way. Also, the responsibility account that requires us to be vigilant of our process's reliability cannot help us make sense of seamless cases. We know, therefore, that the agent must be connected to the reliability of her belief-forming processes, but not in an overly demanding way. She must be sensitive to her process's reliability, but she does not need to reflect on reliability to use the process responsibly.

Virtue reliabilism (Greco 1999, 2010; Pritchard 2010) presents an account that makes sense of the way an agent ought to be sensitive to the reliability of her process. In general, virtue epistemologists argue that we acquire knowledge by manifesting virtue. For virtue reliabilists, such virtues are mainly our cognitive faculties, such as memory, perception, and so on, and since these faculties are well-integrated (discussed in more detail in the next section) into our cognitive systems, we can manifest cognitive ability when we employ them. Virtue reliabilism is different from process reliabilism, in that she does not just need a reliable faculty but manifest ability when employing such a faculty. When perceiving (employing our reliable faculty of perception), an agent can manifest cognitive ability because it is an integrated disposition of her cognitive system. She is connected to the reliability of

[5] Temp is a version of Lehrer's Mr TrueTemp (Lehrer 1990). See Pritchard (2010) and Palermos (2011) for a more thorough discussion on Temp, specifically related to extended cognition of Temp's belief-forming process.

her faculty in the right way. Our internal biological faculties, however, are not the only cognitive abilities we have.

We can acquire new cognitive abilities by connecting to new, reliable belief-forming processes (such as forming beliefs with an AI system) in the required way.[6] For example, Temp's genie-mediated reliable process can become Temp's cognitive ability if Temp employs it frequently and integrates the cognitive ability (to form beliefs about ambient temperature with his process). Such an integration will provide him with a sensitivity to the reliability of his process. I will explore the details of this proposal in the next section—for now, let's explore the notion of sensitivity to the reliability of a belief-forming process.

Virtue reliabilism establishes an appropriate connection between the agent and her process's reliability. It doesn't require that the agent is always aware that her process is reliable (which helps us understand seamless cases), but the virtue reliabilist account does require that there is some connection to the reliability (unlike process reliabilism). An agent can responsibly employ her process if she is (in some way) sensitive to her process's reliability. More specifically, the idea is that the agent uses the process for a significant period, and in this period, she becomes counterfactually sensitive to her process's reliability. This means that she comes to be in a position where, if the process were to stop being reliable, she would become aware that something is amiss. All in all, then, Temp's reliable genie-mediated process can become a cognitive ability when Temp is in a position where, if his genie-mediated belief-forming process were to turn unreliable, he would notice that something is wrong.

When an agent becomes counterfactually sensitive to a new belief-forming process (using an AI to form beliefs, for instance), she can epistemically responsibly employ the said process. In this way, epistemic agents acquire new cognitive abilities (or knowledge-conducive belief-forming processes) (Pritchard 2010, 2012). These abilities may be skills of employing new technologies, new habits of thought, and so on. When an agent becomes sensitive to these processes' reliabilities, they become knowledge-conducive abilities integrated into the agent's cognitive system.

Virtue reliabilism therefore has a solution to how medical practitioners can learn to epistemically responsibly use triage support systems even when they seamlessly rely on these AI technologies. What is required of medical practitioners is that they become counterfactually sensitive to the reliability of their belief-forming processes. The next section unpacks how a medical practitioner can come to be in such a desired relation to her belief-forming process.

---

[6]Greco (1999) explains how our biological cognitive abilities as well as our acquired habits of thoughts make up our cognitive character. In Greco's words, "...knowledge and justified belief are grounded in stable and reliable cognitive character. Such character may include both a person's natural cognitive faculties as well as her acquired habits of thought. Accordingly, innate vision gives rise to knowledge if it is reliably accurate. But so can acquire skills of perception and acquired methods of inquiry, including those involving highly specialized training or even advanced technology. So long as such habits are both stable and successful, they make up the kind of character that gives rise to knowledge." (Greco 1999, 287)

The *cognitive ability* account is a minimal account of the epistemic responsibility required for knowledge.[7] When an agent becomes sensitive to her process's reliability, she can learn to responsibly employ it to potentially generate knowledge with the said process. However, just because a minimal account of epistemic responsibility is possible, we shouldn't dismiss the benefits stemming from more reflective kinds of connection to the reliability of one's processes. While responsibility and knowledge are possible in cases where agents rely on technologies seamlessly, these don't make for ideal responsibility cases. To be in a better position to generate knowledge, the agent may carefully employ her process while reflecting on its reliability. This means that, preferably, medical practitioners ought to understand how triage support systems work and what makes them reliable. To make sure that they use these AI technologies epistemically responsibly, medical practitioners should employ these AI systems while reflecting on their reliability.

Most people, however, do not employ technologies while constantly reflecting on the reliabilities of these technologies. In most cases, users of technology will become familiar with how the technology works and learn to employ it seamlessly. In these cases, they can form beliefs responsibly, and their beliefs may be in the running for knowledge if they are counterfactually sensitive to the reliability of their processes. In what follows, I explicate more thoroughly how an agent becomes counterfactually sensitive to her process's reliability and how we can influence the responsible seamless employment of technology.

10.5 Cognitive Integration

As we've seen in the previous section, the virtue reliabilist account of epistemic responsibility requires that an agent become counterfactually sensitive to the process's reliability. I have not yet explained how this happens. The one-liner is that for an agent to become sensitive to her process's reliability, her process ought to integrate into her cognitive system. In this section, I unpack the concept of cognitive integration and how virtue reliabilists use it. Understanding integration will give us an idea of what we can do to promote an epistemically responsible and seamless use of technology.

[7] I have one more important reason for not limiting the seamless use of technology in terms of the extended cognition theory. Clark (2015) argues that extension and epistemic responsibility are in tension. Extension requires a very strong kind of seamlessness. Virtue reliabilists think that the agent can responsibly employ a process if she is counterfactually sensitive to the process's reliability. Clark finds this account of responsibility demanding and inconsistent with cognitive extension. He argues that only a subpersonal epistemic responsibility is consistent with using technology seamlessly in cases of extended cognition. On this account, a subpersonal cognitive mechanism (specifically, the precision estimation function of the predictive brain model) makes sure that the agent employs a reliable process (or learns to subpersonally reject it over time). I am not on board with this analysis and also feel that seamless use of technology may or may not be an extended cognition case.

Cognitive integration is the "function of cooperation and interaction" within the agent's cognitive system (Greco 2010, 152). A new process integrates into the agent's cognitive system when it has made the necessary interconnections with existing processes and beliefs in her cognitive system. These cooperations and interactions occur at the level of processes as well as beliefs. The beliefs that the agent forms with the new process (of, say, employing an AI system) must cohere with her existing beliefs, and the new process needs to cooperate with existing processes. In sum, cognitive integration is a function of cooperation and interaction of beliefs and processes.

Such cooperative interactions allow the agent to become sensitive to the reliability of her process. Here is how: As described above, newly formed beliefs cohere with pre-existing beliefs, and the new process interacts with pre-existing processes. The new beliefs also become input for existing processes, which in turn form more beliefs, and in this way, the cognitive loops continue forward. When these interactions reach a high degree of interconnectedness, the cognitive system can monitor (so to speak) the reliability of the new process. The high degree of interconnectedness allows the cognitive system to alert the agent when the integrated process turns unreliable. In other words, the agent is alerted if her integrated process turns unreliable.

There is both a reflective and non-reflective route to interaction,[8] and both can result in responsible and seamless employment of technology. Let's start with the non-reflective route. Imagine Temp's genie-mediated process of forming beliefs about temperatures is implemented in a microchip that is implanted in his brain. He's in a coma when the doctors implant this device, and they do not tell him about the surgery.[9] Temp may come to rely on his new process of forming beliefs. If this process is reliable and he employs it for a significantly long time, it may integrate into his cognitive system: With his new device, Temp forms various beliefs that cohere with his existing beliefs, and his new process heavily interacts with existing processes, forming various interconnections. If such a high degree of interconnection is established, Temp becomes counterfactually sensitive to the reliability of the new process. His new process is now integrated and, hence, has become a cognitive ability that Temp can employ responsibly.

Of course, it's unlikely that doctors implant devices in our heads and forget to tell us about them. Typically, we have at least heard of the technologies we learn to seamlessly rely on. We also live in societies where our family, friends, and many others use the same technologies, and in one way or another, we usually hear about the technologies we employ. Many of us purchase the technologies we like after looking them up on the internet and reading about them. Moreover, once we acquire some technology, we tend to begin by interacting with it carefully and consciously. Therefore, while a non-reflective route to integration is possible, we integrate most

[8] See Naeem and Hauser (2024) for a more detailed account of these routes to integration.

[9] This variation of the Temp case is from Pritchard (2010).

of our belief-forming processes via the reflective route to integration. In short, the reflective route to integration is more common.

At first glance, we may think that the reflective route is inconsistent with the seamless use of technology. However, the result of the reflective route, just like the non-reflective route, is integration. That is, the newly acquired belief-forming process has formed a high degree of interconnection with existing processes in the agent's cognitive system. On the reflective route, the agent at first attends to the resource, understands how it works, what makes it useful, and if it is reliable, etc. Once she has employed the process for a long time and formed many beliefs about it, it becomes her integrated cognitive ability. She can then responsibly employ it and generate knowledge with it. In short, the reflective route, just like the non-reflective route we looked at above, leads to integration, and once the belief-forming process is integrated, the agent can use the process responsibly even when relying on it seamlessly. Imagine, for instance, that Temp's doctor tells Temp that they have implanted a chip in his brain. They also tell him how the chip works, what makes it reliable, how to make sure that it runs reliably, and so forth. Temp then frequently employs this new process (of forming beliefs with an implant) for some time, and it integrates into his cognitive system as a new cognitive ability. He can learn to responsibly employ his integrated process, even when he uses it seamlessly.

Consider another example: a scientist thoroughly understands how her laboratory instrument functions, what makes it reliable, how to check if it's not working optimally, and so on. If she works with her instrument every day for years and takes hundreds of readings with it, she is likely to stop reflecting on the reliability of her process or the way she is using her device. Even if she understands her device, the scientist learns to rely on it seamlessly. Her process (of using her instrument to form beliefs) has integrated into her cognitive system and become a cognitive ability for her.

On the reflective route to integration, our acquired processes can integrate faster. The reason is simple: when you have reflective knowledge about the workings of the technology, you already know something about when the technology is likely to go astray. This knowledge can help you develop the sort of counterfactual sensitivity that also operates while you employ it seamlessly. On the non-reflective route, you start from scratch, so to speak. You do not have any pre-existing knowledge that can guide your seamless interaction with the technology, and instead, you will have to learn through trial and error. This is likely to take substantially more time. Simply put, while you may learn to responsibly use a reliable process even if you don't carefully pay attention, it can integrate faster if you, at least at first, use it carefully. This means that (1) Temp can integrate his process even when his doctors forget to tell him that they implanted a device in his head. Also, (2) his process can integrate much faster if they tell him about the device in his head, how it works, and how to spot problems with it.[10]

[10] For a more thorough analysis, look at Naeem and Hauser (2024), who give an account of this in terms of *epistemic defeaters*.

We are now in a position to see the road ahead. The responsible seamless use of technology requires cognitive integration, and such integration can be achieved through a reflective or non-reflective route. The goal is to travel along the routes quickly (see Naeem and Hauser 2024). As I've pointed out, the reflective route tends to be faster than the non-reflective route, and this is because agents embark on it with some prior knowledge about the technology. Thus, the recommendation is simple: find ways to provide agents with more knowledge that can help them detect when the AI becomes unreliable. This is easier said than done, given the famous blackboxness of such technologies. Note, however, that there are specific ways that AI systems fail and teaching practitioners to detect these is therefore an important first step.

We can also learn from the non-reflective route. This route relies entirely on the agent developing a feel for when the technology becomes unreliable. Now, if AI systems were better at communicating their own uncertainty to users, integration could happen much more quickly. We ought to combine user interface research with an in-depth understanding of AI to make progress on this front.

10.6 Conclusion

In this essay, I discuss how we can epistemically responsibly form beliefs with technology even when we rely on it seamlessly. If our belief-forming process is reliable and we are counterfactually sensitive to its reliability, we can employ it responsibly even when using it seamlessly. The chapter illustrates the significance of epistemic responsibility and the minimal responsibility required for knowledge. I have also shown how meeting this requirement allows the agent to employ her process responsibly, even when she uses the technology seamlessly.

An agent can become counterfactually sensitive to the reliability of her process via either the reflective or the non-reflective route. An agent can learn responsible belief formation through the non-reflective route, but she must form beliefs with her process regularly for a long time. On the reflective route, the agent's process can integrate faster, but she ought to start with knowledge about her process and what makes it reliable. She needs sufficient information about the process so that even a short period of use makes her counterfactually sensitive to its reliability.

I recommend we use the reflective route to integrate AI systems so we can learn to use such systems responsibly as soon as possible. To this end, one obvious recommendation is to train users and help them understand AI systems better. But we can also learn from the non-reflective route. For instance, engineers ought to design AI systems so the systems can communicate their confidence to the users, helping them become sensitive to the AI systems' reliabilities more easily. These measures can help us use AI systems responsibly when we employ them seamlessly.

The subject here was the minimal epistemic responsibility required for knowledge (in seamless cases). I outlined how an agent's reliable belief-forming process becomes a knowledge-conducive cognitive ability and that when this is the case, an agent can responsibly use technology seamlessly. This doesn't exhaust the subject of forming beliefs responsibly (with technology). Understanding how to responsibly form beliefs with AI systems is a much broader project with some of the following important considerations: First, knowledge is just one of the epistemic goals and not the only goal worth pursuing. We must also consider how epistemic agents acquire *understanding* when using an AI, how they pursue a *good inquiry*, and so forth. Second, this opens up the topic of intellectual virtues as a means to epistemic responsibility. For instance, an agent may be epistemically responsible because she is open-minded, curious, and creative. While she employs her resources seamlessly, she may manifest virtuous character traits that allow her to form beliefs responsibly, understand ideas, pursue inquiries, and so on. Third, people have epistemic responsibilities or duties based on their social roles. For instance, doctors must know the newest scientific developments in their fields and guide patients accordingly. Medical professionals using triage support systems should stay updated on the latest advancements in triage support algorithms and their limitations.

With this chapter, I hope to have given a decent start to the topic. As previously mentioned, there is much more to learn about responsibly forming beliefs using AI tools. Furthermore, there is an additional layer to explore regarding how to responsibly collaborate with AI as quasi-agents.

References

Alston, William P. 1986. Internalism and Externalism in Epistemology. *Philosophical Topics* 14 (1): 179–221. https://doi.org/10.5840/philtopics198614118.

Andrada, Gloria. 2020. Transparency and the Phenomenology of Extended Cognition. *Límite: Revista de Filosofía y Psicología* 15:1–17.

BonJour, Laurence. 1988. *The Structure of Empirical Knowledge*. Cambridge, MA: Harvard University Press.

Cassinadri, Guido. 2024. ChatGPT and the Technology-Education Tension: Applying Contextual Virtue Epistemology to a Cognitive Artifact. *Philosophy & Technology* 37:14. https://doi.org/10.1007/s13347-024-00701-7.

Champagne, Marc, and Ryan Tonkens. 2015. Bridging the Responsibility Gap in Automated Warfare. *Philosophy & Technology* 28 (1): 125–137. https://doi.org/10.1007/s13347-013-0138-3.

Clark, Andy. 2008a. *Supersizing the Mind: Embodiment, Action, and Cognitive Extension*, Philosophy of Mind. Oxford: Oxford University Press.

Clark, Andy. 2008b. Pressing the Flesh: A Tension in the Study of the Embodied, Embedded Mind? *Philosophy and Phenomenological Research* 76 (1): 37–59. https://doi.org/10.1111/j.1933-1592.2007.00114.x.

Clark, Andy. 2015. What 'Extended Me' Knows. *Synthese* 192 (11): 3757–3775. https://doi.org/10.1007/s11229-015-0719-z.

Clark, Andy, and David Chalmers. 1998. The Extended Mind. *Analysis* 58 (1): 7–19. https://www.jstor.org/stable/3328150.

Farina, Mirko, and Andrea Lavazza. 2022. Incorporation, Transparency and Cognitive Extension: Why the Distinction Between Embedded and Extended Might Be More Important to Ethics Than to Metaphysics. *Philosophy & Technology* 35 (1): 10. https://doi.org/10.1007/s13347-022-00508-4.

Goldberg, Sanford C. 2010. *Relying on Others: An Essay in Epistemology*. Oxford: Oxford University Press.
Greco, John. 1990. Internalism and Epistemically Responsible Belief. *Synthese* 85 (2): 245–277. https://doi.org/10.1007/BF00484794.
Greco, John. 1999. Agent Reliabilism. *Nous* 33 (s13): 273–296. https://doi.org/10.1111/0029-4624.33.s13.13.
Greco, John. 2010. *Achieving Knowledge: A Virtue-Theoretic Account of Epistemic Normativity*. Cambridge: Cambridge University Press.
Hauser, J., Naeem, H. Phenomenal transparency and the boundary of cognition. Phenom Cogn Sci (2024). https://doi.org/10.1007/s11097-024-10025-8
Heersmink, Richard. 2018. The Narrative Self, Distributed Memory, and Evocative Objects. *Philosophical Studies* 175 (8): 1829–1849. https://doi.org/10.1007/s11098-017-0935-0.
Heidegger, Martin. 1976. *Sein und Zeit*. 13. unveränd. Aufl. Tübingen: Niemeyer.
Himmelreich, Johannes. 2019. Responsibility for Killer Robots. *Ethical Theory and Moral Practice* 22 (3): 731–747. https://doi.org/10.1007/s10677-019-10007-9.
Königs, Peter. 2022. Artificial Intelligence and Responsibility Gaps: What Is the Problem? *Ethics and Information Technology* 24 (3): 36. https://doi.org/10.1007/s10676-022-09643-0.
Lehrer, Keith. 1990. *Theory of Knowledge*. London: Westview Press.
Matthias, Andreas. 2004. The Responsibility Gap: Ascribing Responsibility for the Actions of Learning Automata. *Ethics and Information Technology* 6 (3): 175–183. https://doi.org/10.1007/s10676-004-3422-1.
Merleau-Ponty, Maurice, and Donald A. Landes. 2012. *Phenomenology of Perception*. Abingdon: Routledge.
Molineaux, Matthew, Rosina O. Weber, Michael W. Floyd, David Menager, Othalia Larue, Ursula Addison, Ray Kulhanek, et al. 2024. Aligning to Human Decision-Makers in Military Medical Triage. In *Case-Based Reasoning Research and Development*, ed. Juan A. Recio-Garcia, Mauricio G. Orozco-del-Castillo, and Derek Bridge, 371–387. Cham: Springer. https://doi.org/10.1007/978-3-031-63646-2_24.
Naeem, Hadeel, and Julian Hauser. 2024. Should We Discourage AI Extension? Epistemic Responsibility and AI. *Philosophy & Technology* 37 (3): 91. https://doi.org/10.1007/s13347-024-00774-4.
Palermos, Spyridon Orestis. 2011. Belief-Forming Processes. *Extended. Review of Philosophy and Psychology* 2 (4): 741–765. https://doi.org/10.1007/s13164-011-0075-y.
Pritchard, Duncan. 2010. Cognitive Ability and the Extended Cognition Thesis. *Synthese* 175 (S1): 133–151. https://doi.org/10.1007/s11229-010-9738-y.
Pritchard, Duncan. 2012. Anti-Luck Virtue Epistemology. *The Journal of Philosophy* 109 (3): 247–279. https://www.jstor.org/stable/43820700.
Pritchard, Duncan. 2018. Neuromedia and the Epistemology of Education. *Metaphilosophy* 49 (3): 328–349. https://doi.org/10.1111/meta.12295.
Rupert, Robert D. 2004. Challenges to the Hypothesis of Extended Cognition. *The Journal of Philosophy* 101 (8): 389–428. https://www.jstor.org/stable/3655517.
Sutton, John. 2010. Exograms and Interdisciplinarity: History, the Extended Mind, and the Civilizing Process. In *The Extended Mind*, ed. Richard Menary, 189–225. Cambridge, MA: MIT Press. https://doi.org/10.7551/mitpress/9780262014038.003.0009.
Sutton, John, Doris McIlwain, Wayne Christensen, and Andrew Geeves. 2011. Applying Intelligence to the Reflexes: Embodied Skills and Habits Between Dreyfus and Descartes. *Journal of the British Society for Phenomenology* 42 (1): 78–103. https://doi.org/10.1080/00071773.2011.11006732.
Wheeler, M. 2022. Entre la transparence et l'intrusion des machines intelligente (Between Transparency and Intrusion in Smart Machines). In *Intelligence artificielle. Que faire de la transparence technique?* ed. T. Reigeluth and S. Benlaksira, 13–30. Special issue of Pistes. Revue de philosophie contemporaine.

Hadeel Naeem is a research fellow at PAIR (Centre for Philosophy and AI Research) at the Friedrich-Alexander-Universität Erlangen-Nürnberg, where her research is on how we can responsibly form beliefs with AI systems. She is also a member of the Era-Net Neuron project COMPAIN, which examines AI-based pain assessment tools and their impact on our understanding of pain. Before PAIR, Naeem was a research fellow at the Käte Hamburger Kolleg at RWTH Aachen University and a visiting fellow at Boğaziçi University. She has a PhD in philosophy from the University of Edinburgh.

Part III
Ethics of AI and Big Data in Humanitarian Contexts

The third part of the volume focuses on the ethics of AI and Big Data in humanitarian contexts.

Chapter 11
Humanitarian Healthcare, Digital Infrastructure, and AI: An Ethics Talk Diagnostic

Kristin Bergtora Sandvik

11.1 Introduction

Globally, the health sector continues to undergo rapid digitization. While many ethical issues and challenges related to this digital transformation are common across various professional fields in healthcare and medicine, situations of humanitarian crisis—including armed conflict, natural disasters, and man-made disasters—present specific dilemmas and quandaries with respect to digital tools and infrastructures. This chapter aims to contribute to discussions on humanitarian healthcare ethics by asking: What are the ethical implications of integrating humanitarian healthcare into digital infrastructures? What type of new or additional ethical issues arise with the adoption of new technology, such as artificial intelligence tools? To reflect on these questions, this chapter provides an ethics talk diagnostic. This entails identifying and distinguishing sector-specific discussions from a broader background context.[1]

[1] This chapter is based on a presentation called 'Black Boxes/Blackouts/Blackened Out: Gen-AI And the Implications Of Wrapping Humanitarian Health Care Around Digital Infrastructures' given at the 13th ICMM Workshop on Military Medical Ethics *Artificial Intelligence and Big Data Ethics in Military and Humanitarian Healthcare* 20–22 June 2024 | Hybrid Workshop Jongny, Switzerland, for the panel 'The Ethics of AI and Big Data in Humanitarian Contexts'. The chapter also draws on Sandvik (2025). The research for this chapter was funded by the PRIO strategic initiative KnowingAid led by Maria Gabrielsen Jumbert.

K. B. Sandvik (✉)
Peace Research Institute, Oslo, Norway
e-mail: k.b.sandvik@jus.uio.no

B. Koch, D. Winkler (eds.), *Artificial Intelligence Ethics in Military Medicine and Humanitarian Healthcare*, Military and Humanitarian Health Ethics,
https://doi.org/10.1007/978-3-032-11331-3_11

The background context for this exercise is the interplay between humanitarian space, technology, and ethics. As of 2025, the humanitarian sector is experiencing unprecedented turbulence: longstanding internal discontent about the sector's unfitness for purpose dovetails with loss of funding, public and political support, and a proliferation of violence and emergencies on the ground. Whereas the adoption and adaptation of new digital tools has long been seen as a way for the sector to become more fit for purpose, this digital transformation has also brought many new challenges. Today, ethics remains an important frame for discussions about historical legacies, current ills, and pathways for change, as well as a frame for analyzing technological change in the sector. Within the broader context of the humanitarian system, the field of humanitarian healthcare faces challenges in gaining access to and delivering services to communities in need. The point of departure for this chapter is that discussions in the domain of humanitarian healthcare, including those involving ethics, have different drivers, interests, and objectives than those grappling with the humanitarian sector as such. Furthermore, societal discussions about the ethical problems posed by new technologies overlap with but are not identical to ethics conversations dealing with field-specific challenges in the humanitarian sector, or humanitarian healthcare specifically.

This chapter interrogates how these different debates relate to each other and overlap. It does so by considering how ethical problems and challenges are framed. Frames refer to the construction of meaning and the structuring of issues through images, messages, metaphors, etc. (Goffman 1974). Frames can be diagnostic (identification of a problem), prognostic (articulating a plan/strategy for dealing with the problem), or motivational (creating messages and vocabularies to garner support and get actors and audiences involved) (Benford and Snow 2000). The focus in this chapter will be largely on interrogating diagnostic framing. This entails asking about the assumptions and ideas underpinning the representation of the problem, the relationship between the problem and intended solutions, the calibration of tradeoffs, and the range of stakeholders involved. To undertake an 'ethics talk diagnostic', the chapter examines how issues are problematized in humanitarian action, humanitarian healthcare, technology, and ethics, respectively. Broadly, the methodology of this chapter can be described as one of laying out concentric and overlapping circles to study interrelationships. At the same time, the term 'diagnostic' is a medical term for determining the cause or nature of a problem. The chapter investigates the relationship between humanitarian healthcare ethics and digital transformation by identifying, detecting, and characterizing the attributes of technology-driven ethics issues in these intersecting fields of practice. The following considerations guide the discussion:

- Humanitarian healthcare is not subject to existential criticism. The humanitarian sector is facing foundational questions concerning its nature, purpose, and function. Debates on the ethics of the digital transformation are in part framed around these existential challenges. In comparison, debates on the problems of humanitarian healthcare are more instrumental, focusing on the need to improve services.

- The ethical stakes of humanitarian healthcare are enormously high and unique. As a field of practice, humanitarian healthcare is solely focused on 'saving lives' through providing a critical service. This frequently entails unpredictable contexts of resource scarcity, hostile or absent local/national government actors, or hostile non-state actors, and dealing with vulnerable patients and underserved communities. It may also entail a monopoly on providing health services. These interventions entail highly sector-specific uses of technology and involve distinctive registers of risk and harm.
- The norms governing the digital transformation of aid and humanitarian healthcare are not the same. The normative frameworks of governing health-related humanitarianism intersect with but do not overlap with humanitarian ethics or technology ethics.

The task for this chapter is thus to map out a humanitarian ethics assemblage, allowing us to identify, understand, and characterize the problems arising for humanitarian healthcare as it is being wrapped around digital infrastructure. The chapter aligns with the other chapters in the book in its aim to continue the engagement with academics and practitioners in the humanitarian and military medical ethics field. The concept 'humanitarian healthcare' is used broadly as a descriptive label. For readability by practitioners, the chapter adopts a conversational rather than a formal academic tone. The chapter proceeds in three parts: The first part lays out the humanitarian state of play. The second part focuses on the healthcare aspect. The third part sets out to illustrate some of the problems of the digital transformation of humanitarian healthcare in terms of technofailure, risk, and harm, using the terms 'black box,' 'blackouts,' and blackening out as prisms. A brief conclusion follows.

11.2 Humanitarian State of Play: A Rough Sketch

11.2.1 What Is Wrong with Humanitarianism: 'From Fit for Purpose' to 'Is There a Purpose?'

An influential conceptualization of humanitarian governance sees it as the 'increasingly organized and internationalized attempt to save the lives, enhance the welfare, and reduce the suffering of the world's most vulnerable populations' (Barnett 2013, 379). Focus has been given to the management of risk and order (Dijkzeul and Sandvik 2019), as well as the move towards bureaucratization, professionalization, and specialization —factors that contribute to the top-down nature of aid (Coghlan et al. 2024). Already before 2025, the sector had been shrinking rapidly, shredding jobs, portfolios, legitimacy, and losing political clout. After 30 years of humanitarian accountability discussions (Tanguy and Terry 1999; Dufour et al., 2004; Sandvik and Jacobsen 2016; Hilhorst et al. 2021), a widespread sense of discord had evolved into a strong call for a 'humanitarian reset'. Many commentators disagreed that the sector was savable—or that it should be saved: the question was no longer 'how can humanitarianism be fit for purpose' but 'Can humanitarianism at all, ever, be fit for purpose?' While the upheaval of early 2025 has somewhat shifted the dynamics of these discussions, this more fundamental doubt remains and has implications for how we think about both the role and importance of technology in improving humanitarianism and the potential for ethics to 'save' humanitarianism, including digital humanitarianism from itself.

11.2.2 The Digital Transformation: Adoption, Adaptation, and AI

The context for this chapter is the digital transformation of aid, entailing the adoption and adaption of various technological tools, most recently AI. From the late 2000s, the humanitarian enterprise was characterized by considerable optimism regarding the possibility of improving humanitarian action through new, digital technologies as well as through innovation processes. The expanding toolbox grew to include global connectivity, mobile phones, social media platforms, geospatial technologies, various forms of crowdsourcing, drones, big data, digital cash, biometrics, and the blockchain. Together, they reshaped how humanitarian emergencies are understood and addressed and by whom (Sandvik et al. 2014). These technologies gave rise to discrete mini-literatures focusing on their positive but more often their negative potential impact on aid (Sandvik, 2023; Sandvik et al. 2017). There is a large scholarship critiquing specific types of technology adoption (Sandvik and Lohne 2014), the governance of data (Madianou 2019), and the problematic relationship between humanitarians and market/security actors in the domain of technology (Martin 2023).

Looking back a decade, it seems clear that as the innovation paradigm folded into a generalized engagement with the digital transformation of global society, the focus on tinkering with smaller humanitarian goods gave way to considerations of how humanitarian supply chains integrated into the global data economy. This digital transformation encompasses both tools and systems, involving profound changes in the infrastructure, approaches, and objectives of the sector. The term 'digital transformation' refers to the assimilation of ICTs, which transforms how an organization operates, delivers on its mission, achieves more impact, and with whom it collaborates. This encompasses the digitization and datafication of governance, citizenship, and commercial transactions through the proliferation of digital goods as well as the rapid growth of a sprawling digital infrastructure, conceptualized as 'objects that create the grounds on which other objects operate, and when they do so they operate as systems' (Donovan 2015; Iazzolino 2021; Jacobsen and Sandvik 2018; Sandvik 2017, 2023). A key feature of digital transformation is the continuous flow of data, which enables the systematic monitoring of individuals or groups through personal data systems designed to influence or govern their behavior. The monitoring of digital ecosystems is not only becoming central to aid work—it is increasingly important as aid work in its own right (Sandvik 2023). This transformation broadens the group of stakeholders involved in aid delivery to involve technology startups, established market players, individuals or groups with digital, skills and ordinary citizens mobilized and organized through technology platforms.

Decades in the making, artificial intelligence is the ability of a computer system to imitate human thinking processes for problem-solving purposes. ChatGPT—short for Chatbot Generative Pre-Trained Transformer—by OpenAI was officially released in late 2022. Highly experimental and arriving in an unprepared regulatory landscape, generative AI achieved rapid global uptake. Generative AI uses natural language processing and machine learning methods to mimic human communication. Using AI and machine learning algorithms, generative AI allows users to generate new content—words, images, videos—by giving prompts to the system to create specific outputs. The role and importance of ethics as a way of gauging the impact of AI on humanitarianism has engendered significant interest among agencies and practitioners (McElhinney and Spencer 2024; OCHA 2024; Raftree 2024; Spencer 2024) as well as academic commentators (Pizzi et al. 2020; Coppi et al. 2021; Madianou 2021; Beduschi 2022; Devidal 2024; Jaff 2024; Sandvik 2025). As of 2025, the experimental development of AI continues apace, engendering new ethical and regulatory controversies, with undetermined institutional and operational consequences for the aid sector.

11.2.3 Perspectives on Technology

Setting the stage for a critique of the digital transformation, the chapter maps out key perspectives on technology often referenced in debates in the humanitarian sector. While the most technology-friendly might be inclined to overlook the negative sides of technology, seeing only the negative sides or assuming that everything is just bad might also be ethically problematic. The framing of technology interventions is often characterized by technological solutionism, foregrounding problem framings amenable to technological innovation and intervention and the interests of technology stakeholders (Jasanoff 2004). Discussions on emergent technologies frequently exhibit strong tendencies toward technological determinism. From a deterministic view, the potential and pitfalls of digital goods are inherent within the technology itself. For the technological utopianist, digital goods have inherent and infinite (positive) possibilities and can be a 'game changer' for a raft of problems (or, as above, can *revolutionize* them) — from insecurity to resource inequality and injustice. In the cybersecurity field, *cyber-utopianism* refers to a naïve belief in the emancipatory nature of online communication, along with a refusal to acknowledge any negative impact of the internet on society (Morozov and Docksai 2011). For the extreme sceptics ('the Luddites'), technology is 'bad' (or 'stupid') and will inevitably engender disastrous consequences. Though opposed, both perspectives assume that digital goods will function as planned, without major frictions, malfunctions, security incidents, regulatory stoppages, low uptake, problematic user practices, or commercial problems that will compromise their function or importance. These differences and similarities underpin how technology is perceived, what the problems are, who is responsible and thus also fundamentally shape the approach to ethics (Sandvik 2023).

11.2.4 Ethics as a Tool for Grappling with Tech

In the motivational framing proposed by Hugo Slim, humanitarian ethics can be construed as a powerful language of political persuasion, providing a moral rationale for humanitarian intervention. Taking this framing of ethics as a starting point, this chapter conceives of ethics as a form of soft regulation whereby problems are identified and acknowledged, and normative ways forward are provided. Over the last decade, ethics have become an important way of framing debates on values, tradeoffs, and responsibility in the humanitarian sector, often in the context of discussions of humanitarian accountability (Sandvik 2023).

Why has the engagement with ethics been so relatively intense in the aid sector? This is, of course, partly because the moral infrastructure of the sector—the humanitarian imperatives and principles—are about ethics. However, for the fragmented and transnational aid sector, ethics provide a familiar and legitimate way of taking issues seriously. Ethics has also been a highly useful vehicle for convening stakeholders around conversations about the identification and ranking of critical problems related to digital transformation. Ethics offers a platform for framing and foregrounding values, tradeoffs, and pathways. Ethics are good for problematizing techno solutionism (reducing issues to the question of new tools) but also for grappling with deflationism (introducing false problems) and fatalism (bowing before the intractability of the problem) (Santoni de Sio and Mecacci 2021). Ethics are also useful as we have conversations about the type of risks that might arise and how these risks are pertinent to the specific area of intervention. Ethics help us calibrate and articulate focused critiques of how specific digital tools, including AI, may threaten humanitarian imperatives and principles. Yet, humanitarian ethics talk also serves a different professional function: as noted concerning humanitarian principles, they serve as identity markers and 'interpersonal glue' that provides common purpose and goals for team members (Hilhorst and Schmiemann (2002) cited in Hunt (2011)). Because the topic of this chapter is humanitarian healthcare, it is worth noting the significant difference between ethics as an identity marker and ethics as foundational to professional medical credentials and practice.

What kind of ethics do we discuss? A pared-down notion of humanitarian ethics includes the imperatives of doing no harm and assisting according to need, and principles of humanity, neutrality, universality, impartiality, etc. (see, for example, the International Review of the Red Cross Code of Conduct, ICRC 2018). Yet, concerning the aims of the digital transformation— and the landscape in which this chapter situates itself—ethics discussions also involve digital humanitarian norms, societal AI norms, generalized criticisms of 'ethics washing,' and the codification of technology ethics in hard law (such as the EU AI Act). While the sector seems to have converged around the slightly limp 'do no digital harm' and the need to double down on humanitarian principles and restatements of data responsibility, there has been an enormous amount of 'ethics-crafting' initiatives over the past decades, focusing on humanitarian technology (Sandvik et al. 2014), innovation (Hunt et al. 2019), specific digital tools (Wang 2020) and particular communities of practice. The burgeoning field of societal AI norms is often propelled forward by industry actors and represents soft power industry standard initiatives. The global proliferation of AI ethics initiatives that preceded the first drafts of the EU AI Act culminated in a critique of 'ethics washing' where criticism was given to what is a structural deficit yet also a source of freedom: ethics frameworks lack sanctions and implementation tools (Wagner 2018). This type of critique has been rendered somewhat moot by the adoption, in 2024, of two foundational international legal instruments: the EU AI Act and the Council of Europe Framework Convention on Artificial Intelligence and Human Rights, Democracy and the Rule of Law. As of 2025, the main debates have now moved on to the challenge of implementing hard law in the context of a global backsliding of human rights, climate considerations and the rule of law.

11.3 Humanitarian Healthcare

11.3.1 Digital Infrastructure and AI: Usages in Humanitarian Health

The early phase of the digital transformation of humanitarian healthcare focused on information gathering and analysis. This included early warning technologies, and real-time epidemiological and humanitarian maps created by satellite, drone, and geographic information systems (GIS) imagery. Digital tools also changed clinical work by allowing for portable point-of-care testing, aiding disease screening and diagnostic testing, as well as telemedicine and teleconsulting from cell phone calls to integrated cameras and remote (robot) surgical interventions. Coordination, data collection and sharing, information sharing, and evaluation have been and can still be greatly improved by digital tools. The potential for predictive modeling for epidemics, staff selection, training, and deployment in emergencies was seen as particularly important (Hunt et al. 2016).

Applications of AI for health include diagnosis, clinical care, research, drug development, healthcare administration, public health, and surveillance. While applications may not represent novel uses of AI per se, clinicians, patients, laypeople, health-care professionals and workers access and use AI for diagnosis and care in ways that reshape how healthcare is understood, accessed and delivered. At the same time, many applications and uses are still unproven and may ultimately not deliver the benefits that have been advertised, or worse, do harm to patients, exacerbate infrastructural vulnerabilities, erode clinical expertise, and waste resources.

For example, AI may assist in imaging cases, reviewing routine diagnoses, and reducing communication workload. AI may also help with writing up clinical notes, filing patient electronic health records, etc. Among potential risks are inaccurate, incomplete, or false responses, poor quality training data, or bias of training data and responses ('garbage in, garbage out'). Another important issue is the risk of skill degradation of healthcare personnel. While AI may provide virtual assistants for communicating with patients, this may erode the clinician-patient relationship, entail undetected instances of outdated, false, or incomplete information, compromise privacy, compromise trust in medical expertise in favor of unskilled 'experts outside the health system, and even lead to the emotional manipulation of the patient by AI. From a health system perspective, risks range from the overestimation of the benefits of large language models to digital shadows, automation of bias, poor maintenance, cyberinsecurity, and unstable connectivity (Rejali and Heiniger 2020). In the domain of healthcare, so-called 'humanitarian intelligence' may be particularly problematic due to the multiple sites of intimate data collection (Stellmach et al. 2023). Going beyond data privacy challenges, the potential merger of individualized and group-level health data engenders particular vulnerabilities (Sandvik and Raymond 2017).

11.3.2 What Is Special About 'Humanitarian Tech Health Ethics'?

Humanitarian healthcare aims to save and safeguard the lives of people caught up in situations of crisis. The settings are diverse, from primary care and field hospitals to vaccination and feeding programs to treatment centers during infectious disease outbreaks (Hunt et al. 2018). From the humanitarian healthcare perspective, issues arise at the interface of the humanitarian ethics and humanitarian technology ethics described above and medical ethics. Medical ethics is a tool for health professionals in decision-making, patient care, and collaboration with other humanitarians, including healthcare workers. The four pillars of medical ethics include beneficence (doing good); non-maleficence (doing no harm), autonomy (patient self-determination), and justice (ensuring fairness). In everyday practice, principles of medical ethics draw attention to key moral considerations of medical practice such as avoiding harm, promoting the good of individual patients, maintaining patient confidentiality, focusing on individual consent and individual decision-making ability, and grappling with issues of justice and equity, including conflicts of interest. For the individual health worker, challenges include, among other, those related to the clinical skills required in the humanitarian environment, where clinical care concerns direct consequences of a disaster; the care of underlying chronic conditions that present during a disaster; and the management of coincidental emergencies that occur alongside the response and still require clinical management. Systemic challenges include service delivery, the management of the health workforce and health information systems, access to essential medicines, financing, and leadership and governance (Hunt et al. 2018).

What is special with respect to humanitarian healthcare ethics? Perhaps no other field of humanitarian practice has such an enormous gap between globalized professional and clinical ethical norms and standards and the reality of humanitarian crisis. As such, emergencies confront clinicians with an operational environment posing a different 'moral landscape' than what they are used to or have been trained to expect. Ethical dilemmas emerge from this moral landscape of resource scarcity and constraints on clinical service, including diagnostic, referral, and intervention options. Levels of achievable care may be low. Instability and insecurity make it harder to provide health care while increasing health care needs. Aid agencies may adopt policies detrimental to necessary ethical action (Hunt 2011; Schwartz et al. 2010, 2012).

Importantly, this means that much of the absolutist criticism against humanitarian ethics in general fits poorly when applied to humanitarian healthcare. From the perspective of critics of the humanitarian turn to ethics, professional ethics cannot be dismissed as 'ethics washing' with calls for it to go away. At the same time, while calls for dismantling the humanitarian system generally do not extend to the field of humanitarian healthcare, and radical contestations over bio-medical knowledge and health care systems are seen as problematic (conspiracy theories, religious extremism), there are demands for structural reform for example, in terms of addressing persistent problems of equity and bias. As observed by Coghlan et al. (2024) to decolonize humanitarian health means contesting structural racism and power imbalances and placing agency in the hands of those whose lives are being impacted by crisis.

Furthermore, the questions animating the generalized humanitarian technology ethics debate and the ones shaping the conversation about healthcare ethics continue to shift and evolve. Importantly, similar questions may often refer to different debates. For example, for humanitarian technology ethics, the line of argument around consent in GDPR has seen a move towards giving up on meaningful consent. For healthcare professionals, questions about consent are fundamentally different: patient autonomy and consent cannot be given up in the same manner. At the same time, humanitarian ethics remain a critical prism for grasping crosscutting changes across the sector.[2]

By the mid-2020s, an important recalibration in how ethics questions are framed seems to go in the direction of requiring an understanding of the underlying

[2] To that end, Hunt et al. 2018 offers the following set of helpful guiding questions to bring out the ethical dilemmas inherent in humanitarian technology adoption and adaptation:

- How does ICT interact with the ethical values and norms of aid organizations and their workers
- What is the impact on distributive justice and equality?
- How does ICT influence relationships in humanitarian operations?
- How may ICTs alter relationships between medical workers, patients, and communities?
- What new relationships, including private sector technology providers and ICT specialists, are becoming important in these relationships?

technology of the specific digital tool instead of just its usage. For example, when discussing autonomy, the WHO consensus ethical principles for use of AI for health (2021) foreground issues of transparency, safety, fairness, discrimination, and bias, underscoring that 'humans should remain in control of health-care systems and medical decisions'. As digital humanitarian infrastructure is transformed by AI, critical problem framings and problematizations will become increasingly important for capturing and analyzing accountability, justice, and ethics issues at stake. The last part of this chapter tries to 'think with' this insight.

11.4 Framing Problems: Technofailure, Fragility and the Risks of Hyperconnectivity

As the focus has shifted from the humanitarian nature of digital tools to the humanitarian nature of their shortcomings, risks, and failures, problem framing shifts too. This third and final part of the chapter focuses on problem-framing at the interface of the humanitarian emergency context, the healthcare delivery, and the digital transformation. Key here are the concepts of technofailure, structural risk, and infinite vulnerability. This cluster will be used in the three problem framings ending this chapter (on the black box, blackouts, and processes of blackening out). *Technofailure* is linked to the technology industry and is an attribute of global digital infrastructures. As noted by Taylor (2023) concerning the role of technofailure in the global digital economy, new technologies produce new opportunities for technological failure but also capitalize on this failure. This is a business model focused on constant updating and obsolescence rather than maintenance and repair. Failure is naturalized and commodified. The objective is not to reduce device failure but the impact of device failure. Taylor observes that

> In the hyperconnected parts of the world, Big Tech is 'working to ensure that device failure does not result in downtime or data loss, cloud backup and restore services strive to reconfigure breakdowns and malfunctions into uneventful and forgettable moments, rather than traumatic or catastrophic data loss events' (Taylor 2023).

Systemic risk is the attendant effect of the digital transformation of aid. Infinite vulnerability is the compounded vulnerability emerging from a specific emergency context, the problems of humanitarian digital management, and the political economy of cybersecurity and protection (Sandvik 2016). 'Infinite' speaks both to the as yet uncertain and undetermined types of harm that may occur and the unpredictable scope and impact of harm. Over the last two decades, the aid sector has engaged in a form of digital transformation whereby the sector has mainstreamed technofailure and embedded systemic risk and infinite vulnerability at the heart of its operational infrastructure (Sandvik 2023). Perhaps nowhere are the consequences of technoproblems more urgent and the ethical dilemmas greater than in the field of humanitarian healthcare, and perhaps nowhere are the future unknown unknowns of AI more important to tangle with and try to unpack.

11.4.1 Black Box Experimentation in Humanitarian Healthcare

The first framing is the notion of 'black box experimentation.' Across policy discussions on AI, concepts such as transparency, explainability, and intelligibility feature prominently. For example, the WHO (2021) notes that AI technologies should be intelligible or understandable to developers, medical professionals, patients, users, and regulators. Sufficient information must be published or documented before the design or deployment of AI, and the information should facilitate meaningful public consultation and debate on how the AI is designed and how it should or should not be used. In contexts where literacy and digital literacy are critically low, attempting to ensure that 'AI is explainable according to the capacity of those to whom it is explained' (WHO 2021) will be extremely challenging. While discussions on the dilemmas of artificial intelligence have much in common with previous generations of conversations on the ethics of humanitarian health technology, the first-order problems are built into products in a different way. Recalling the reflection on experimentation above, the problem is that without knowing about and understanding the design and content of the tool or infrastructure in question, it is not possible to assess its use. A key issue is automation bias and the potential for false, inaccurate, or biased responses due to flawed or incomplete training data or poorly crafted algorithms. In the case of health care, the concern is that AI bias may translate into real-life bias by health care professionals. Trusting too much in the machine, they may also overlook diagnostic, clinical, and therapeutic errors they should have spotted but were not alert to. Moreover, AI doesn't have morality and makes an inconsistent moral advisor. In sum, this may lead to skill degradation, moral de-skilling, and abdication of responsibility vis-à-vis decision-making algorithms.

11.4.2 The Impact of Blackouts on Health Care Delivery

Much attention has been given to external threats to humanitarian health care. Yet, from a sectoral perspective, we need to more carefully consider the logistical (not only the political) implications of wrapping services, including health care around digital infrastructures in humanitarian settings. On a basic everyday level, a potentially serious consequence of so-called AI deskilling is that clinicians become increasingly unable to complete an ever-growing range of medical tasks in the event of network failures or critical security breaches. Furthermore, connectivity is not equal, stable, or infinite. While we are currently discussing digital shadows and strategic underserving of populations (through 3G), the increased climate and disaster risk, coupled with decoupled and/or disrupted global supply chains or resource scarcity, might mean that the humanitarian sector is setting itself up for serious access problems. While attention has belatedly been given to the sustainability of generative AI and other resource-intensive systems and tools, there is also a problematic tiering between 3G, 4G, and 5G systems. Additionally, disruptions and resilience are also not equally distributed. For emergency care, disruptions in a digitally dependent system will have a catastrophic impact on the ability to respond. Yet, the degree of vulnerability of these systems depends on how technofailure is mediated and repaired. Financial costs, geopolitical considerations (such as the Chinese-American trade war or the sanctions regime and the impact on supply chains), and the 'status' of the emergency (forgotten conflict, deserving or undeserving victims, geopolitical allies) also play important roles.

11.4.3 Blackening Out Health Care Responses: Surveillance, Mis/Disinformation and Censorship Risks

The final problem relates to AI as a system for medical knowledge and care provision. In the best of worlds, AI has the potential for improving and improving the effectiveness of health data collection, analysis, and programming across linguistic and cultural barriers. Yet, we are not living in the best of worlds. As exemplified by HIV/AIDS, Ebola and Covid-19 but also reproductive health interventions, mis and disinformation about health emergencies and about care and medical personnel not only erodes trust but engenders threats and violence against healthcare personnel and attacks against health-care facilities The continuously growing ability of malicious actors (including governments, universities and civil society actors) to produce and disseminate false imagery, films, sounds, and to manipulate and interfere with for example the integrity of medical records, the infrastructure and workflows of health bureaucracies or the dissemination of public health advice means that for humanitarian actors, there is a challenge with maintaining truth 'at scale' across humanitarian space but also to avoid the creation of localized sites of information anarchy, where the lack of accurate health information, widespread mis and disinformation and the paucity of viable paths for fixing this means 'blackening out' pockets of reality (Sandvik 2025).

11.5 Conclusion

This chapter has attempted to articulate an 'Ethics talk diagnostic' to sort issues and set the agenda for better discussions on ethics and technology in humanitarian healthcare. While digital and AI ethics issues are frequently generalizable throughout the humanitarian sector, they are not the same everywhere. The chapter has attempted to identify, detect, and characterize the differences between ethics, technology uses, and problem framings common to the humanitarian sector as such and in humanitarian healthcare more specifically. Amid much generalized talk about AI in the humanitarian sector, this chapter has argued for more specific and situated conversations on the ethics of AI in the humanitarian healthcare field. As illustrated by the brief thematic discussions offered, the risks relate to black box experimentation (skill degradation, moral de-skilling, and abdication of responsibility vis-à-vis decision-making algorithms), digital disruptions, and the problematic impact of AI on the knowledge systems underpinning medical knowledge and humanitarian healthcare.

References

Barnett, Michael N. 2013. Humanitarian governance. *Annual Review of Political Science* 16 (1): 379–398.

Beduschi, A. 2022. Harnessing the potential of artificial intelligence for humanitarian action: opportunities and risks. *International Review of the Red Cross* 104 (919): 1149–1169.

Benford, R. D., and D. A. Snow. 2000. Framing processes and social movements: an overview and assessment. *Annual Review of Sociology* 26 (1): 611–639.

Coghlan, Rachel, et al. 2024. The "new-old" dimensions of caring in humanitarian response: the opportunity for public health palliative care to advance the humanitarian-development nexus, decoloniality, and localization thought. *INQUIRY: The Journal of Health Care Organization, Provision, and Financing* 61:00469580241277443.

Coppi, G., R. M. Jimenez, and S. Kyriazi. 2021. Explicability of humanitarian AI: a matter of principles. *Journal of International Humanitarian Action* 6 (1): 19.

Devidal, P. 2024. Lost in digital translation? The humanitarian principles in the digital age. *International Review of the Red Cross* 1–35.

Dijkzeul, Dennis, and Kristin Bergtora Sandvik. 2019. A world in turmoil: governing risk, establishing order in humanitarian crises. *Disasters* 43:S85–S108.

Donovan, K. P. 2015. Infrastructuring aid: materializing humanitarianism in northern Kenya. *Environment and Planning D: Society and Space 33* (4): 732–748.

Dufour, Charlotte, et al. 2004. Rights, standards and quality in a complex humanitarian space: is Sphere the right tool? *Disasters* 28 (2): 124–141.

Goffman, Erving. 1974. *Frame analysis: An essay on the organization of experience*. Harvard University Press.

Hilhorst, Dorothea, et al. 2021. Accountability in humanitarian action. *Refugee Survey Quarterly* 40 (4): 363–389.

Hunt, Matthew R. 2011. Establishing moral bearings: ethics and expatriate health care professionals in humanitarian work. *Disasters* 35 (3): 606–622.

Hunt, Matthew, et al. 2016. Ethics of emergent information and communication technology applications in humanitarian medical assistance. *International Health* 8 (4): 239–245.

Hunt, Matthew, et al. 2018. Moral experiences of humanitarian health professionals caring for patients who are dying or likely to die in a humanitarian crisis. *Journal of International Humanitarian Action* 3 (1): 1–13.

Hunt, M., et al. 2019. Ethics at the intersection of crisis translation and humanitarian innovation. *Journal of Humanitarian Affairs* 1 (3): 23–32.

Iazzolino, G. 2021. Infrastructure of compassionate repression: making sense of biometrics in Kakuma refugee camp. *Information Technology for Development 27* (1): 111–128.

ICRC. 2018. The International Review of the Red Cross Code of Conduct, ICRC, 2018.

Jacobsen, Katja Lindskov, and Kristin Bergtora Sandvik. 2018. UNHCR and the pursuit of international protection: accountability through technology? *Third World Quarterly* 39 (8): 1508–1524.

Jaff, D. 2024. The use of AI for humanitarian response during conflict: do no digital harm. *Medicine, Conflict and Survival* 40 (3): 273–275.

Jasanoff, Sheila. 2004. The idiom of co-production. In *States of knowledge: The co-production of science and the social order*, ed. Sheila Jasanoff, 1st ed., 12. London: Routledge.

Madianou, Mirca. 2019. Technocolonialism: Digital innovation and data practices in the humanitarian response to refugee crises. *Social Media+ Society* 5 (3): 2056305119863146.

Madianou, M. 2021. Nonhuman humanitarianism: When 'AI for good' can be harmful. *Information, Communication & Society* 24 (6): 850–868.

Martin, Aaron. 2023. Aidwashing surveillance: Critiquing the corporate exploitation of humanitarian crises. *Surveillance & Society* 21 (1): 96–102.

McElhinney, H., and S. W. Spencer. 2024. The clock is ticking to build guardrails into humanitarian AI, March 11. https://www.thenewhumanitarian.org/opinion/2024/03/11/build-guardrails-humanitarian-ai.

Morozov, Evgeny, and Rick Docksai. 2011. Technology's role in revolution: internet freedom and political oppression. *The Futurist; Washington* 45 (4): 18–21.

OCHA. 2024. Briefing note on artificial intelligence and the humanitarian sector. https://www.unocha.org/publications/report/world/briefing-note-artificial-intelligence-and-humanitarian-sector.

Pizzi, M., M. Romanoff, and T. Engelhardt. 2020. AI for humanitarian action: Human rights and ethics. *International Review of the Red Cross* 102 (913): 145–180.

Raftree, L. 2024. Do humanitarians have a moral duty to use AI to reduce human suffering? Four key tensions to untangle, 11 June 2024. https://alnap.org/humanitarian-resources/publications-and-multimedia/do-humanitarians-have-a-moral-duty-to-use-ai/.

Rejali, Saman, and Yannick Heiniger. 2020. The role of digital technologies in humanitarian law, policy and action: charting a path forward. *International review of the Red Cross* 102 (913): 1–22.

Sandvik, Kristin Bergtora. 2017. Now is the time to deliver: looking for humanitarian innovation's theory of change. *Journal of International Humanitarian Action* 2:1–11.

Sandvik, Kristin Bergtora. 2023. *Humanitarian extractivism: The digital transformation of aid.* Manchester: Manchester University Press.

Sandvik, Kristin Bergtora. 2025. Calibrating AI/d talk: framing perceptions, reframing policy and deframing knowledge. *Journal of International Humanitarian Action*. https://doi.org/10.1186/s41018-025-00173-0.

Sandvik, Kristin Bergtora, and Katja Lindskov Jacobsen, eds. 2016. *UNHCR and the struggle for accountability: technology, law and results-based management*. Routledge.

Sandvik, Kristin Bergtora, and Kjersti Lohne. 2014. The rise of the humanitarian drone: Giving content to an emerging concept. *Millennium* 43 (1): 145–164.

Sandvik, Kristin, and Nathaniel Raymond. 2017. Beyond the protective effect: Towards a theory of harm for information communication technologies in mass atrocity response. *Genocide Studies and Prevention: An International Journal* 11:1.

Sandvik, Kristin Bergtora, et al. 2014. Humanitarian technology: a critical research agenda. *International Review of the Red Cross* 96 (893): 219–242.

Sandvik, Kristin Bergtora. 2016. The humanitarian cyberspace: shrinking space or an expanding-frontier? *Third World Quarterly* 37 (1): 17–32.

Sandvik, Kristin Bergtora, Katja Lindskov Jacobsen, and Sean Martin McDonald. 2017. Do no harm: A taxonomy of the challenges of humanitarian experimentation. *International Review of the Red Cross* 99 (904): 319–344.

Santoni de Sio, F., and G. Mecacci. 2021. Four responsibility gaps with artificial intelligence: Why they matter and how to address them. *Philosophy & Technology* 34:1057–1084.

Schwartz, L., C. Sinding, M. Hunt, et al. 2010. Ethics in humanitarian aid work: learning from health worker's narratives. *AJOB Primary Research* 1:45–54.

Schwartz, Lisa, et al. 2012. Models for humanitarian health care ethics. *Public Health Ethics* 5 (1): 81–90.

Slim, Hugo. 2015. *Humanitarian ethics: A guide to the morality of aid in war and disaster*. Oxford University Press.

Spencer, S. 2024. Seizing the potential and sidestepping the pitfalls. *Humanitarian Practice Network* 89: https://odihpn.org/wp-content/uploads/2024/05/HPN_Network-Paper89_humanitarianAI.pdf.

Stellmach, Darryl, et al. 2023. Problematising medical data in humanitarian response. *Journal of Humanitarian Affairs* 5 (2): 3–12.

Tanguy, Joelle, and Fiona Terry. 1999. Humanitarian responsibility and committed action. *Ethics & International Affairs* 13:29–34.

Taylor, A. R. E. 2023. The infrastructure of digital failure. In *Routledge international handbook of failure*, ed. A. Mica, M. Pawlak, A. Horolets, and P. Kubicki. Abingdon: Routledge.

Wagner, B. 2018. Ethics as an escape from regulation. From 'ethics-washing' to ethics-shopping? In *Being profiled: cogitas ergo sum : 10 years of 'profiling the European 3 citizen'*, ed. E. Bayamlioglu, I. Baraliuc, L. A. W. Janssens, and M. Hildebrandt, 84–89. Amsterdam: Amsterdam University Press.

Wang, N. 2020. We live on hope...: Ethical considerations of humanitarian use of drones in post-disaster Nepal. *IEEE Technology and Society Magazine* 39 (3): 76–78.

WHO consensus ethical principles for use of AI for health. 2021. https://www.who.int/publications/i/item/9789240029200.

Kristin Bergtora Sandvik is a professor of legal sociology at the Faculty of Law, University of Oslo and a Research Professor in Humanitarian Studies at PRIO. Sandvik is Candidata Juris from the University of Oslo and Doctor of Juridical Sciences (S.J.D) from Harvard Law School (2008). She works on the digital transformation of humanitarian action and refugee management with a focus on legalization, accountability, ethics and rights. She also has a long-standing focus on global health, engaging with the entanglements between HIV/AIDS, Ebola and more recently Covid-19 and human rights. Her book *Humanitarian Extractivism: the Digital Transformation of Aid* was published by Manchester University Press in 2023.

Chapter 12
Navigating Risks in Data Collection on Attacks Against Healthcare: New Technologies and Ethical Considerations Stemming from the Insecurity Insight's Practical Experience

Ana Elisa Barbar and Christina Wille

12.1 Introduction

Attacks against healthcare are defined by the World Health Organization as "*any act of verbal or physical violence, threat of violence or other psychological violence, or obstruction that interferes with the availability, access and delivery of curative and/ or preventive health services*" (World Health Organization 2018). These violent events disrupt healthcare delivery wherever they occur, as a consequence of staff shortages when health workers are killed or injured, when access to care is directly obstructed or denied, and when medical supplies and infrastructure are looted or destroyed (Safeguarding Health in Conflict Coalition—SHCC 2024).

The detrimental effects of attacks justify the surveillance and closely monitoring of the events. This data can be used to prepare and react in an appropriate way to incidents, to reinforce preventive and mitigating measures and finally strengthening protection of healthcare by better protecting people (health workers, patients) and the healthcare services (equipment and supplies, structure, referral pathways and systemic aspects that enable access to care) (ICRC 2016). In the past decade, data about attacks on healthcare has been growing, as different stakeholders agree upon added value of collecting information about the incidents, structuring those in functional databases and, when relevant, disclosing publicly the information. While differences arise in the way data is collected, the indicators applied, and the usability of each dataset, academics, practitioners and authorities agree that, without

A. E. Barbar (✉)
Geneva, Switzerland

C. Wille
Vaud, Switzerland
e-mail: christina.wille@insecurityinsight.org

B. Koch, D. Winkler (eds.), *Artificial Intelligence Ethics in Military Medicine and Humanitarian Healthcare*, Military and Humanitarian Health Ethics,
https://doi.org/10.1007/978-3-032-11331-3_12

systematic information it is difficult to reduce or stop the violence (ICRC 2020; Haar and Sirkin 2022; WHO 2023).

Data collection mechanisms range from national level initiatives, led by governments or national professional associations (e.g. see in ICRC 2020, the systems developed by the Colombian health authorities, and the data collection carried out by the Spanish Medical Association) to international datasets hosted by global organizations and covering multiple States or regions across the globe. Amongst these global data collection systems, there are the System of Surveillance of Attacks, managed by the World Health Organization (WHO 2018), and the Global Health Map[1] with the associated data shared via the Humanitarian Data Exchange (HDX), managed by Insecurity Insight. Each system provides its own overview of frequency and type of attacks, often using different definitions to frame inclusion criteria. Also with high degree of variation are the indicators related to impact of incidents (e.g. number and group of people wounded or killed, destruction of assets, cancellation or postponing of healthcare activities, etc.). Finally, access to the systems and the information, both to input information as well as to verify and use the output analysis, may vary significantly, depending on the purpose of the system and the regulations put forward by the organization holding it. Some systems are closed off to selected users and only consolidated, yearly reports are offered to the public, whereas other systems may receive input from a variety of stakeholders and provide regularly updated overviews, often accessible online from any computer.

The issue of data collection on attacks on healthcare has been subject of heated debate, given the mentioned multiplicity of processes, indicators and uses that may frame each data system (Meier et al. 2021). The International Committee of the Red Cross co-hosted an event in 2019 only to discuss the issue (ICRC 2020), and the International Peace Institute recently published a report on the same topic (Haar and Sirkin 2022). The authors of this chapter defend that, while it is impossible to develop and implement one single global system that would be perfectly responding to all needs of data use regarding attacks on healthcare, it may be possible to constructively debate what elements can or may be enhanced to ensure each system has the most ethical, useful, and efficient methodology possible, considering its primary purposes, in line with the debate on Good Practices presented by the World Health Organization (2023). There remains a need for further efforts by organizations and academia to investigate to what extent system are achieving the intended impact and to identify improvements for protection through data collection and analysis.

This chapter aims at presenting lessons learned from Insecurity Insight, to describe and debate the use of artificial intelligence (AI) tools to support data collection on attacks against healthcare. The discussion will be centered around whether AI tools have enhanced or mitigated protection risks related to such data collection, and what other benefits or risks may be observed with the introduction of this technology. Section 12.2 will present the operational framework of Insecurity Insight, while Sect. 12.3 presents the ethical standards and limits surrounding this

[1] https://mapaction-maps.herokuapp.com/health

work. Finally Sect. 12.4 explores the leading ethical questions, debating them against the experience of Insecurity Insight, following by the final section with conclusions. The authors of this chapter hope to contribute through the discussion of Insecurity Insight's experience to a wider debate on ethical and protection concerns to strengthening the protection of healthcare.

12.2 Ethical and Practical Questions Related to Data Collection on Attacks on Healthcare

According to ethical guidance on collection and use of data for research and clinical interventions, information should generate benefits to an individual or a group and reduce potential risks or effects of harmful elements. These concepts, borrowed from bioethics and research ethics, are also similar to some of the principles applicable in humanitarian action: it shouldn't do harm, should respect dignity and autonomy of people, and should impartially distribute benefits (Inter-Agency Standing Committee—IASC 2016; International Committee of the Red Cross 2012; Protection Information Management—PIM 2017). Many of these concerns, as well as the ones described ahead, are brought forward and thoroughly debated in guidelines that addressed collection and use of protection information (IASC 2016; ICRC 2024).[2]

Guidelines also clearly indicate that data collection must be non-maleficent to the people at risk of violence or affected by it: it must not increase likelihood of violence, neither through misuse of data for further violence (attacks or blockages), nor due to reprisals against reporting. This seems to be particularly important as a concern when data is attached to personal, individual information (ICRC 2012), such as name of the person who provided the report, characteristics of individual perpetrators who might seek to retaliate at personal level, or when it entails information that could support a criminal case (ICRC 2024).

In addition, the use of data should bring clear benefits: by supporting warring parties in exerting precaution and proportionality when conducting military operations, by informing health system stakeholders in their risk analysis (and thus reducing chances of indiscriminate negative consequences of hostilities, supporting mitigation measures to limit the impact of violence on the delivery of health care), or by favouring accountability. These positive effects of the use of data are normally understood as the very reason why data is collected. Nonetheless, the direct use of data about attacks to inform protective actions, e.g. better contingency plans or

[2] Is it to note that Insecurity Insight does not work with protection data in the strict sense of the term: the incident data is collected and analysed not for protection follow-up, but for generating useful information for humanitarians, as previously stated. Nonetheless, given the sensitivity of the topic, Insecurity Insight strives to adjust and adapt to formal guidance in the area, with the aim of consolidating ethical and reliable informational products.

crisis response, is often overlooked as a benefit, given that most systems would not explicitly declare these as intended outcomes of the work.

It is important to notice that, while these benefits are sought through ethical data collection and analysis, they might not all be possible under the same information system, given that indicators to best support one or other beneficial action may not all be present in a single data collection protocol. The guidance offered by the International Labor Organization and the World Health Organization (2022) on surveillance of violence and harassment against health workers presents different layers of data that need to be incorporated in an efficient information system. Moreover, expectations on driving accountability might differ, as some stakeholders might aim at having data readily presentable to legal authorities, other stakeholder might expect to use overarching, less granular data to mobilize peers and others who seek accountability, in an advocacy-facing purpose (Haar and Sirkin 2022).

At present, data collection on adverse events is surrounded by a very strong hypothesis of potential harmdoing. Unlike for other fields of protection work, for which these concerns are addressed through guidelines and other relevant material, no such guidance exists on the attacks on health care. At present, there is no clearly agreed purpose for data collection and no shared set of possible indicators to measure impact, benefit and harm. In addition to that, a history of de-confliction mechanisms failing to protect health sites,[3] has left a mark on humanitarian agencies (The New Humanitarian 2018). The lack of respect demonstrated by warrying parties when knowingly attacking protected (and de-conflicted) sites and violating basic rules of International Humanitarian Law, raises even more preoccupation and concern around potential risks of reporting and public advocacy using incident data.

Most protection practices were shaped before the internet, mobile phones and social media profoundly altered the visibility of modern conflicts. Adaption to new realities takes time and guidance is still to be fully adjusted. The concept of real-time survivor reporting has only recently been incorporated into the discussion on how to treat this circulating information (ICRC 2024). Between the fear of causing harm and the intention to protect, organizations are still defining how to use the opportunity to look at social media as an empowered and first-person space of dialogue. Paid bots, hate speech and disinformation add to the complexity of how to approach these spaces, the content circulating there, and maintain reliability.

While a significant expansion is seen, over the past 10 years, in the capacity of humanitarians to internally manage their own security and risks, there was no comparable growth in addressing attacks on data. The general guidance still goes in the line of restricted circulation and limited information-sharing, as a promise of efficiency towards safer humanitarian operations, and the work on data attacks on healthcare is driven by the same thinking. Interestingly, this is not documented by research comparing, for example, outcomes of incidents reported privately through official channels, and incidents self-reported publicly, online.

[3] To de-conflict means to inform warrying parties the precise location of protected sites, hoping they will be spared from fighting and kept in safety.

On the practical side of things, there are many issues about data collection that are repeated as key limitations to expansion: lack of an ethical framework for protecting persons when reporting, lack of trained personnel for adequate and ethical reporting, lack of protected reporting systems, lack of outreach to explain and engage people in reporting. WHO, in its 2023 Good Practices document, highlights these points, but these challenges are not particular to this area of work. They are also present in other overarching systems of documentation of "incidents", such as the discussion about mandatory report of infectious diseases (Sert et al. 2022), sexual violence (British Red Cross and International Committee of the Red Cross 2020) or attacks against educational facilities (Global Coalition to Protect Education from Attack 2024). The more comprehensive, detailed, or "global" the system, the more it would be expected that it underreports, given the multiple layers to collect and filter information. A high number of reported events may also represent a high burden in data treatment, therefore it demands bigger teams and budget to enter, verify and classify events.

12.3 Incorporating New Technologies in the Work of Insecurity Insight

As a humanitarian-to-humanitarian association, Insecurity Insight supports the work of aid agencies, providers of healthcare, education, and protection services, amongst other civil society organisations, by providing publicly available information for evidence-based policies. Insecurity Insight carries out its work by structuring activities in different pillars, from development and implementation of standards for event-based data collection, to provision of actionable and freely accessible information about patterns of violence and other harmful events, such as damage and destruction of food systems. It also supports, advises and exchanges with organizations who deliver aid, in technical partnerships that support their work, and works in coalition with other partners and organizations whose aim is to prevent violence through evidence-based actions, mitigate its impact or strengthen accountability, at operational or policy level.

The values of Insecurity Insight are Humanity, Independence, Neutrality, "Do no harm" and Professionalism,[4] as well as "Balancing transparency and access with Data Protection". This last value, combined with the principle of non-maleficence, is particularly important for the discussion in this chapter as it denotes part of the ethical challenges faced by Insecurity Insight in carrying out its work: while publicizing information on incidents of violence to the public may involve certain risks, care is taken to prevent harm and to provide reliable information, accessible to those who might benefit from it.

[4] For a full description of each value, as well as an overview of Insecurity Insight's various products and working topics (also beyond Health in Danger), please consult Insecurity Insight's website.

As for its products, Insecurity Insight produces independent reports, short briefings, thematic factsheets, amongst other documents that compile and analyse events and trends on violence against healthcare. Insecurity Insight initially started collecting information on attacks on healthcare using individual search in international media and newspapers, back in 2008 while testing methods in a project driven, at the time, by the International Committee of the Red Cross. These newspapers and reports came through diplomatic pouch or personal delivery from different areas of the world, and were individually processed, with information manually inserted in digital databases. This process served the initial years of Insecurity Insight's work and constituted an initial approach to the data collection, limited by many aspects: firstly, the news of the attack would have to be caught by a local journalist and reported in an accessible media outlet, secondly Insecurity Insight would need to receive the publication material, and thirdly, the understanding of the incident would be limited to the information presented in that accessible material.

In subsequent years, starting around 2015, as more and more media articles moved online, Insecurity Insight systematically followed media outlets, like IRIN,[5] and OSAC[6] using RSS feeds and used LexisNexis searches for more information. Researchers read through articles to identify relevant information. The number of identified information remained limited as was shown by a study using the publicly available data collected for the calendar year 2017, that compared the information identified by Insecurity Insight and the World Health Organisations using online searches. The study only found a minimal overlap between the incidents identified which suggested information on attacks on health care remained significantly underreported (Parada et al. 2023).

Following this assessment, Insecurity Insight embarked on a process of training artificial intelligence into the search process to support and facilitate the collection, classification and processing of the data on attacks on healthcare with a view to developing an automatic data collection and AI-backed classification framework aligned with humanitarian objectives. The challenge was to increase access to relevant information while remaining on a very limited budget and without exposing researchers to security risks. Artificial intelligence-supported methods are currently also used for social media sentiment analysis, as one of the products currently developed by Insecurity Insight to its partners.

Artificial intelligence (AI) is utilized through classification models, natural language processing (NLP), and machine learning, with the latter trained on in-house annotations. These algorithms enable the rapid identification of reported incidents across various sources, using classifiers to prioritize information based on relevance. This system presents human researchers with the most pertinent data, significantly reducing the time spent sifting through irrelevant content.

The verification of information trustworthiness remains a human responsibility. Once verified, text-based reports are converted into structured data, with AI

[5] https://newirin.irinnews.org/

[6] https://www.osac.gov/

assisting in standardizing details such as dates and geographic locations, while human input is essential for interpreting complex content. This approach has increased the identification of relevant information from several hundred cases to thousands of incidents annually.

For years, the algorithms relied solely on English-language NLP, introducing biases and likely continuing the underreporting of critical information. In 2024, the NLP capabilities were expanded to include French and Arabic, addressing these limitations and broadening the scope of data collection (See Lambda et al, 2024 for the debate on DAVINCI: Dataset for Detection of Violent Incidents).

Before examining the specific ethical considerations of using AI tools in the work of Insecurity Insight, it is essential to emphasize that the drive for efficiency never compromises the commitment to data reliability and protection. Insecurity Insight continuously invests in training both staff and algorithms to ensure the system is used to improve the efficiency of humans who maintain the ultimate control over the data collection system. AI tools are continuously adapted to meet the needs of the sensitive topics it addresses, and staff continues to verify content. No data is fully automated for publication; all final decisions regarding the database content are rigorously validated by humans through a multi-layered quality assurance process—details of which are beyond the scope of this chapter.

12.4 AI and Data Collection: Is It Harming or Enhancing Ethical Data Collection and Data Processing, as Carried Out by Insecurity Insight?

The discussion in this section will use three ethical angles for debating whether the use of AI may reduce or harm ethical principles of collecting and publishing data on violence against healthcare. It will approach questions related to: non-maleficence (the principle of "do no harm"), beneficence and justice (in a common "do good" approach), and the problem of reliability of data. These issues are examined using concrete examples from Insecurity Insight practices and work throughout the past 16 years as case studies for debate. Although these points may not be directly replicable to other organizations or other contexts of application of AI, the authors hope this case study approach may encourage public and candid debates on the risks involved in data collection about attacks, and means to scale up on monitoring of incidents, validation mechanisms and ultimately protection measures associated to such knowledge.

12.4.1 Could the Use of AI Bring Harmful Effects to People, Breaking the Principle of Non-maleficence?

In this aspect of the ethical debate, there is a concentration of concerns and protection questions around the possibility of reprisals or further harmdoing towards victims of attacks once data is published (ICRC 2024). Moreover, the data processing speed enabled by the use of AI might shortens the time gap between the occurrence of an incident, and its public exposure. This may be argued as a vulnerability aspect given that conflict dynamics, presence of perpetrators and other harmful elements in the environment might still be ongoing at time of publication, which may "facilitate" reprisals against people who reported. Still on the possibility of maleficence, it has been argued that the identification of granular data (especially regarding the location of events, perpetrators and victims), as well as the exposure of the person or entity who reported the incident might bring potential harm (ICRC 2012).

As the referred manuals explicitly mention, harmful events as potentially criminal data or the issue of protection data from an individual perspective[7] are points that may not be fully applicable to the data collection and publication done by Insecurity Insight: published attack data never contains any personally identifiable information. Yet these remain valid points for the debate on protective and ethical procedures, and therefore should be taken into consideration in other cases and data systems. The ICRC manual on Rights and Responsibilities of healthcare workers responding to conflict and other emergencies (ICRC 2014) suggests that the denunciation of a violation of international humanitarian law, as well as all contacts with media, should be product of a careful decision to avoid harm to patients and other vulnerable stakeholders.

With these points in view, Insecurity Insight argues that its data collection and publication procedures, using AI to capture and classify potential incidents, is not harmful. Firstly, it is to note that Insecurity Insight rarely captures incidents of violence against healthcare by active encouragement of denunciation: although Insecurity Insight is open to receiving spontaneous documentation sent by anyone, the AI-support process described in this chapter is only relevant to capture information that is circulating on public platforms, therefore, already published. Most information is published by edited media outlets that follow their own editorial standards. Increasingly information is also published by representatives of known organisations who pass on via social media platforms, usually LinkedIn, documentation of incidents affecting their programmes, colleagues or work they support. It remains very rare that the information is directly published by survivors of violence. Thus, Insecurity Insight does not increase the risk of harm from publishing information on attacks against healthcare, as it only consolidates existing publicly available information through comprehensive AI tools. By standardizing incident information into structured data, any personally identifiable information present in the original

[7] That is, when data is collected with a single individual providing data about what happened to oneself, as a victim of violence.

reports is removed before publication, ensuring data protection and privacy. The shared information does not include any information on the person or organization who provided the information.

Humanitarian organisations usually refrain from mentioning specific conflict parties or perpetrators of violence to adhere to standards of neutrality and impartiality. Insecurity Insight includes information on the reported perpetrators in its datasets based on publicly reported information that has been verified by a human researcher for plausibility or signs of disinformation. Therefore, Insecurity Insight does report first on assumed perpetrators of violence against health care. Insecurity Insight makes clear that it is neither investigating or validating accusations against a particular perpetrator, it only curates and collates the information that is being reported through public channels. Any denial by accused conflict parties is taken into account.

As geocoordinates are increasingly used to target health facilities, concerns have arisen that publishing the exact locations of affected facilities could trigger further attacks. The rise in targeted attacks, particularly airstrikes using guided weapon systems capable of in-flight adjustments based on programmed coordinates, has heightened these fears. While the AI technology behind such weapon systems is a serious concern for various reasons, there is no evidence to suggest that conflict parties with access to this technology would use geolocation data from reports on healthcare attacks to programme their weapons. To mitigate any potential risks, Insecurity Insight ensures that geolocated data on healthcare attacks is of an approximate accuracy that is appropriate for information mapping and visual representation and remains insufficient for programming weapon systems.

In addition, there are fears that information on attacks on health care may be used by conflict parties to assess the extent of damage they caused with a view to repeating attacks. While most conflict parties systematically carry out post-battle damage assessments, most have their own satellite and other observation tools to assess damage. There is no evidence that conflict parties access spreadsheets on incident descriptions as part of their targeting planning. Yet, out of fear of causing harm, the Humanitarian Data Exchange bars publication of geolocation of attacks on health care while at the same time publishing the geolocation of health facilities.

However, evidence suggests that consistent incident reporting—especially when accompanied by media and political attention on violence against healthcare—can prompt governments in affected countries to restrict internet access, media rights, and freedom of speech. These measures often have far-reaching and detrimental effects on populations in conflict-affected areas, including healthcare professionals and their patients. Such patterns have been observed in the past year in Ethiopia, Sudan, the Occupied Palestinian Territories, and Myanmar (Safeguarding Health in Conflict Coalition 2024) and seem to appear regardless of the form of reporting.

12.4.2 *Could the Use of AI Strengthen the Application of the Beneficence Principle Towards Affected Population, and Enhance Justice in the Distribution of Resources?*

This section addressed the issue of potential positive ("do good") impact of incorporating AI tools onto the collection and processing of data. As initial hypothesis, one could argue that the use of AI would not bring enhanced benefits, as it doesn't capture "novel" events, relying on incidents that are already circulating, and it doesn't necessarily provide immediate applications for security management and other beneficial acts. Another hypothesis of neutral beneficence would be related to justice, if assumed that the use of mentioned AI tools is not aimed at enhancing the accountability against perpetrators.

Insecurity Insight's decade-long experience in collecting and sharing data on attacks against healthcare shows that, while AI does not generate new information in the way that methods like on-the-ground interviews or population sampling can, it effectively captures a much larger share of existing data. This includes a significant increase in both the quantity and quality of already known information, drawing from lesser-known languages and local media sources beyond mainstream international outlets. This expanded capacity not only enhances the scope of data collection by incorporating diverse sources, but also reduces reliance on potentially biased international media, offering a more comprehensive and balanced understanding based on a greater diversity of sources.

As an example, in 2016, while using entirely manual information searches by reading through a range of internationally available sources, Insecurity Insight worked with a database of average 40 incidents per month. With the help of AI tools, Insecurity Insight now produced in 2023 on average of 256 verified incidents of violence against health care per month, using only about double the staff hours than in 2016. This is in line with the recommendation of the Inter-Agency Standing Committee on protection in humanitarian action: "*Data and information collection and sharing should be timely to support early warning mechanisms and enable rapid and potentially life-saving interventions*" (2016). Undoubtedly, the use of AI has brought greater visibility to incidents of violence against healthcare, even though many cases remain unreported on public platforms and therefore go undetected by AI tools.

In addition to NLP and classifier AI tools, APIs (Application Programming Interfaces) play a crucial role in disseminating AI-identified information more widely and promptly to a diverse range of humanitarian stakeholders. Selected categories of Insecurity Insight's data, securely stored in the Security in Numbers Database (SiND), are systematically and automatically shared with the broader humanitarian community through API functionality, connecting to the Humanitarian Data Exchange. This integration enables the generation of tailored datasets to meet the specific needs of various stakeholders, whether focused on a particular country or topic, thereby maximizing the benefits of AI for a wider community.

The data and products developed by Insecurity Insight can support global advocacy efforts and structured, historical analysis of the problem based on a larger pool of available information (Safeguarding Health in Conflict Coalition 2024). However, the advocacy calendar of the humanitarian community has largely remained unchanged by the potential speed of AI in data processing. It continues to prioritize annual reports, typically published in May during the United Nations' Protection of Civilians Week, rather than embracing more timely discussions of trends in addition to individual incidents that attract high media attention.

In relation to the ethical principle of justice, Insecurity Insight's use of AI is supportive of a broader distribution of space and power in the communities affected by violence, as it gives opportunity to voices unheard by traditional media to be captured, empowers local reporting, and provides up-to-date information based on first-person sharing of experiences. When capturing communication shared directly by community members, health workers and local authorities, the AI tools amplify the initial call for attention that these persons have autonomously decided to publish. Since 2023, a growing number of global legal accountability organizations have turned to Insecurity Insight's data to evaluate the overall scale of damage and identify potential case studies of incidents. The brief summaries produced by Insecurity Insight often indicate unlawful attacks on healthcare personnel or facilities, prompting further investigation for accountability purposes.

12.4.3 Does the Use of AI Compromise or Enhance Reliability of the Knowledge Produced by Insecurity Insight?

The ethical standards represented by the concept of reliability, when publishing data related to violence against healthcare, is the key to ensure data is taken up by stakeholders as useful and relevant. In this case study, the authors understand reliability as directly interlinked to the principles of impartiality and neutrality, valued by Insecurity Insight. Moreover, reliability denotes the trustworthiness in ensuring data collection and publication are processed through structured, accountable processes, regardless of the use of AI tools—but especially with the inclusion of such new technologies.

In this perspective, it could be argued that AI may be more objectively focused on formal criteria in data processing, and that AI tools may in fact remove subjective human biases. At the same time, several questions remain on whether AI tools could lead to greater susceptibility in mis- or dis-information campaigns, and whether AI language processing tools, more specifically, can acknowledge and filter AI-generated information. Finally, it may be suggested that AI-led data collection could be falling short of alignment with the principle of impartiality.

Considering the previous concerns, Insecurity Insight trains its own algorithms to ensure a maximum of control over the features, model prediction techniques, and decision-trees used. Insecurity Insight regularly tests and validates results to identify potential biases in decision-making, including ethical considerations, and takes measures to ensure that the focus of the algorithms remains aligned to the principal purpose of Insecurity Insight's work of monitoring violence affecting the aid sector. Human researchers continue to validate and oversee final decisions at all times.

Insecurity Insight continues to test publicly available AI-supported tools, but as of 2024, significant concerns remain regarding the reliability of results, particularly when using less common global languages. For instance, a tested AI tool mistranslated an incident of military occupation of a health facility in Myanmar as a "raid with looting." This misrepresentation likely stemmed from insufficient language training material in Burmese, which failed to capture crucial distinctions between "occupation" and "raid," as outlined in International Humanitarian Law (IHL). Without human verification and tailored training of AI tools to address the specific needs of humanitarian perspectives on violence in conflict, off-the-shelf AI solutions remain inadequate for such sensitive work making investment in training of classifications by experts a necessity.

While this approach of training and developing AI for Insecurity Insight's purpose does not eliminate biases inherent in online reporting—such as the decision on which stories are detailed or overlooked, and who has or not not access to internet reporting—, it ensures that incident identification is based on clear IHL-informed defined criteria of harm, without being influenced by commercial, political, or other interests in the identification of publicly reported incidents.

This highlights the critical lesson learned in recent years: the ethical application of AI tools necessitates a deep understanding of the assumptions underlying the algorithms. This understanding enables focused verification of the algorithm's gaps and helps maintain reliability by creating a feedback loop of data and knowledge informed by AI. Human oversight and expert knowledge in the subject matter is essential to ensure quality-driven processes and accountability in the final validation of incidents.

12.5 Conclusions

Drawing from Insecurity Insight's experience in integrating AI technologies for collecting and processing data on attacks against healthcare, it is evident that as of 2024, off-the-shelf AI tools are not suitable for accurate classification of sensitive conflict-related information for humanitarian purposes. These tools often fail to account for the biases present in various media channels, their own "hallucinations," and the limited visibility of local reporting in international media. To effectively address these challenges, AI tools must be trained with specific priorities that reflect the nuances of data collection and processing. This requires ongoing investment and human oversight to ensure quality and accountability throughout the processes.

At Insecurity Insight, AI tools are employed alongside complementary human oversight, providing significant benefits in terms of capturing a broader scope of available information. This approach expands the range of sources and enhances access to local reporting channels. By using AI in this manner, we can effectively share the experiences of diverse populations with a global audience and humanitarian practitioners.

Protection risks often expressed by humanitarian actors, such as the risks of reprisals and further harm due to reporting, do not materialize in the experience of Insecurity Insight. No personal identifiable information is shared and geolocated information only enables information maps, but remains insufficient for the use in geo-precise weapon systems. High resolution satellite images or reconnaissance drones provide more accurate battle impact assessments than a line in a data file on the Humanitarian Data Exchange databases. The primary (and sole) harm observed in Insecurity Insight's experience stems from increasing restrictions on internet use and information sharing, as perpetrators of violence recognize the influence of publicly reported incidents.

While AI has led to an increase in documented information, it also raises the risk that such growing volume of information will be mistaken for a complete picture. This perception can result in the neglect of violence in areas with limited internet access or stricter restrictions on public platforms, overshadowed by the flood of information from better-connected regions. Consequently, the enhanced availability of information through AI tools may inadvertently harm communities whose voices remain unamplified.

Finally, it is acknowledged that social media may bring forward unfiltered content, which means that more information is available, but the narrative maybe be easily controlled and/or influenced by interested stakeholders. Beyond the risks of hate speech, dis- and misinformation, use of AI tools should be careful to not perpetuate information that cannot pass through quality and reliability verification checks.

Insecurity Insight is dedicated to continuously enhancing the methods and processes for data collection, processing, and the publication of information aimed at preventing, mitigating, or advocating for a cessation of violence against healthcare. In this spirit, the authors welcome ongoing discussions arising from the experiences shared in this chapter, particularly regarding the biases and limitations inherent in any data system.

References

British Red Cross and International Committee of the Red Cross. 2020. Forced to report—the humanitarian impact of mandatory reporting on access to health care for victims/survivors of sexual violence in armed conflict and other emergencies. Report. https://www.redcross.org.uk/-/media/documents/about-us/international/forced-to-report-sexual-violence-final-policy-paper.pdf. Accessed 15 Sept 2024.

Global Coalition to Protect Education from Attack. 2024. Education under attack. Report. https://protectingeducation.org/wp-content/uploads/eua_2024.pdf. Accessed 15 Sept 2024.

Haar, R., and S. Sirkin. 2022. Strengthening data to protect healthcare in conflict zones. International Peace Institute report. https://www.ipinst.org/2022/11/strengthening-data-to-protect-healthcare-in-conflict-zones. Accessed 15 Sept 2024.

Inter-Agency Standing Committee. 2016. Policy on protection in humanitarian action. Policy document. https://interagencystandingcommittee.org/iasc-protection-priority-global-protection-cluster/iasc-policy-protection-humanitarian-action-2016. Accessed 15 Sept 2024.

International Committee of the Red Cross—ICRC. 2012. Health care in danger: the responsibilities of health-care personnel working in armed conflicts and other emergencies. Reference document. https://healthcareindanger.org/wp-content/uploads/2015/09/icrc-002-4104-the-responsibilities-health-care-personnel.pdf. Accessed 15 Sept 2024.

International Committee of the Red Cross—ICRC. 2016. Protecting health care—Key recommendations. Report. https://www.icrc.org/sites/default/files/document/file_list/protecting-healthcare_recommendations.pdf. Accessed 15 Sept 2024.

International Committee of the Red Cross—ICRC. 2020. Promoting peer-to-peer exchanges on data collection systems to analyse violence against health care. Report. https://www.icrc.org/en/publication/4508-promoting-peer-peer-exchanges-data-collection-systems-analyse-violence-against. Accessed 15 Sept 2024.

International Committee of the Red Cross—ICRC. 2024. Professional standards for protection work by humanitarian and other human rights actors during armed conflict and other violence. Reference document. https://shop.icrc.org/professional-standards-for-protection-work-pdf-en.html. Accessed 15 Sept 2024.

International Labor Organization and World Health Organization. 2022. Caring for those who care: guide for the development and implementation of occupational health and safety programmes for health workers. Guide. https://www.ilo.org/publications/caring-those-who-care-guide-development-and-implementation-occupational-0. Accessed 15 Sept 2024.

Lamba, Hemank, et al. 2024. HumVI: A multilingual dataset for detecting violent incidents impacting humanitarian aid. https://arxiv.org/abs/2410.06370. Accessed 24 Oct 2024.

Meier, B. M., H. Rice, and S. Bandara. 2021. Monitoring attacks on health care as a basis to facilitate accountability for human rights violations. *Health and Human Rights Journal* 23 (1): 55–70.

Parada, V., L. Fast, C. Briody, C. Wille, and R. Coninx. 2023. Underestimating attacks: comparing two sources of publicly-available data about attacks on health care in 2017. *Conflict and Health* 17:3. https://doi.org/10.1186/s13031-023-00498-w.

Protection Information Management. 2017. PIM Matrix. Guidance material. http://pim.guide/essential/principles-matrix-process-quick-reference-flyer/. Accessed 15 Sept 2024.

Safeguarding Health in Conflict Coalition. 2024. Critical condition—Violence against health care in conflict. Report. https://insecurityinsight.org/wp-content/uploads/2024/05/2023-SHCC-Critical-Conditions.pdf. Accessed 15 Sept 2024.

Sert, G., E. Mega, and A. K. Dedeoğlu. 2022. Protecting privacy in mandatory reporting of infectious diseases during the COVID-19 pandemic: perspectives from a developing country. *Journal of Medical Ethics* 48:1015–1019.

The New Humanitarian. 2018. What is humanitarian deconfliction?—How aid agencies try to avoid getting bombed in Yemen and Syria. Analysis. https://www.thenewhumanitarian.org/analysis/2018/11/13/humanitarian-deconfliction-syria-yemen. Accessed 15 Sept 2024.

World Health Organization—WHO. 2018. Surveillance system for attacks in health care (SSA): methodology. Technical document. https://www.who.int/publications/i/item/surveillance-system-for-attacks-on-health-care-(-ssa). Accessed 15 Sept 2024.

World Health Organization—WHO. 2023. Prevention and protection against attacks on healthcare—Good practices. Report. https://iris.who.int/bitstream/handle/10665/375802/9789240019461-eng.pdf?sequence=1. Accessed 15 Sept 2024.

Ana Elisa Barbar is an expert on protection of healthcare, worked with the Red Cross and Red Crescent Movement in Latin America, Middle East and Africa. Ana was advisor to policy and operations of the International Committee of the Red Cross on issues of protection of healthcare and currently works as a consultant to international organizations (including the World Health Organization) in the same topic. She is the Chair of the Executive Board to Insecurity Insight, and holds a Bachelor's in Psychology, with a clinical license and a full residency in Primary Health Care, as well as an Executive Master's in Policy Making and International Negotiations.

Christina Wille is Director and founding member of Insecurity Insight and has developed Insecurity Insight's AI supported data collection processes on violence and its consequences for humanitarian work. She is the editor of the Safeguarding Health in Conflict Coalition Report and a board member of the Explosive Weapons Monitor and the h2h network. Previously, she worked for the Small Arms Survey and the European Commission. She studied International Relations at the University of Cambridge, UK.

Chapter 13
Ethical Capacities and Organizational Infrastructure: Navigating Opportunities and Challenges of Artificial Intelligence in Humanitarian Project Closure

Isabel Muñoz Beaulieu, Handreen Mohammed Saeed, and Matthew Hunt

13.1 Introduction

Humanitarian organizations are increasingly adopting artificial intelligence (AI) technology for their programming and operations (Spencer 2024; OCHA 2024a). Artificial intelligence is not a single technology but a broad term that covers various tools and capabilities aimed at emulating aspects of human intelligence. It uses large data sets to train models and algorithms in conducting a wide range of resource-intensive tasks. Examples of adoption in the humanitarian aid field include report drafting, monitoring and assessment activities, and enhancing early warning capabilities (Spencer 2024; OCHA 2024a). Many commentators see great potential for the use of AI models in humanitarian aid that can learn from data, recognize patterns, make predictions, and even generate new information, enabling humanitarian actors to achieve greater outputs with fewer resources (Spencer 2021; Beduschi 2022; Pizzi et al. 2020; Zarei et al. 2024; OCHA 2024a). AI is described as having the potential of enhancing humanitarian organizations' capabilities in preparedness, response, and recovery by efficiently analyzing and interpreting vast amounts of data (Beduschi 2022). AI can also streamline decision-making processes, especially in situations that require rapid or large-scale actions (Pizzi et al. 2020).

The rapid uptake of AI technologies has been a source of active debate in the humanitarian sector, including discussion of the best ways to harness its potential while avoiding negative impacts on humanitarian operations (Spencer 2024;

I. Muñoz Beaulieu (✉) · M. Hunt
McGill University, Montreal, QC, Canada
e-mail: isabel.munozbeaulieu@mail.mcgill.ca; matthew.hunt@mcgill.ca

H. Mohammed Saeed
McMaster University, Hamilton, ON, Canada
e-mail: mohamh35@mcmaster.ca

B. Koch, D. Winkler (eds.), *Artificial Intelligence Ethics in Military Medicine and Humanitarian Healthcare*, Military and Humanitarian Health Ethics,
https://doi.org/10.1007/978-3-032-11331-3_13

Beduschi 2022). These concerns are clustered around issues with security and confidentiality, potential bias and discrimination, and a lack of accountability in the use of new AI technology. The large amounts of data required to train AI models raises significant concerns around privacy, security, and confidentiality for data sharers (Beduschi 2022). In humanitarian contexts, this data often comes from recipients of assistance—people already facing higher degrees of vulnerability. The adoption of AI in these contexts raises critical questions about how security and confidentiality risks are distributed and who bears the burden when personal and sensitive information are involved in humanitarian operations (Kreutzer et al. 2024). Additionally, if AI is used to support decisions about resource allocation but is trained on historically biased data, it may reinforce existing inequalities—potentially resulting in the unfair distribution of life-saving resources or perpetuating the discriminatory practices embedded in the original data collection processes (Kreutzer et al. 2024; Spencer 2021).

More broadly, the emergence of AI applications within the humanitarian sector over the past decade has been highly experimental, potentially raising questions about accountability and good governance for its responsible implementation and oversight (Jacobsen and Steinacker 2021; Sandvik and Liden 2023). Remaining accountable towards local actors is further complicated by the responsive, emergency-driven nature of humanitarian aid which often limits consideration of AI's long-term impacts and risks, especially on populations affected by disaster and conflict (Eckenwiler et al. 2023). These uncertainties highlight the need for humanitarian agencies to address the ethical implications of AI adoption, particularly in terms of its long-lasting effects on crisis-affected groups and individuals.

The short-term emergency nature of humanitarian aid entails that humanitarian projects will eventually close once the crisis subsides, project objectives are met or due to budgetary and security constraints (Hunt et al. 2020). Humanitarian projects may also be shifted to developmental approaches or handed over to local or international partners (Pal et al. 2019). When closures are conducted abruptly or with insufficient planning, affected communities may experience harms if they are left without assistance on which they depended upon for survival (Abramowitz 2016). They may also experience increased tensions, insecurity, or a sense of abandonment (Ashley and Jayousi 2006). To minimize and mitigate harms following the closure of humanitarian projects, humanitarian organizations will need to consider the long-term impact of their interventions and examine what it means to close well (Eckenwiler et al. 2023; Hunt et al. 2020).

In this chapter, we examine the ethical issues associated with using AI in the closure of humanitarian projects. Our aim is to foster discussion and reflection about these issues, identify ethical capacities that can support ethical AI use by humanitarian organizations and staff, and propose ways that organizations can establish ethical infrastructure that supports the enactment of these capacities. We begin by outlining the context of humanitarian project closure and reviewing the current uses of AI in project closure and their ethical implications. We then build on the ethical capacities proposed by Pal et al. (2019)—attentiveness, responsiveness, and foresighting—to explore how these capacities can support the responsible implementation of AI in project closure and serve as a means to assess its risks and opportunities. Additionally, we discuss the importance of a strong organizational ethical infrastructure, including ethical resources, practices, and expertise, to support the enactment of attentiveness, responsiveness and foresighting related to AI during project closure.

13.2 Background

13.2.1 Humanitarian Project Closure

Humanitarian action's primary goals are to save lives, alleviate suffering and promote human dignity during and in the immediate aftermath of an emergency (Pringle and Hunt 2016). This focus on addressing immediate life-saving needs, oriented by the principles of neutrality, humanity, impartiality, and independence, contrasts sharply with the longer-term, political, and rights-based strategies often employed in other types of assistance, such as development assistance (Ford et al. 2010; Lie 2020). In the context of humanitarian aid, when the objectives of a project are met or once the emergency abates, humanitarian organizations will ideally exit, often redirecting their efforts and resources to respond to other urgent crises (Lee and Özerdem 2015). Projects are likely to be phased down (gradually decreasing operations, occasionally maintaining minimal presence in case the crisis re-emerges), handed over to local or international partners, or phased over to a development approach (Lee and Özerdem 2015; Pal et al. 2019; Hunt et al. 2020). The exit of a humanitarian organization might also happen abruptly due to security considerations, budgetary constraints, or the local government rescinding permission for humanitarian organizations to operate (Hunt et al. 2020). Most forced closures are sudden, limiting the ability to implement phased or gradual closure approaches or handover of project activities.

In a study of national and international humanitarian workers' experiences of 'closing well', the closure and handover of projects was described by a participant as one of the "hardest parts" of an intervention (Hunt et al. 2020). The numerous logistical, financial, and human resource capacities to successfully handover project activities to local authorities require humanitarian organizations have sufficient resources to support these transitions (Sitali et al. 2023). Moreover, closure processes that lack transparency, accountability, and adequate planning can generate feelings of frustration and disappointment in affected populations due to the potential loss of essential services (Abu-Sada and Mambetova 2012). Determining when the right time is to exit is a critical but difficult task, as exiting prematurely can trigger conflict recurrence by neglecting long-term needs, while a delayed exit can increase aid dependency (Lee and Özerdem 2015). This dynamic can function as a form of "moral entanglement" that requires careful attention to the obligations of humanitarian organizations, especially where projects are longer in duration and more comprehensive in nature, and where communities have few other means of support (Hunt and Miao 2018). An additional concern for project closure is the careful management of administrative and financial data, including attention to ethical considerations of privacy, security, and accountability that must be addressed. Thus, responsible data management has been highlighted as a crucial aspect of an ethical project closure (Hunt et al., 2023). In sum, successful exit and project handover are complex processes that require diligent planning, coordination, and availability of resources, along with attention to ethical hazards during and following closure (Hunt et al. 2020; Pal et al. 2019; Sitali et al. 2023).

13.2.2 AI Applications During and for Humanitarian Project Closure

The employment of digital technologies and artificial intelligence in the humanitarian sector has become widespread over the past two decades (Beduschi 2022; Kreutzer et al. 2024; Spencer 2024). The context of the COVID-19 pandemic and the emergence of data-driven interventions for contact tracing and pandemic surveillance hastened the transition to digital technologies and placed AI at the forefront of these interventions (Pizzi et al. 2020; Spencer 2021; Beduschi 2022). Increasing computational power coupled with greater data availability and new developments in Large Language Models (LLMs) and generative AI, such as ChatGPT, have further accelerated the adoption of AI (Sandvik 2023; Beduschi 2022; Spencer 2024). For example, Mercy Corps has developed its own LLM for monitoring and evaluation, allowing staff to easily scan organizational reports and request support in writing executive summaries and emails (Weber 2025). Despite the wide adoption of AI for humanitarian practice, to our knowledge, no report has specifically addressed the actual and potential uses of AI in humanitarian project closure and handover processes. With the goal of beginning to map this terrain, we present three potential use cases for the application of AI for humanitarian project closure.

First, AI offers the potential to enhance humanitarian operation efficiency by automating resource-intensive tasks such as gathering, organizing, and synthesizing large sets of project documents (Spencer 2021; Pizzi et al. 2020). It can also assist in drafting reports and grant applications, as well as performing monitoring and assessment activities through data collection and analysis (Spencer 2024; OCHA 2024a). These capabilities could be employed as part of project closure, including the compilation of project data to support handover processes or the creation of end-of-project reports. For example, AI tools can support the development of needs assessment reports, flag services that may require sustained support, and produce checklists to orient resource allocation discussions. In doing so, AI can contribute to more timely, informed, and effective closure processes—helping organizations better balance urgent demands with long-term responsibilities (Spencer 2021). More broadly, by reducing the time that project staff need to dedicate to these time-consuming tasks, the use of AI can enhance the capacity for organizations to direct attention on other critical tasks—such as managing project closure in a thoughtful and ethical manner. AI's potential to increase the bandwidth of humanitarian practitioner's involved in project closure to attend to other tasks is particularly important given the current global context, where the scale and frequency of crises exceeds the system's ability to respond (Development Initiatives 2023; OCHA 2024b). In such settings, humanitarian organizations often face "tragic choices"—decisions where, regardless of the option taken, something of moral significance is lost (Calabresi and Bobbitt 1978; Heyse 2013). Decisions to close or hand over projects with the intention that humanitarian organizations can shift their operations to address other crises are often of this nature, requiring difficult choices about which services and activities can be sustained and what will be given up (Abramowitz 2016). They may also lead to decisions to close projects earlier or more abruptly so that humanitarian resources can be redeployed more quickly. These choices can have significant consequences for communities and populations who had received this assistance, particularly in contexts with a large probability of recurrence of the disaster or conflict. In this context, AI's ability to streamline some operations and reduce inefficiencies can help humanitarian actors navigate these challenges more strategically (Beduschi 2022; Pizzi et al. 2020).

Second, AI has the ability to support proactive planning and allocation of resources based on predictions of how a crisis is likely to evolve and, in turn, support decision-making about when and how to close a project (Beduschi 2022; Margffoy 2023). Predictive analytics powered by AI can support more informed decision-making around the timing and strategy of the handover or phasing down of a project. By analyzing large and complex datasets, predictive models can identify trends and behavioral patterns, offering insights into when a crisis is likely to recur or escalate (Berea 2022; Dixon et al. 2024). In contexts where humanitarian crises are cyclical or where future instability is anticipated, predictive tools could help make decisions whether certain project components should be maintained in standby mode, allowing for a more rapid reactivation if the crisis flares up again. In other cases, predictive analytics can guide the development of phased transition plans by identifying optimal timelines or suggesting gradual steps based on risk indicators, contextual changes, or service utilization patterns. Several examples already demonstrate the practical utility of such models. Project Jetson, an initiative by the United Nations High Commissioner for Refugees, uses AI predictive analytics to forecast future trends in forced displacement, helping humanitarian actors prepare for and respond to emerging and future needs (UNHCR, n.d.). Similarly, the Cholera Prediction Modelling System developed by NASA uses AI to identify regions at high risk of cholera outbreaks, enhancing the ability of humanitarian organizations to prioritize and allocate resources for disease prevention (NASA 2020). By enabling earlier and more strategic planning, predictive analytics can contribute to more adaptive and resilient project transitions—helping ensure that support can be sustained or scaled based on anticipated and emerging needs.

Third, AI tools can support processes for receiving and sharing multi-lingual information with affected populations who may be spread across a broad geographic area. For example, chatbots offer promising opportunities to support more inclusive and responsive handover and closure processes by gathering real-time feedback from community members about their ongoing needs, preferences, and concerns (OCHA 2024a). These insights can inform key decisions about which services could be sustained, reduced, or handed over to other actors. AI technology allows chatbots to support and translate multiple languages, adapt to different contexts, and function at scale, thereby expanding the reach and responsiveness of humanitarian responses (Spencer 2021, 2024). Chatbots can also help facilitate two-way communication by answering common questions, providing updates, and guiding affected populations through next steps—whether that involves accessing new service providers or understanding the timeline for withdrawal (Beduschi 2022; OCHA 2024a). By enabling more consistent and accessible communication, chatbots can contribute to accountability and transparency during closure phases. They offer a scalable and cost-effective tool for supporting a form of community consultation and the gathering of perspectives of affected populations which can contribute to shaping project closure.

13.2.3 AI and Data Ethics in Humanitarian Project Closure

Humanitarian projects often gather vast amounts of personal and sensitive information, which necessitates critical decisions about whether and how to share, return, destroy, or retain this data during project closure or handover stages (Hunt et al. 2023). The employment of sensitive and personal information could pose security and confidentiality risks that continue to be experienced by people affected by the humanitarian crisis, despite humanitarian organizations having ended their projects in a particular setting (Spencer 2021). These risks are exacerbated by a lack of regulation and accountability measures for AI's usage in humanitarian contexts (Sandvik and Liden 2023). Moreover, AI algorithms rely on large data sources, which may be incomplete or inaccurate, leading to biased decision-making that can perpetuate marginalization and inequality, ultimately increasing harm to already vulnerable populations (Spencer 2021; Beduschi 2022; Kreutzer et al. 2024).

Despite these known risks, there are few to no requirements for humanitarian actors to audit their AI systems to ensure data collection is done accurately or to mitigate bias (McElhinney and Spencer 2024; Spencer 2021; CDAC Network 2025). Additionally, there is no systematic regulation of how humanitarian organizations process data to train these algorithms or store and share it in the long-term (Beduschi 2022; Hunt et al. 2023). This lack of oversight creates uncertainty about how data collected for financial purposes, healthcare, human resources, or program operations are processed and applied in humanitarian programs and closure or handover processes (Spencer 2021). The absence of traceability and regulation in

AI systems can lead to a lack of explainability of AI outputs, weakening accountability and redress mechanisms (Spencer 2021; Sandvik and Liden 2023). Even if harm caused by AI models can be established, enforcing accountability for data management practices remains challenging due to accountability gaps in the humanitarian sector (Alexander 2021; Spencer 2021). These concerns are further heightened by the lack of community consultation on the use of AI and algorithmic models in these contexts (Spencer 2024).

Guidelines and policies on AI and data responsibility in humanitarian action have been developed by organizations such as the International Committee of the Red Cross (ICRC), the United Nations Office for the Coordination of Humanitarian Affairs, and the Inter-Agency Standing Committee (IASC) (IASC 2023; OCHA 2019; ICRC 2020, 2024). In parallel, collaborative efforts among clusters of organizations—such as those convened by the CDAC Network—have emerged to develop responsible AI frameworks tailored to humanitarian contexts (CDAC Network 2025). These guidelines and initiatives aim to help humanitarian actors strengthen data protection practices and prioritize privacy across their operations. The ICRC Policy on AI, in particular, offers specific guidance on how to incorporate humanitarian principles into the organization's approach to AI (ICRC 2024). Hunt et al. (2023) suggest that to manage data responsibly during humanitarian closure, humanitarian organizations should consider principles of data purpose limitation, data rights, duties of care, harm minimization, and alignment with existing laws and regulations. However, despite growing attention, guidance on the ethical and responsible use of AI in humanitarian settings remains limited. Scholars and practitioners are calling for the development of clear guardrails, principles, or minimum standards to ensure that AI use aligns with the core humanitarian principles of humanity, impartiality, neutrality, and independence, as well as with key operational commitments like "do no harm," accountability, and localization (McElhinney and Spencer 2024; Spencer 2024). Without robust accountability and governance measures for the ethical use of AI in humanitarian aid and during project closures, tackling persistent issues of bias, security, confidentiality, and responsibility becomes increasingly difficult.

13.3 Ethical Capacities for "Closing Well"

In the following section we examine how humanitarian organizations, and their staff can think and act regarding the responsible use of AI in humanitarian project closure. We draw on an analysis of ethical capacities for humanitarian project closure proposed by Pal et al. (2019). They define ethical capacities as "*the ability and disposition to think and act in ways that are consistent with one's normative commitments.*" The ethical capacities proposed for humanitarian project closure focus on the need for *attentiveness*, *responsiveness*, and *foresight* for closing well. We build on this framing to consider ways for humanitarian organizations and staff to strengthen their ability to address AI-related challenges such as bias and discrimination, mechanisms for accountability, and issues of security and confidentiality. It is important to underline the individual and collective levels of these ethical capacities, which in turn are shaped by institutional and structural features which can support or constrain them.

13.3.1 Attentiveness

Attentiveness in humanitarian project closure entails attending and being open to the needs and concerns of individuals and groups who are involved in or affected by a closure or handover of project activities. Attentiveness involves bearing in mind the existing relationships, expectations, and perceptions of closure and handover processes, and how these relationships shape the way humanitarian aid operates (Pal et al. 2019; Brun and Horst 2023). Attentiveness can help humanitarian organizations and staff consider how relationships are affected by AI deployment and orients those involved to recognize the needs and concerns of those impacted at the closure stage of projects. This orientation encourages humanitarian organizations and their staff to consider the broader, interconnected, and relational contexts from which algorithmic systems emerge and are deployed, all while aiming to protect the welfare of vulnerable individuals and groups affected by crisis (Birhane 2021).

The ability of AI tools to perform well relies on the quality of the data upon which they are trained (OCHA 2024a). Yet, because these data are shaped by societal structures and dynamics which often exclude marginalized populations, AI is prone to reproduce, reinforce, and amplify bias and discrimination (Leslie 2019; Spencer 2021). For example, when chatbots and virtual assistants are used to streamline needs assessments and draft exit reports, or when predictive analytics are employed to determine the appropriate time for closure or handover, there is a risk of perpetuating structural discrimination by relying on biased data sets that are not representative of the entire population, particularly the most vulnerable (Spencer 2021; Beduschi 2022). As AI learns to recognize patterns in existing data, the limitations of the sourced data could lead AI to confidently produce outputs that do not align accurately with the local context (OCHA 2024a).

A different example of how AI tools could perpetuate bias is illustrated in a case study of the handover of a humanitarian medical project to local authorities, where electronic and paper records in both Arabic and English needed to be transferred to local partners (Hunt et al. 2023). AI translation tools could greatly enhance the efficiency of the handover process, ensuring language accessibility and the accurate transfer of records. However, since language models are primarily trained on English data (OCHA 2024a), there is a risk of mistranslating health records, which could pose significant risks to patient health, especially given the lack of traceability in AI decision-making processes (Beduschi 2022).

Various techniques and tactics have been proposed to mitigate bias, avoid discrimination, and reduce risk of harm. However, many of these solutions focus on "fixing the technology" rather than prioritizing and centering the needs of individuals and communities who are most affected (Birhane 2021). By being vigilant about potential for bias and discrimination in AI usage, humanitarian actors enact attentiveness towards those people who are involved in or impacted by their programs, recognizing their needs and concerns. They can ask: *how are others' perspectives being included or excluded in how we collect data and employ AI in closure processes? How have existing relationships informed the way AI tools are designed and implemented to attend to the ongoing and long-term needs of affected groups?* And *what additional spaces for discussion can be created among humanitarian actors, partners, and communities to collaboratively design inclusive strategies for data collection and AI implementation for project closure?* This includes considerations for who is involved in discussions of what and why data is collected, how it is managed during and after the exit of an organization, and how it will inform and train AI models. Establishing communities of practice and collaboration for various types of AI could help the sector work alongside partners and communities to identify both good practices and potential harms that may arise from AI implementation for closure processes (Raftree 2024).

13.3.2 Responsiveness

Being responsive involves humanitarian organizations and workers seeking to tailor project closure approaches to the local context, including capacities, resources and coping strategies of affected communities, and demonstrating adaptability as situations evolve and shift (Pal et al. 2019). Responsiveness recognizes that all project contexts are different and dynamic, demanding continuous adaptation to meet the needs of crisis-affected and vulnerable groups, particularly given the lasting impacts of AI and humanitarian interventions (Spencer 2024). This approach points humanitarian organizations to proactively address changing needs and priorities and fine-tune plans to ensure that closure activities are context sensitive. AI tools can support responsiveness by making resource-intensive decision-making tasks more efficient, synthesizing large amounts of relevant information to support project closure at a faster speed and larger scale than is possible for humans (Spencer 2021; Pizzi et al. 2020). For example, AI can enhance the ability to carry out rapid needs assessments, allowing for quick adjustments to the project closure process. Depending on what is identified during these assessments, the phase-out can be slowed, or extra resources can be allocated to communities experiencing the loss of essential services after an organization leaves.

As AI technologies are adopted to scale up resource-intensive processes in the humanitarian sector, it is crucial to ensure they can conduct tasks efficiently while maintaining accountability to affected populations (Sandvik and Liden 2023;

Spencer 2024). Pizzi et al. (2020) highlight the issue of AI as a "black box," where the opaque nature of AI systems obstructs transparency and accountability in how data is processed and makes it impossible to fully comprehend and explain how data is used by AI models to make decisions. This opaqueness in the functioning of AI models can conflict with key considerations that have been identified as important for ethical project closure, such as transparency and harm minimization (Pal et al. 2019). For example, a predictive model's ability to forecast conflict flare-ups or disaster risks can inform decisions on whether to close a project, transfer resources elsewhere, or phase down while leaving enough remnants to restart the project later. However, if there's a lack of transparency about the data used, how it was processed, and how well it reflects local contexts, this can significantly impact the ability to execute a responsible and effective project closure that adequately reflects local needs and priorities (Pal et al. 2019). The lack of explainability leaves individuals unaware of when and how AI influences decisions affecting their rights, making it very challenging to seek redress when harm occurs (Pizzi et al. 2020). These issues of accountability are compounded by the fact that the development of AI tools requires a long chain of actors who are sometimes far-removed from the humanitarian context, including funders, technology developers, contractors, and private sector vendors (Kreutzer et al. 2024; Pizzi et al. 2020). A mismatch of knowledge, expectations, and desired outputs between technology developers, humanitarian actors, and affected populations can create gaps in adapting tools that are responsive to local needs and capacities (Kreutzer et al. 2024).

As we have described, responsiveness, as an ethical capacity, requires accountability guardrails to ensure AI solutions are aligned and adapted to the evolving needs of the affected population. Remaining accountable is rendered more challenging due to the lack of safeguards and standards in the sector to ensure ethical and responsible AI use (Spencer 2021; McElhinney and Spencer 2024; Kreutzer et al. 2024). Nevertheless, responsiveness can prompt humanitarian actors to consider '*what is owed*' to affected populations. In other words, they might ask, *how can the employment of AI tools for closure be tailored to better align with the local context, including resources and coping strategies for communities? How can AI be designed and applied to respond to the needs of people who are especially vulnerable at the closure stage of a project? What opportunities do affected populations have to influence, adapt to, or seek redress in relation to AI tools used in closure processes?* These considerations may call for the development of guidelines and best practices at both the organizational and sectoral levels to ensure responsible and context sensitive AI adoption in humanitarian aid.

13.3.3 Foresighting

Foresighting is anticipatory. As an ethical capacity, it involves the ability and commitment to identify possible outcomes, anticipate contingencies, and be diligent in planning (Pal et al. 2019). It orients humanitarian actors to carefully plan for project closure in ways that seek to anticipate risks and act to mitigate or minimize potential for harm. It can lead humanitarian workers to model different scenarios and anticipate how they might unfold. This capacity is crucial for protecting the security and confidentiality of data sharers, as it supports humanitarian actors to adapt to evolving contexts and to act in ways that address the potential creation or exacerbation of vulnerabilities within crisis-affected populations (Pal et al. 2019; Hunt et al. 2023).

Ethical issues associated with the humanitarian use of biometrics have been widely discussed, particularly for the registration of refugees and other migrants by organizations such as the UN High Commissioner for Refugees (UNHCR) (Jacobsen and Steinacker 2021; Jacobsen 2021; Kreutzer et al. 2024; Guo and Noori 2021). Similar to AI, biometric use requires large data sets and is experimental in nature. Biometric data is generally collected through fingerprint and iris scanning for the purpose of identification and verification (Gelb and Clark 2013). Using biometric applications, humanitarian organizations can assist deduplication processes to easily remove identical and repeated files from databases, identify groups in need of aid by verifying their identity, and confirm their eligibility for multiple types of assistance (Açıkyıldız 2024). Despite the benefits of quickly amassing identification data, critics of biometrics argue that its collection and storage imposes a significant burden on organizations to consistently uphold high standards of technical and organizational security (OXFAM 2018).

The use of biometrics by humanitarian organizations has been described as perpetuating a state of surveillance for the most vulnerable with the potential for malicious targeting of data sharers if data security is not adequately safeguarded (Latonero 2019). These risks became starkly visible in the abrupt aid withdrawal from Afghanistan in 2021. At the time, the data of approximately 7.4 million Afghans was stored in large biometric databases belonging to military and humanitarian organizations (Jacobsen 2021; Guo and Noori 2021). Humanitarian and military organizations had no established protocols for how to manage sensitive data during an abrupt project exit, leading to an increased state of vulnerability for the affected population (Guo and Noori 2021; Jacobsen and Steinacker 2021). When these organizations abruptly withdrew and the Taliban regained control of key infrastructure, the absence of robust contingency planning left sensitive data exposed, posing severe security and confidentiality risks (Jacobsen and Steinacker 2021; Guo and Noori 2021). These consequences illustrate the importance of anticipating potential harms and taking action to avoid them. The collection and storage of biometric data for displaced populations in Afghanistan exposed a lack of preparation and contingency planning to safeguard the most vulnerable (Jacobsen and Steinacker 2021).

Through enacting foresighting, humanitarian organizations can better prepare for both abrupt and planned project closures. Foresighting, as an ethical capacity, involves careful attention to the long-lasting nature of data and its implications for the organization's eventual exit. From this perspective, humanitarian organizations might ask, *how can we minimize and mitigate potential for harm with the design and implementation of AI and other types of technology in closure processes? What mechanisms exist at the organizational level to manage data responsibly during and after a project ends? And what processes exist to plan for and adapt AI tools as circumstances change?* Project closure, especially when abrupt, requires that organizations anticipate and plan for the lasting impact of their departure. This approach includes considering what will remain and endure—such as data and technology—and addressing the associated risks.

13.4 An Organizational Ethical Infrastructure

Ethical capacities encompass the ability and disposition to think and act in ways that align with normative commitments. For humanitarians, these include commitments to do no harm, to be impartial, to practice accountability, to treat people with dignity and respect, and to alleviate suffering, amongst others (Anderson 1999; Slim 2015; Pringle and Hunt 2016; Core Humanitarian Standards 2024). To help promote these capacities amongst their staff, humanitarian organizations should seek to create an environment that is supportive of developing and practicing the capacities of *attentiveness, responsiveness, and foresight* in the use of AI for humanitarian project closure. To do so, reviewing organizations' existing ethical resources, practices, and expertise can be beneficial (Hunt et al. 2024). These features have been described as an organization's *ethical infrastructure* and contribute to its ethical climate which, in turn, supports value-driven decision-making (Silverman 2000; Hunt et al. 2024). The following section will explore how resources, practices and expertise at the organizational level create conditions that promote *attentiveness, responsiveness*, and *foresight* in the implementation of AI tools for project closures.

13.4.1 Ethical Resources

An organization's ethical resources include the array of policies, codes and tools that are established to articulate and advance its mission and guiding values. Core ethical resources may include an organization's mission statement, code of conduct or code of ethics. It may also include policies for accountability or priority setting. In the context of AI in humanitarian aid, policies may be established which draw from sectoral guidelines such as the United Nations Principles of Ethical Use of AI (United Nations 2022) or the IASC's operational guidance on data responsibility (IASC 2023). Additionally, government policies or regulations, such as the European Union's General Data Protection Regulation (GDPR) may shape an organization's normative commitments to ensure the protection of data sharers' rights (European Parliament and Council of the European Union 2016). The adoption of such policies can enhance the ability of humanitarian organizations to be attentive to the needs and concerns of vulnerable groups and reduce risks of bias and harm. For example, organizational policies that provide guidance for collecting data in ways that are impartial and promote fairness, and that include monitoring to verify that vulnerable groups are not excluded, can help reduce the risks of bias and discrimination often perpetuated by AI models (Pizzi et al. 2020; Spencer 2021). Moreover, humanitarian organizations may develop policies for project closure that include attention to how AI tools will be used to support closure processes in ways that enable responsiveness and foresight. These strategies can include best practices on collaborating with local partners, funders, and technology developers, to ensure AI tools are adapted to the local context and respond to communities' lasting needs and priorities. Additionally, these strategies can incorporate considerations to minimize or mitigate potential harms. It is also possible to highlight principles such as accountability, which humanitarian organizations should uphold when collecting and storing personal and sensitive information, or when experimenting with new AI technology.

13.4.2 Ethical Practices

Organizations can implement a range of ethical practices, such as staff onboarding, training, and routinized spaces for feedback and reflection, to guide both individual and collective actions. These procedures and activities can also help reinforce key elements of what it means to close well and guide staff to design closure processes with attentiveness, responsiveness and foresight. An example of such an ethical practice is the establishment of onboarding procedures to introduce new staff to the organization's principles and ethical commitments, such as accountability, managing data responsibly, and doing no harm. Onboarding can also prepare new staff to address challenges such as bias, confidentiality and security risks associated with data collection and AI usage. Another practice that can contribute to building a strong ethical climate for AI usage is the establishment of spaces for asynchronous and anonymous feedback on how the incorporation of new AI tools is being experienced by staff, as well as for affected populations. Providing spaces for feedback, dialogue and sharing of experiences can create opportunities for learning, as well as improve accountability for impacts resulting from the use of AI tools. As the use of AI in humanitarian aid rapidly increases (McElhinney and Spencer 2024; Beduschi 2022), humanitarian organizations will benefit from establishing structured practices to document and learn from experiences. These practices may include regularly revising ethical resources, such as guidelines and best practices, and collaborating with local experts and technology developers to update staff training and resources. By reflecting on past experiences, humanitarian organizations can adapt their practices to the evolving nature of AI and anticipate potential issues or needs that may hinder effective and ethical project closure.

13.4.3 Ethical Expertise

Ethical expertise encompasses the abilities and knowledge of all members of an organization to address and respond to the ethical aspects of humanitarian activities. In the context of AI, this may include developing an understanding of what responsible AI use entails in various closure processes. Building this expertise may involve designating lead staff responsible for supporting others when questions arise about how best to uphold the organization's ethical commitments to affected communities, with a focus on minimizing potential harm from AI use. Limited technical capacities may hinder the effective use of AI systems and ability to protect the rights of vulnerable groups (Pizzi et al. 2020; Kreutzer et al. 2024). A lack of expertise or training among those deploying AI and other data-driven tools can lead to significant risks, such as failing to properly audit the system, over-reliance on it, or misinterpreting its insights. These errors can result in serious consequences, including the failure to deliver critical aid to the most vulnerable or breaches to security and confidentiality that may lead to discrimination and persecution of data sharers (Pizzi et al. 2020). To promote an enabling climate for the adoption of ethical capacities and mitigate potential harms of AI, organizations could establish AI and data stewards as part of humanitarian project closures. Stewardship fosters action-oriented approaches to managing data, and AI tools, in ways that align with an organization's commitments and responsibilities towards others (Statistics Canada 2020). In humanitarian project closure, data stewardship involves fiduciary responsibilities to ensure responsible AI practices that address bias, security, confidentiality, and accountability systematically within an organization (Rosenbaum, 2010; Hunt et al. 2023). AI and data stewards can develop ethical resources, such as guidelines and best practices for AI use during closure and facilitate training and workshops to promote ethical AI practices. They are responsible for overseeing the organization's adherence to these commitments, encouraging staff to follow established resources and practices that are attentive and responsive to the needs of affected communities. Additionally, stewards can help define roles and responsibilities to foresight and address any impacts of AI use during closure. Strengthening the capacities of data stewards, through training, resourcing and institutional support, helps ensure that the organization's ethical infrastructure is equipped to guide attentive, responsive, and foresighted AI implementation. Table 13.1 offers an overview of how these capacities interact with the different dimensions of organizational ethical infrastructure.

Table 13.1 Ethical capacities, guiding questions and organizational ethical infrastructure related to AI and project closure

Ethical capacities	Guiding questions	Examples of organizational ethical infrastructure
Attentiveness	1. How are others' perspectives being included or excluded in how we collect data and employ AI in closure processes? 2. How have existing relationships informed the way AI tools are designed and implemented to attend to the ongoing and long-term needs of affected groups? 3. What additional spaces for discussion can be created among humanitarian actors, partners, and communities to collaboratively design inclusive strategies for data collection and AI implementation for project closure?	• *Ethical resources:* Create organizational policies that guide the collection of data fairly, and monitoring of bias and potential for discrimination • *Ethical practices:* Invite local experts to collaborate in designing inclusive strategies for the implementation of AI tools • *Ethical expertise:* Establish stewardship roles to uphold commitments to attend to the needs of affected populations
Responsiveness	1. How can the employment of AI tools for closure be tailored to better align with the local context, including resources and coping strategies for communities? 2. How can AI be designed and applied to respond to the needs of people who are especially vulnerable at the closure stage of a project? 3. What opportunities do affected populations have to influence, adapt to, or seek redress in relation to AI tools used in closure processes?	• *Ethical resources:* Design and implement policies and guidelines that highlight commitments to accountability when implementing new technology • *Ethical practices:* Create channels for affected populations to provide asynchronous and anonymous feedback and identify ways they can influence, adapt, or redress AI tools used for closure • *Ethical expertise:* Identify data stewards with the mandate to ensure the organization remains accountable to those they are assisting
Foresighting	1. How can we minimize and mitigate harm with the design and implementation of AI and other types of technology in closure processes? 2. What mechanisms exist at the organizational level to manage data responsibly during closure and after a project ends? 3. What processes exist to plan for and adapt AI tools as circumstances change?	• *Ethical resources:* Develop exit strategies that demand contingency planning for AI's role in both abrupt and planned exits • *Ethical practices:* Leverage past experiences in AI design and implementation to prepare and anticipate potential issues or needs at closure • *Ethical expertise:* Define roles and responsibilities to prepare for closure and to proactively address risks associated with AI tools

13.5 Conclusion

AI adoption in humanitarian aid is accelerating (Spencer 2024), yet there is a notable gap in discussions about its ethical implications, especially concerning project closure. In this chapter, we examine how the ethical capacities of attentiveness, responsiveness, and foresighting can inform the use of AI in these contexts. We analyze how these capacities can help address biases and discrimination, promote accountability to affected populations despite AI's opaque nature, and protect the security of individuals and confidentiality of their data by anticipating potential harms and taking steps to mitigate risks. Additionally, we argue that a robust organizational ethical infrastructure is crucial for realizing these capacities. Humanitarian organizations must invest in developing ethical resources, practices, and expertise to lay the groundwork (Hunt et al. 2024) for the responsible implementation of AI and to support ethical project closure. Supporting the development and practice of these ethical capacities, including through the development of a solid ethical infrastructure, will support humanitarian organizations to harness AI's potential while upholding their commitments to promote the well-being of affected communities during and after project closure.

References

Abramowitz, Sharon. 2016. Chapter 7. What Happens When MSF Leaves? Humanitarian Departure and Medical Sovereignty in Postconflict Liberia. In *Medical Humanitarianism*, ed. Sharon Abramowitz and Ichiro Kawaki, 137–154. Philadelphia, PA: University of Pennsylvania Press. https://www-degruyter-com.proxy3.library.mcgill.ca/document/doi/10.9783/9780812291698-009/html?lang=en.

Abu-Sada, Caroline, and Khurshida Mambetova. 2012. Reversing the Optics. In *Dilemmas, Challenges, and Ethics of Humanitarian Action*, Reflections on Médecins Sans Frontières' Perception Project, ed. Caroline Abu-Sada, 11–28. Montreal: McGill-Queen's University Press. http://www.jstor.org/stable/j.ctt1pq12z.5.

Açıkyıldız, Çağlar. 2024. 'I Know You like the Back of My Hand': Biometric Practices of Humanitarian Organisations in International Aid. *Disasters* 48 (2): e12612. https://doi.org/10.1111/disa.12612.

Alexander, Jessica. 2021. 25 Years of Aid Accountability. *The New Humanitarian* (blog). April 27, 2021. https://www.thenewhumanitarian.org/feature/2021/4/27/then-and-now-25-years-of-aid-accountability.

Anderson, Mary B. 1999. *Do No Harm How Aid Can Support Peace or War*. Boulder, CO: Lynne Rienner. https://www.rienner.com/title/Do_No_Harm_How_Aid_Can_Support_Peace_or_War.

Ashley, John, and Nedal Jayousi. 2006. Setting a Palestinian National Food Security Strategy. *Palestine-Israel Journal of Politics, Economics & Culture* 13 (3): 112–118.

Beduschi, Ana. 2022. Harnessing the Potential of Artificial Intelligence for Humanitarian Action: Opportunities and Risks. *International Review of the Red Cross* 104 (919): 1149–1169. https://doi.org/10.1017/S1816383122000261.

Berea, Anamaria. 2022. Predictive Analytics. In *Encyclopedia of Big Data*, ed. Laurie A. Schintler and Connie L. McNeely, 760–764. Cham: Springer. https://doi.org/10.1007/978-3-319-32010-6_170.

Birhane, Abeba. 2021. Algorithmic Injustice: A Relational Ethics Approach. *Patterns* 2 (2): https://doi.org/10.1016/j.patter.2021.100205.

Brun, Cathrine, and Cindy Horst. 2023. Towards a Conceptualisation of Relational Humanitarianism. *Journal of Humanitarian Affairs* 5 (1): 62–72. https://doi.org/10.7227/JHA.103.

Calabresi, Guido, and Philip Bobbitt. 1978. Tragic Choices. *Faculty Books*, January. https://scholarship.law.columbia.edu/books/83.

CDAC Network. 2025. FCDO SAFE AI Roundtable: Building a Responsible AI Framework for Humanitarian Action in a Rapidly Changing Landscape. U.K. https://static1.squarespace.com/static/60996b757eb6521a42f3839d/t/6800cd407493ab2ba92ce146/1744883009243/FCDO+SAFE+AI+Roundtable+-+Read+Out.pdf.

Core Humanitarian Standards. 2024. Core Humanitarian Standard. https://handbook.hspstandards.org/en/chs/2024/#ch001.

Development Initiatives. 2023. Global Humanitarian Assistance Report 2023.

Dixon, Diny, Hina Sattar, Natalia Moros, Srija Reddy Kesireddy, Huma Ahsan, Mohit Lakkimsetti, Madiha Fatima, et al. 2024. Unveiling the Influence of AI Predictive Analytics on Patient Outcomes: A Comprehensive Narrative Review. *Cureus* 16 (May): https://doi.org/10.7759/cureus.59954.

Eckenwiler, Lisa, Matthew R. Hunt, Jan Joy Louise, G. Crismo, Elyse Conde, Shelley-Rose Hyppolite, Mayfourth Luneta, Isabel Munoz-Beaulieu, Handreen Mohammed Saeed, and Lisa Schwartz. 2023. Viewing Humanitarian Project Closure Through the Lens of an Ethics of the Temporary. *Disaster Prevention and Management: An International Journal* 32 (2): 311–322. https://doi.org/10.1108/DPM-11-2022-0226.

European Parliament and Council of the European Union. 2016. *Regulation (EU) 2016/ 679 of the European Parliament and of the Council - of 27 April 2016 - on the Protection of Natural Persons with Regard to the Processing of Personal Data and on the Free Movement of Such Data, and Repealing Directive 95/46/EC (General Data Protection Regulation).* https://eur-lex.europa.eu/legal-content/EN/TXT/PDF/?uri=CELEX:32016R0679.

Ford, Nathan, Rony Zachariah, Ed Mills, and Ross Upshur. 2010. Defining the Limits of Emergency Humanitarian Action: Where, and How, to Draw the Line? *Public Health Ethics* 3 (1): 68–71. https://doi.org/10.1093/phe/php026.

Gelb, Alan, and Julia Clark. 2013. *Identification for Development: The Biometrics Revolution*, SSRN Scholarly Paper. Rochester, NY: Social Science Research Network. https://doi.org/10.2139/ssrn.2226594.

Guo, Eileen, and Hikmat Noori. 2021. This Is the Real Story of the Afghan Biometric Databases Abandoned to the Taliban. *MIT Technology Review* (blog). https://www.technologyreview.com/2021/08/30/1033941/afghanistan-biometric-databases-us-military-40-data-points/.

Heyse, Liesbet. 2013. Tragic Choices in Humanitarian Aid: A Framework of Organizational Determinants of NGO Decision Making. *VOLUNTAS: International Journal of Voluntary and Nonprofit Organizations* 24 (1): 68–92. https://doi.org/10.1007/s11266-012-9292-y.

Hunt, Matthew, and Jingru Miao. 2018. Moral entanglement and the closing of humanitarian projects. In, Humanitarian ethics and action. Eds. A Ahmad, J Smith. Zed Books: London, UK. p 22-39.

Hunt, Matthew, Lisa Eckenwiler, Shelley-Rose Hyppolite, John Pringle, Nicole Pal, and Ryoa Chung. 2020. Closing Well: National and International Humanitarian Workers' Perspectives on the Ethics of Closing Humanitarian Health Projects. *Journal of International Humanitarian Action* 5 (1): 16. https://doi.org/10.1186/s41018-020-00082-4.

Hunt, Matthew, Isabel Muñoz Beaulieu, and Handreen Mohammed Saeed. 2023. What Does 'Closing Well' Entail for Humanitarian Project Data? Seven Questions as Humanitarian Health Projects Are (Being) Closed or Handed Over. *Journal of Humanitarian Affairs*. November. https://doi.org/10.7227/JHA.106.

Hunt, M., A. Okhowat, G. Krishnaraj, I. McClelland, and L. Schwartz. 2024. Laying the Groundwork: Insights from Organisational Ethics for Humanitarian Innovation. *Journal of Humanitarian Affairs 5* (3): 32–38. https://doi.org/10.7227/JHA.115.

IASC. 2023. Data Responsibility in Humanitarian Action. IASC. https://interagencystanding-committee.org/sites/default/files/migrated/2023-04/IASC%20Operational%20Guidance%20on%20Data%20Responsibility%20in%20Humanitarian%20Action%2C%202023.pdf.

ICRC. 2020. Handbook on Data Protection in Humanitarian Action. ICRC. https://shop.icrc.org/handbook-on-data-protection-in-humanitarian-action-pdf-en.html.

ICRC. 2024. Building a Responsible Humanitarian Approach: The ICRC's Policy on Artificial Intelligence. November 18, 2024. https://www.icrc.org/en/publication/building-responsible-humanitarian-approach-icrcs-policy-artificial-intelligence.

Jacobsen, Katja Lindskov. 2021. Biometric Data Flows and Unintended Consequences of Counterterrorism. *International Review of the Red Cross* 103 (916–917): 619–652. https://doi.org/10.1017/S1816383121000928.

Jacobsen, Katja, and Karl Steinacker. 2021. Contingency Planning in the Digital Age: Biometric Data of Afghans Must Be Reconsidered. August 26, 2021. https://blogs.prio.org/2021/08/contingency-planning-in-the-digital-age-biometric-data-of-afghans-must-be-reconsidered/.

Kreutzer, Tino, James Orbinski, Lora Appel, Aijun An, and Patrick Vinck. 2024. Ethical Implications Related to Processing of Personal Data and Artificial Intelligence in Humanitarian Crises: A Scoping Review. *Research Square*. https://doi.org/10.21203/rs.3.rs-4224535/v1.

Latonero, Mark. 2019. Opinion | Stop Surveillance Humanitarianism. *The New York Times*, July 12, 2019, sec. Opinion. https://www.nytimes.com/2019/07/11/opinion/data-humanitarian-aid.html.

Lee, S. Y., and A. Özerdem. 2015. Exit Strategies. In *The Routledge Companion to Humanitarian Action*, ed. Roger Mac Ginty and Jenny H. Peterson, 1st ed., 372–384. New York: Routledge. https://www-taylorfrancis-com.proxy3.library.mcgill.ca/chapters/edit/10.4324/9780203753422-36/exit-strategies-sung-yong-lee-alpaslan-%C3%B6zerdem.

Leslie, David. 2019. Understanding Artificial Intelligence Ethics and Safety: A Guide for the Responsible Design and Implementation of AI Systems in the Public Sector. Zenodo. https://doi.org/10.5281/ZENODO.3240529.

Lie, Jon Harald Sande. 2020. The Humanitarian-Development Nexus: Humanitarian Principles, Practice, and Pragmatics. *Journal of International Humanitarian Action* 5 (1): 18. https://doi.org/10.1186/s41018-020-00086-0.

Margffoy, Mayra. 2023. AI for Humanitarians: A Conversation on the Hype, the Hope, the Future. *The New Humanitarian*, September 5, 2023. https://www.thenewhumanitarian.org/feature/2023/09/05/ai-humanitarians-conversation-hype-hope-future.

McElhinney, Helen, and Sarah Spencer. 2024. Humanitarian AI Guidelines: The Clock Is Ticking to Create Minimum Standards. *The New Humanitarian*, March 11, 2024. https://www.thenewhumanitarian.org/opinion/2024/03/11/build-guardrails-humanitarian-ai.

NASA. 2020. Predicting Cholera Risk in Yemen. Text. Article. NASA Earth Observatory. August 12, 2020. https://earthobservatory.nasa.gov/images/147101/predicting-cholera-risk-in-yemen.

OCHA. 2019. OCHA Data Responsibility Guidelines. OCHA. https://centre.humdata.org/wp-content/uploads/2019/03/OCHA-DR-Guidelines-working-draft-032019.pdf.

OCHA. 2024a. Briefing Note on Artificial Intelligence and the Humanitarian Sector. Centre for Humanitarian Data. https://www.unocha.org/publications/report/world/briefing-note-artificial-intelligence-and-humanitarian-sector.

OCHA. 2024b. World Humanitarian Overview 2024. OCHA. https://www.unocha.org/publications/report/world/global-humanitarian-overview-2024-enarfres.

OXFAM. 2018. Biometrics in the Humanitarian Sector. The Engine Room. https://www.theengineroom.org/wp-content/uploads/2018/03/Engine-Room-Oxfam-Biometrics-Review.pdf.

Pal, Nicole E., Lisa Eckenwiler, Shelley-Rose Hyppolite, John Pringle, Ryoa Chung, and Matthew Hunt. 2019. Ethical Considerations for Closing Humanitarian Projects: A Scoping Review. *Journal of International Humanitarian Action* 4 (1): 17. https://doi.org/10.1186/s41018-019-0064-9.

Pizzi, Michael, Mila Romanoff, and Tim Engelhardt. 2020. AI for Humanitarian Action: Human Rights and Ethics. *International Review of the Red Cross* 102 (913): 145–180. https://doi.org/10.1017/S1816383121000011.

Pringle, John, and Matthew Hunt. 2016. Humanitarian Action. In *Encyclopedia of Global Bioethics*, ed. Henk ten Have, 1562–1571. Cham: Springer. https://doi.org/10.1007/978-3-319-09483-0_235.

Raftree, Linda. 2024. Do Humanitarians Have a Moral Duty to Use AI to Reduce Human Suffering? Four Key Tensions to Untangle. ALNAP. June 11, 2024. https://alnap.org/humanitarian-resources/publications-and-multimedia/do-humanitarians-have-a-moral-duty-to-use-ai/.

Rosenbaum, S. 2010. Data Governance and Stewardship: Designing Data Stewardship Entities and Advancing Data Access. *Health Services Research* 45(5p2) 1442-1455 https://doi.org/10.1111/hesr.2010.45.issue-5p2; https://doi.org/10.1111/j.1475-6773.2010.01140.x

Sandvik, Kristin. 2023. Taking Stock: Generative AI, Humanitarian Action, and the Aid Worker. *Global Policy Journal*. https://www.globalpolicyjournal.com/blog/28/07/2023/taking-stock-generative-ai-humanitarian-action-and-aid-worker.

Sandvik, Kristin, and Kristoffer Liden. 2023. Ungovernable or Humanitarian Experimentation? Generative AI as an Accountability Issue. *Global Policy Journal*. https://www.globalpolicyjournal.com/blog/24/08/2023/ungovernable-or-humanitarian-experimentation-generative-ai-accountability-issue.

Silverman, Henry J. 2000. Organizational Ethics in Healthcare Organizations: Proactively Managing the Ethical Climate to Ensure Organizational Integrity. *HEC Forum* 12 (3): 202–215. https://doi.org/10.1023/A:1008985411047.

Sitali, Norman, Emily Briskin, Jonathan Foday, Caroline Walker, Kees Keus, Francis Smart, Engy Ali, and Katherine Whitehouse. 2023. What It Takes to Get It Right: A Qualitative Study Exploring Optimal Handover of Health Programmes in Tonkolili District, Sierra Leone. *Global Public Health* 18 (1): 2058047. https://doi.org/10.1080/17441692.2022.2058047.

Slim, Hugo. 2015. *Humanitarian Ethics: A Guide to the Morality of Aid in War and Disaster*. Oxford: Oxford University Press. http://ebookcentral.proquest.com/lib/mcgill/detail.action?docID=4454177.

Spencer, Sarah. 2021. Humanitarian AI: The Hype, the Hope and the Future. HPN Network Paper. Humanitarian Practice Network. https://odihpn.org/wp-content/uploads/2021/11/HPN-Network-Paper_AI_web_181121.pdf.

Spencer, Sarah. 2024. Humanitarian AI Revisited: Seizing the Potential and Sidestepping the Pitfalls. HPN Network Paper. Humanitarian Practice Network. https://odihpn.org/wp-content/uploads/2024/05/HPN_Network-Paper89_humanitarianAI.pdf.

Statistics Canada. 2020. Statistics Canada Data Strategy. March 13, 2020. https://www.statcan.gc.ca/en/about/datastrategy.

UNHCR. n.d. Project Jetson. https://jetson.unhcr.org/. Accessed 10 Oct 2024.

United Nations. 2022. Principles for the Ethics. New York. https://unsceb.org/sites/default/files/2023-03/CEB_2022_2_Add.1%20%28AI%20ethics%20principles%29.pdf.

Weber, Daniela. 2025. Safe Generative AI Chatbots. *United Kingdom Humanitarian Innovation Hub* (blog). https://www.ukhih.org/news/safe-generative-ai-chatbots-mercy-corps/.

Zarei, Hossein, Hossein Baharmand, Mahdi Bashiri, and Samaneh Madanian. 2024. Technological Advancements in Humanitarian Aid. *International Journal of Disaster Risk Reduction* 109 (July): 104527. https://doi.org/10.1016/j.ijdrr.2024.104527.

Isabel Muñoz Beaulieu is conducting her PhD at McGill University. Her work and research on humanitarian and global health ethics builds upon collaborations with the Center for Disaster Preparedness in the Philippines and the Canadian Red Cross. Isabel has gained field experience working in the humanitarian and development field with the United Nations High Commissioner of Refugees in Guatemala and The Hunger Project. She also works as a research associate for the Lancet Commission on Racism, Structural Discrimination and Global Health and is a member of the Humanitarian Health Ethics Research Group.

Handreen Mohammed Saeed is a family physician currently completing a fellowship in primary HIV care at the University of Toronto and a Master of Public Health (MPH) at McMaster University. From 2016 to 2018, he served as Head of Medical Activities with Médecins Sans Frontières (MSF) in Iraqi Kurdistan, where he led multiple clinical and health-related projects, and later coordinated health programs for Syrian refugees with Syria Relief. As a member of the Humanitarian Health Ethics Research Group, Handreen has contributed to studies on humanitarian ethics, data management, and the ethical considerations involved in closing humanitarian projects.

Matthew Hunt is a professor at McGill University's School of Physical and Occupational Therapy, and a researcher at the Centre for Research on Ethics and the Centre for Interdisciplinary Research in Rehabilitation. Matthew conducts research at the intersections of ethics, rehabilitation, and humanitarian action. Current research projects include investigations of ethical considerations in how humanitarian projects are closed, the place of sustainability in humanitarian action, disability inclusion in disaster risk reduction and climate change adaptation, as well as a living laboratory based at a rehabilitation hospital in Montreal. He co-leads the Humanitarian Health Ethics Research Group (humanitarianhealthethics.net).

MIX
Papier aus verantwortungsvollen Quellen
Paper from responsible sources
FSC® C105338

If you have any concerns about our products,
you can contact us on
ProductSafety@springernature.com

In case Publisher is established outside the EU,
the EU authorized representative is:
Springer Nature Customer Service Center GmbH
Europaplatz 3, 69115 Heidelberg, Germany

Printed by Libri Plureos GmbH
in Hamburg, Germany